JERRY LEE LEWIS

BREATHLESS!

EVERY SONG FROM *EVERY* SESSION, 1952-2022

PETER CHECKSFIELD

Copyright © 2023 Peter Checksfield
All rights reserved.

The editorial arrangement, analysis, and professional commentary are subject to this copyright notice. No portion of this book may be copied, retransmitted, reposted, duplicated, or otherwise used without the express written approval of the author, except by reviewers who may quote brief excerpts in connection with a review. All images are used in accordance to Fair Use copyright laws.

DEDICATION

JERRY LEE LEWIS

[29th September 1935 - 28th October 2022]

I'd also like to dedicate this to Jerry's extended family, including wife Judith, former wives Myra and Kerrie, children Ronnie, Phoebe, Lori and Lee (aka Jerry Lee Lewis III), and sister Linda Gail Lewis.

INTRODUCTION

"Talk about it one time, yeah!" (Jerry Lee Lewis, 1964)

In the summer of 1952, a 16 year-old Jerry Lee Lewis, with his best friend Cecil Harrelson, traveled from Ferriday, Louisiana, to New Orleans, and cut a Demo record at Cosimo Matassa's J&M Recording Studios. In April 2022, a frail 86 year-old Jerry Lee Lewis, suffering from the debilitating effects of a stroke 3 years earlier, recorded a Gospel album with his cousin Jimmy Lee Swaggart in Baton Rouge. It was his final recording. Almost inevitably, the obituaries focused on his often controversial personal life. This book is about THE MUSIC, music which encompasses Rock 'n' Roll, Country, Blues, Pop standards, Gospel and just about everything in between. Included is every *available* song Jerry recorded in the studio, as well as those that were only taped in concert.

"Well, I ain't braggin', it's understood!" (Jerry Lee Lewis, 1957)

I met Jerry Lee Lewis several times over the years, even getting to ask him a few questions once; I stayed at his sister Linda Gail Lewis' home, twice; I hung out with his then wife Kerrie and his daughter Phoebe, separately; I traveled around the UK with his band on tour buses; I was an extra in the 'Great Balls of Fire!' movie, getting paid to heckle Dennis Quaid; and I played guitar on his niece Mary Jean's album which she recorded with UK Country star Jonny Williams. I've also chatted with more than 20 musicians associated with Jerry Lee Lewis, from his early days at Sun to his road bands of the '80s, '90s and beyond. I say all this NOT as a boast, but because I have occasionally drawn on those experiences when writing this book.

"I love ya like a hog loves slop!" (Jerry Lee Lewis, 1969)

I've learnt from and sometimes met many other fans over the years, and although I'm sure I've overlooked some, these include: Stephen Ackles, Terry Adams, Martin Bates, Wim de Boer, Joe Bonomo, Trevor Cajiao, Emma Connolly, Chris Davies, Phil Davies, Federico Fichera, Barrie Gamblin, Wolfgang Guhl, Richard Harvey, Peter Hayman, Ian Holton, Tony Houlton, Per Kallin, John Kenyon, Graham Knight, Paul McPhail, Andrew McRae, Kay Martin, Lucio Mendonca, Peter Molecz, Tony Papard, John Pearce, Pierre Pennone, Thomas Rund, Johannes "Tex" Sipkema, Thomas Sobczak, Gary Skala, Tom Sturt, Piet and Els Versteijnen, Dave Webb, Daniel White and Jonny Williams.

Last, but certainly not least, I'd like to thank my better half Heather. Without her love, support and patience, I wouldn't even be an author.

Peter Checksfield (March 2023)

If you have any additional information or interview requests, do not hesitate to get in touch:

peterchecksfieldauthor@gmail.com

The author meets Jerry Lee Lewis for the first time (1983)

CONTENTS

1. A Damn Good Country Song
2. A Little Peace and Harmony
3. A Picture From Life's Other Side
4. After The Fool You've Made Of Me
5. Alabama Jubilee
6. All Night Long [1]
7. All Night Long [2]
8. All Over Hell and Half Of Georgia
9. All The Good Is Gone
10. All-Star Jam
11. Alvin
12. Am I To Be The One
13. Amazing Grace
14. And For The First Time
15. Another Hand Shakin' Goodbye
16. Another Place, Another Time
17. Arkansas
18. Arkansas Seesaw
19. As Long As I Live
20. As Long As We Live
21. Autumn Leaves
22. Baby (You've Got What It Takes)
23. Baby What You Want Me To Do
24. Baby, Baby Bye Bye
25. Baby, Hold Me Close
26. Bad, Bad Leroy Brown
27. Bad Moon Rising
28. Ballad Of Forty Dollars
29. Beautiful Dreamer
30. Be-Bop-A-Lula
31. Because Of You
32. Before The Next Teardrop Falls
33. Before The Night Is Over
34. Before The Snow Flies
35. Better Not Look Down
36. Big Blon' Baby
37. Big Blue Diamonds
38. Big Boss Man
39. Big Legged Woman
40. Big Train (From Memphis)
41. Billy Boy (Charming Billy)
42. Birds and The Bees (Boy Meets Girl)
43. Black Bottom Stomp
44. Black Mama
45. Blue Christmas
46. Blue Suede Shoes
47. Blueberry Hill
48. Bluer Words
49. Blues Like Midnight
50. Bonnie B.
51. Boogie Woogie Country Man
52. Born To Be A Loser
53. Born To Lose
54. Bottles and Barstools
55. Bottom Dollar
56. Bread and Butter Man
57. Break My Mind
58. Break Up
59. Breathless
60. Bright Lights, Big City
61. Brown Eyed Handsome Man
62. Burning Memories
63. C.C. Rider
64. Candy Kisses
65. Careless Hands
66. Carry Me Back To Old Virginia
67. Change Places With Me
68. Changing Mountains
69. Chantilly Lace
70. Cheater Pretend
71. Children Go Where I Send Thee
72. Circumstantial Evidence
73. City Lights
74. Cold, Cold Heart
75. Cold, Cold Morning Light
76. Come As You Were
77. Come On In
78. Come Sundown

79. Come What May
80. Comin' Back For More
81. Corrine, Corrina
82. Country Memories
83. Couple More Years
84. Crazy Arms
85. Crazy Heart
86. Crazy Like Me
87. Crown Victoria Custom '51
88. Cry
89. Cryin' Time
90. Danny Boy
91. Daughters Of Dixie
92. Dead Flowers
93. Deep Elem Blues
94. Detroit City
95. Dixie
96. Don't Be Ashamed Of Your Age
97. Don't Be Cruel
98. Don't Boogie Woogie
99. Don't Drop It
100. Don't Let Go
101. Don't Let Me Cross Over
102. Don't Let The Stars Get In Your Eyes
103. Don't Stay Away (Till Love Grows Cold)
104. Don't Take It Out On Me
105. Don't Touch Me
106. Down The Line
107. Down The Road Apiece
108. Down The Sawdust Trail
109. Down Yonder
110. Dream Baby (How Long Must I Dream)
111. Drinkin' Champagne
112. Drinkin' Wine Spo-Dee-O-Dee
113. Dungaree Doll
114. Early Mornin' Rain
115. Earth Up Above
116. Easter Parade
117. Echoes
118. Eight By Ten
119. End Of The Road
120. Evening Gown
121. Every Day I Have To Cry
122. Faded Love
123. Falling To The Bottom
124. Fever
125. Filipino Baby
126. Five Foot Two, Eyes Of Blue
127. Flip, Flop and Fly
128. Folsom Prison Blues
129. Foolaid
130. Foolish Kind Of Man
131. Fools Like Me
132. For The Good Times
133. Forever Forgiving
134. Four Walls
135. Frankie and Johnny
136. Fraulein
137. Friday Night
138. From A Jack To A King
139. Funny How Time Slips Away
140. Games People Play
141. Gather 'Round Children
142. Georgia On My Mind
143. Get Out Your Big Roll Daddy
144. Give Me Some Action
145. Goldmine In The Sky
146. Good Golly Miss Molly
147. Good Love (Shouldn't Feel So Bad)
148. Good News Travels Fast
149. Good Rockin' Tonight
150. Good Time Charlie's Got The Blues
151. Goodnight Irene
152. Goosebumps
153. Got You On My Mind
154. Got You On My Mind Again
155. Gotta Travel On
156. Great Balls Of Fire
157. Great Speckled Bird
158. Green, Green Grass Of Home
159. Hadacol Boogie
160. Hallelujah, I Love Her So

161. Hand Me Down My Walkin' Cane
162. Handwriting On The Wall
163. Hang Up My Rock 'N' Roll Shoes
164. Harbor Lights
165. Have I Got A Song For You
166. Have I Told You Lately That I Love You
167. He Can't Fill My Shoes
168. He Looked Beyond My Fault
169. He Set Me Free - I Saw The Light
170. He Took It Like A Man
171. He'll Have To Go
172. Heartaches By The Number
173. Hearts Were Made For Beating
174. Hello Hello Baby
175. Hello Josephine (My Girl Josephine)
176. Help Me Make It Through The Night
177. Here Comes That Rainbow Again
178. Herman The Hermit
179. Hey Baby
180. Hey Good Lookin'
181. High Blood Pressure
182. High Heel Sneakers
183. High Powered Woman
184. High School Confidential
185. Hillbilly Music (Fever)
186. His Hands
187. Hit The Road, Jack
188. Hold On I'm Coming
189. Hold You In My Heart
190. Holdin' On
191. Home
192. Home Away From Home
193. Homecoming
194. Honey Hush
195. Hong Kong Blues
196. Honky Tonk Heart
197. Honky Tonk Heaven
198. Honky Tonk Rock 'N' Roll Piano Man
199. Honky Tonk Song
200. Honky Tonk Stuff
201. Honky Tonk Wine
202. Honky Tonk Woman
203. Honky Tonkin'
204. (Hot Damn) I'm A One Woman Man
205. Hound Dog
206. How Great Thou Art
207. How's My Ex Treating You
208. I Ain't Loved You
209. I Am What I Am
210. I Believe In You
211. I Betcha Gonna Like It
212. I Can Help
213. I Can Still Hear The Music In The…
214. (I Can't Get No) Satisfaction
215. I Can't Get Over You
216. I Can't Give You Anything But Love
217. I Can't Have A Merry Christmas, Mary
218. I Can't Help It
219. I Can't Keep My Hands Off Of You
220. I Can't Seem To Say Goodbye
221. I Can't Stop Loving You
222. I Can't Trust Me (In Your Arms Anymore)
223. I Could Never Be Ashamed Of You
224. I Don't Do It No More
225. I Don't Hurt Anymore
226. I Don't Know Why (I Just Do)
227. I Don't Love Nobody
228. I Don't Want To Be Lonely Tonight
229. I Forgot More Than You'll Ever Know
230. I Forgot To Remember To Forget
231. I Get The Blues When It Rains
232. I Got A Woman
233. I Hate Goodbyes
234. I Hate You
235. I Know That Jesus Will Be There
236. I Know What It Means
237. I Like It Like That
238. I Love You Because
239. I Love You So Much It Hurts
240. I Only Want A Buddy, Not A Sweetheart
241. I Really Don't Want To Know
242. I Saw Her Standing There

243. I Saw The Light
244. I Sure Miss Those Good Old Times
245. I Think I Need To Pray
246. I Threw Away The Rose
247. I Walk The Line
248. I Was Sorta Wonderin'
249. I Wish I Was Eighteen Again
250. I Wish You Love
251. I Won't Have To Cross Jordan Alone
252. I Wonder Where You Are Tonight
253. I'd Be Talkin' All The Time
254. I'd Do It All Again
255. I'll Find It Where I Can
256. I'll Fly Away
257. I'll Keep On Loving You
258. I'll Make It All Up To You
259. I'll Never Get Out Of This World Alive
260. I'll Sail My Ship Alone
261. I'll See You In My Dreams
262. I'm A Lonesome Fugitive
263. I'm Alone Because I Love You
264. I'm Feelin' Sorry
265. I'm In The Gloryland Way
266. I'm Knee Deep In Loving You
267. I'm Left, You're Right, She's Gone
268. I'm Longing For Home
269. I'm Looking Over A Four Leaf Clover
270. I'm On Fire
271. I'm So Lonesome I Could Cry
272. I'm Sorry, I'm Not Sorry
273. I'm Still Jealous Of You
274. I'm The Guilty One
275. I'm Throwing Rice
276. I'm Using My Bible For A Road Map
277. I'm Walkin'
278. I've Been Twistin'
279. I've Forgot More About You (Than He'll...
280. If I Ever Needed You (I Need You Now)
281. If I Had It All To Do Over
282. If We Never Meet Again-I'll Meet You In...
283. In Loving Memories
284. In The Garden
285. In The Mood
286. Invitation To Your Party
287. It All Depends (Who Will Buy The Wine)
288. It Hurt Me So
289. It Is No Secret
290. It Makes No Difference Now
291. It Was The Whiskey Talkin' (Not Me)
292. It Will Be Worth It All When We See Jesus
293. It Won't Happen With Me
294. It'll Be Me
295. It's A Hang Up Baby
296. It's Been So Long
297. It's The Real Thing
298. Ivory Tears
299. Jack Daniels (Old Number Seven)
300. Jackson
301. Jailhouse Rock
302. Jambalaya (On The Bayou)
303. Jealous Heart
304. Jenny, Jenny
305. Jerry Lee's Rock 'N' Roll Revival Show
306. Jerry Lee's Boogie (New Orleans Boogie)
307. Jerry's Got The Blues
308. Jerry's Place
309. Jesus Hold My Hand
310. Jesus Is On The Mainline
311. John Henry
312. Johnny B. Goode
313. Jukebox
314. Jukebox Junky
315. Just A Bummin' Around
316. Just A Closer Walk With Thee
317. Just A Little Bit
318. Just Because
319. Just Dropped In
320. Just In Time
321. Just Who Is To Blame
322. Keep Me From Blowing Away
323. Keep Me In Mind
324. Keep My Motor Running

325. Keep On The Firing Line
326. Keep Your Hands Off Of It! (Birthday Cake)
327. King Of The Road
328. Lady Of Spain
329. Late Night Lovin' Man
330. Lawdy Miss Clawdy - C.C. Rider
331. Let A Soldier Drink
332. Let Me On
333. Let The Good Times Roll
334. Let's Have A Party
335. Let's Live A Little
336. Let's Put It Back Together Again
337. Let's Say Goodbye Like We Said Hello
338. Let's Talk About Us
339. Lewis Boogie
340. Lewis Workout
341. Life's Little Ups and Downs
342. Life's Railway To Heaven
343. Lincoln Limousine
344. Listen, They're Playing My Song
345. Little Green Valley
346. Little Queenie
347. Live and Let Live
348. Livin' Lovin' Wreck
349. Living On The Hallelujah Side
350. Lonely Weekends
351. Lonesome Fiddle Man
352. Long Gone Lonesome Blues
353. Long Tall Sally
354. Looking For A City
355. Lord, I've Tried Everything But You
356. Lord, What's Left For Me To Do
357. Lost Highway
358. Louisiana Man
359. Love Game
360. Love Inflation
361. Love Letters In The Sand
362. Love Made A Fool Of Me
363. Love For All Seasons
364. Love On Broadway
365. Lovers Honeymoon

366. Lovesick Blues
367. Lovin' Cajun Style
368. Lovin' Up A Storm
369. Lucille
370. Lust Of The Blood
371. Mama, This One's For You
372. Mama's Hands
373. Margie
374. Matchbox
375. Mathilda
376. Maybellene
377. Me and Bobby McGee
378. Me and Jesus
379. Mean Old Man
380. Mean Woman Blues
381. Meat Man
382. Meeting In The Air
383. Melancholy Baby
384. Memories
385. Memory Number One
386. Memory Of You
387. Memphis Beat
388. Memphis, Tennessee
389. Mexicali Rose
390. Middle Age Crazy
391. Milk Cow Blues
392. Milkshake Mademoiselle
393. Milwaukee Here I Come
394. Miss The Mississippi and You
395. Mississippi Kid
396. Mom and Dad's Waltz
397. Mona Lisa
398. Money (That's What I Want)
399. More and More
400. Mother, The Queen Of My Heart
401. Music! Music! Music! - Canadian Sunset
402. Music To The Man
403. My Babe
404. My Blue Heaven
405. My Bonnie
406. My Carolina Sunshine Girl

407. My Cricket and Me
408. My Fingers Do The Talkin'
409. My God Is Real
410. My God's Not Dead
411. My Mammy
412. My Only Claim To Fame
413. My Pretty Quadroon
414. Mystery Train
415. Near You
416. Never Too Old To Rock 'N' Roll
417. Night Train To Memphis
418. No Headstone On My Grave
419. No Honky Tonks In Heaven
420. No Love Have I
421. No More Hanging On
422. No More Than I Get
423. No One But Me
424. No One Knows Me
425. No One Will Ever Know
426. No Particular Place To Go
427. No Traffic Out Of Abilene
428. North To Alaska
429. Number One Lovin' Man
430. Oh Lonesome Me
431. Oklahoma Hills
432. Old Black Joe
433. Old Glory
434. Old Sweet Music (Sweet Jesus)
435. Old Time Christian
436. Old Time Religion
437. Old Time Rock and Roll
438. Ole Pal Of Yesterday
439. On The Back Row
440. On The Jericho Road
441. Once More With Feeling
442. One Has My Name
443. One Minute Past Eternity
444. One More Time
445. One Of Them Old Things
446. Only Love Can Get You In My Door
447. Only You (And You Alone)

448. Ooby Dooby
449. Out Of My Mind
450. Over The Rainbow
451. Parting Is Such Sweet Sorrow
452. Pass Me Not, O Gentle Savior
453. Peace In The Valley
454. Peach Picking Time Down In Georgia
455. Pee Wee's Place
456. Pen and Paper
457. Personality
458. Pick Me Up On Your Way Down
459. Pink Cadillac
460. Pink Pedal Pushers
461. Play Me A Song I Can Cry To
462. Please Don't Talk About Me When I'm…
463. Pledging My Love
464. Poison Love
465. Precious Memories
466. Pride Don't Mean A Thing
467. Promised Land
468. Pumping Piano Rock
469. Put Me Down
470. Ragged But Right
471. Raining In My Heart
472. Ramblin' Rose
473. Red Hot Memories (Ice Cold Beer)
474. Release Me
475. (Remember Me) I'm The One Who…
476. Restless Heart
477. Reuben James
478. Ride Me Down Easy
479. Ring Of Fire
480. Rita May
481. Rock 'N' Roll Funeral
482. Rock 'N' Roll Is Something Special
483. Rock 'N' Roll Medley
484. Rock 'N' Roll Money
485. Rock and Roll
486. Rock and Roll (Fais-Do-Do)
487. Rock and Roll Ruby
488. Rock and Roll Time

489. Rockin' Jerry Lee
490. Rockin' My Life Away
491. Rockin' The Boat Of Love
492. Rockin' With Red
493. Rocking Little Angel
494. Rocking Pneumonia and Boogie Woogie Flu
495. Roll On
496. Roll Over Beethoven
497. Room Full Of Roses
498. Sail Away
499. San Antonio Rose
500. Save The Last Dance For Me
501. Sea Cruise
502. Seasons Of My Heart
503. Secret Places
504. Send Me The Pillow You Dream On
505. Set My Mind At Ease (1962)
506. Settin' The Woods On Fire (1958)
507. Seventeen
508. Sexy Ways
509. Shake, Rattle and Roll
510. Shame On You
511. Shanty Town
512. She Even Woke Me Up To Say Goodbye
513. She Never Said Goodbye
514. She Sings Amazing Grace
515. She Still Comes Around
516. She Sure Makes Leaving Look Easy
517. She Thinks I Still Care
518. She Was My Baby (He Was My Friend)
519. She's Reachin' For My Mind
520. Shoeshine Man
521. Shotgun Man
522. Shoulder To Lean On - Make The World...
523. Shout
524. Sick and Tired
525. Silent Night
526. Silver Threads Among The Gold
527. Since I Met You Baby
528. Singing The Blues
529. Sittin' and Thinkin'

530. Sixteen Candles
531. Sixty Minute Man
532. Skid Row
533. Slippin' and Slidin'
534. Slippin' Around
535. Smoke Gets In Your Eyes
536. So Long I'm Gone
537. Softly and Tenderly
538. Someday (You'll Want Me To Want You)
539. Someone Who Cares For You
540. Sometimes A Memory Ain't Enough
541. Speak A Little Louder To Us Jesus
542. Stagger Lee
543. Stepchild
544. Sticks and Stones
545. Sunday Morning Coming Down
546. Swanee River
547. Sweet Dreams
548. Sweet Georgia Brown
549. Sweet Little Sixteen
550. Sweet Thang
551. Sweet Virginia
552. Swing Down Sweet Chariot
553. Swing Low Sweet Chariot
554. Swinging Doors
555. Take Me Out To The Ball Game
556. Take Your Time
557. Teenage Letter
558. Teenage Queen
559. Tell Tale Signs
560. Tennessee Saturday Night
561. Tennessee Waltz
562. Thanks For Nothing
563. That Kind Of Fool
564. That Lucky Old Sun
565. That Old Bourbon Street Church
566. That Was The Way It Was Then
567. That's My Desire
568. The Alcohol Of Fame
569. The Ballad Of Billy Joe
570. The Closest Thing To You

571. The Crawdad Song
572. The Fifties
573. The Fire Megamix!
574. The Gods Were Angry With Me
575. The Goodbye Of The Year
576. The Haunted House
577. The Hole He Said He'd Dig For Me
578. The House Of Blue Lights
579. The Hurtin' Part
580. The Killer
581. The Last Cheater's Waltz
582. The Last Letter
583. The Lily Of The Valley
584. The Love-In
585. The Marine's Hymn
586. The Mercy Of A Letter
587. The Morning After Baby Let Me Down
588. The Old Country Church
589. The Old Rugged Cross
590. The One Rose That's Left In My Heart
591. The Pilgrim
592. The Return Of Jerry Lee
593. The Revolutionary Man
594. The Urge
595. The Wild Side Of Life
596. There Must Be More To Love Than This
597. There Stands The Glass
598. Things
599. Things That Matter Most To Me
600. Think About It, Darlin'
601. Thirteen At The Table
602. Thirty Nine and Holding
603. This Land Is Your Land
604. This Must Be The Place
605. This Train
606. This World Is Not My Home
607. Time Changes Everything
608. To Make Love Sweeter For You
609. Today I Started Loving You Again
610. Together Again
611. Tomorrow May Mean Goodbye

612. Tomorrow Night
613. Tomorrow's Taking Baby Away
614. Too Many Rivers
615. Too Much To Gain To Lose
616. Too Weak To Fight
617. Too Young
618. Toot, Toot, Tootsie Goodbye
619. Tossin' and Turnin'
620. Touching Home
621. Travelin' Band
622. Treat Her Right
623. Trouble In Mind
624. Tupelo County Jail
625. Turn Around
626. Turn On Your Love Light
627. Turn Your Radio On
628. Tutti Frutti
629. Twenty Four Hours A Day
630. Twilight
631. Ubangi Stomp
632. Until The Day Forever Ends
633. Up On Cripple Creek
634. Waiting For A Train
635. Wake Up Little Susie
636. Walk A Mile In My Shoes
637. Walk Right In
638. Walkin' The Dog
639. Walking The Floor Over You
640. Wall Around Heaven
641. Waymore's Blues
642. We Both Know Which One Of Us…
643. We Live In Two Different Worlds
644. We Remember The King
645. We Three (My Echo, My Shadow and Me)
646. Wedding Bells
647. What A Friend We Have In Jesus
648. What A Heck Of A Mess
649. What Am I Living For
650. What Makes The Irish Heart Beat
651. What My Woman Can't Do
652. What'd I Say

653. What's Made Milwaukee Famous
654. What's So Good About Goodbye
655. When A Man Loves A Woman
656. When Baby Gets The Blues
657. When He Walks On You
658. When I Get My Wings
659. When I Get Paid
660. When I Take My Vacation In Heaven
661. When Jesus Beckons Me Home
662. When My Blue Moon Turns To Gold Again
663. When The Grass Grows Over Me
664. When The Saints Go Marching In
665. When They Ring Those Golden Bells
666. When Two Worlds Collide
667. When You Wore A Tulip and I Wore A...
668. Whenever You're Ready
669. Where He Leads Me
670. Where Would I Be
671. Whiskey River
672. White Christmas
673. Who Will The Next Fool Be
674. Who's Gonna Play This Old Piano
675. Who's Sorry Now
676. Whole Lotta Shakin' Goin' On
677. Why Don't You Love Me
678. Why Me Lord
679. Why Should I Cry Over You
680. Why You Been Gone So Long
681. Wild and Wooly Ways
682. Wild One (Real Wild Child)
683. Will The Circle Be Unbroken
684. Wine Me Up
685. Wolverton Mountain
686. Woman, Woman (Get Out Of Our Way)
687. Won't You Ride In My Little Red Wagon
688. Workin' Man Blues
689. Would You Take Another Chance On Me
690. You Are My Sunshine
691. You Belong To Me
692. You Call Everybody Darling
693. You Can Have Her
694. You Don't Miss Your Water
695. You Don't Have To Go
696. You Helped Me Up
697. You Ought To See My Mind
698. You Went Back On Your Word
699. You Went Out Of Your Way
700. You Win Again
701. (You'd Think By Now) I'd Be Over You
702. You're All Too Ugly Tonight
703. You're The Only Star (In My Blue Heaven)
704. You've Still Got A Place In My Heart
705. Young Blood
706. Your Cheatin' Heart
707. Your Loving Ways

SELECTED USA DISCOGRAPHY

* = Bootleg only, (L) = Live recording

---

[1] **A DAMN GOOD COUNTRY SONG** (1975)
(Donnie Fritts)

Recorded in June 1975 for the 'Odd Man In' album, the lyrics about pills, whisky and women, combined with an involved and world-weary vocal, made this a great choice for a single. Apart from the word "Damn" that is, enough in 1975 for radio to effectively ban the song. Consequently, it stalled at No. 68 in the US Country charts. A version with an alternate and inferior vocal was issued on a 1987 box-set, while writer Donnie Fritts recorded it himself as a duet with Waylon Jennings in 1997. Not a song that has been performed much since, rare exceptions were San Francisco in 1975 and Hollywood in 1983.

First Release: 'Odd Man In' (1975) + Single A-side (1975)

A Damn Good Country Song / When I Take My Vacation In Heaven
(No. 68 Country)

[2] **A LITTLE PEACE AND HARMONY** (1974)
(Ray Griff)

A nice enough mid-tempo Country song with old-time chord changes, it was recorded in October 1974 and issued the following year. Ray Griff recorded his own version in 1977.

First Release: 'Boogie Woogie Country Man' (1975)

[3a] **A PICTURE FROM LIFE'S OTHER SIDE** (1970)
(Traditional)

'A Picture From Life's Other Side' was first released on record by Smith's Sacred Singers in 1926, though Jerry probably knew it via Hank Williams' 1951 single. He first recorded it for a December 1970 session In Memphis, where the song is played at a breakneck speed that doesn't suit it at all.

First Release: 'The Killer: 1969-1972' (box-set, 1986)

[3b] A PICTURE FROM LIFE'S OTHER SIDE (1974)

Performed in ¾ 'waltz' time, this is one of two songs recorded at a February 1974 session for the 'I-40 Country' album. It shows too, as his voice is noticeably rougher than on the July 1973 sessions that provided most of the other songs for the album (Jerry had voice problems for much of 1974-1975, largely due to a sinus problem that was corrected in early 1976). The song was performed very occasionally in later years, including Copenhagen 1978, Hollywood 1979, Rotterdam 1981 and Nottingham 1983.

First Release: 'I-40 Country' (1974)

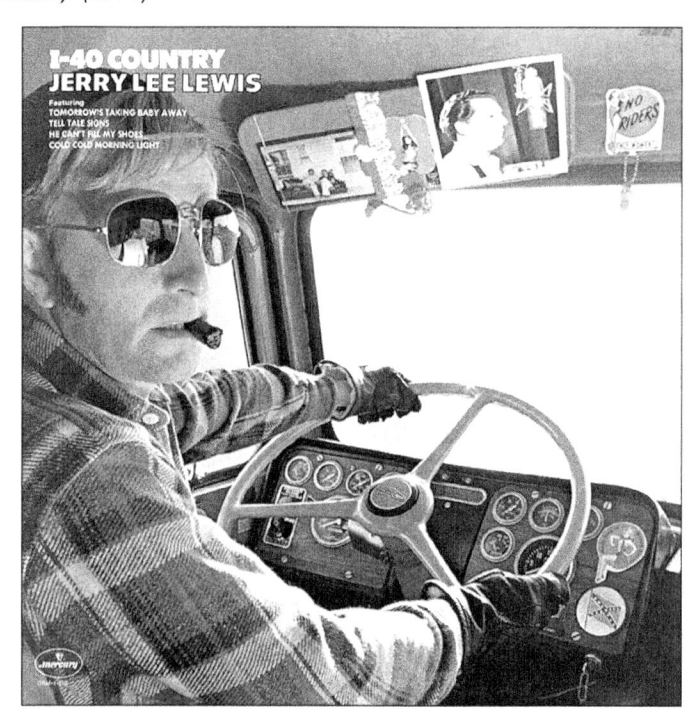

'I-40 Country' (1974)

[4] AFTER THE FOOL YOU'VE MADE OF ME (1975)
(Jerry Foster / Bill Rice)

A mid-tempo Country-Pop song from the appropriately-named 'Country Class', this was recorded in December 1975. Interestingly, along with the 4 songs from the session that were all (eventually) released, Jerry recorded a song called 'I Love It (When You Love All Over Me)', which was wiped the same day. Presumably someone was *very* displeased with it!

First Release: 'Country Class' (1976)

[5] ALABAMA JUBILEE (1979)
(George Cobb / Jack Yellen)

First recorded by Collins and Harlan in 1915, 'Alabama Jubilee' is one of three songs on 1980's 'When Two Worlds Collide' that was given a 'Country-Dixieland' treatment, complete with banjo, fiddle, trumpet, trombone and clarinet. Featuring numerous piano solos in a variety of styles, it is amongst the very highlights, not only of his tenure with Elektra, but of his whole recorded output. It was performed live in Cardiff in 1983.

First Release: 'When Two Worlds Collide' (1979)

[6] ALL NIGHT LONG [1] (1957)
(Traditional)

Jerry actually recorded two, entirely different, songs called 'All Night Long'. This first one is of unknown origin, recorded at Sun circa February 1957, which successfully combines a boogie woogie rhythm with the kind of lyrical detail that Chuck Berry excelled at.

First Release: 'Rockin' & Free' (1974)

[7] ALL NIGHT LONG [2] (1969)
(Don Chapel)

Recorded in April 1968, and included on Jerry's 'Country comeback' album 'Another Place, Another Time', 'All Night Long' [2] was also recorded by writer Don Chapel's then-wife Tammy Wynette around the same time. Beautifully sung and played, Jerry surprised the audience in Augusta, Maine in 1985 by performing a word-and-note-perfect version, the only known performance of the song live.

First Release: 'Another Place, Another Time' (1968)

[8] ALL OVER HELL AND HALF OF GEORGIA (1973)
(Charlie Daniels)

Following the 'All Star' London sessions in January 1973, a similar experiment was conducted in Memphis in the September of that year, this time with such southern luminaries as Steve Cropper, Donald 'Duck' Dunn, Al Jackson, Carl Perkins, Tony Joe White, Augie Meyers and The Memphis Horns. Musically more adventurous than 'The Session', the end results were more mixed thanks to a combination of hard partying and material that sometimes took Jerry too far out of his comfort zone. Ten songs were released as 'Southern Roots', while enough to fill a 2nd album remained unreleased until the mid-'80s - including this one, Charlie Daniels' 'All Over Hell and Half Of Georgia'. A pounding Country-Rocker, lines such as *"Well, its heaven raisin' hell just me and Charlotte!"* and *"Jerry Lee's a rockin' mother-humper!"* clearly weren't on the original lyric sheet (the 'Charlotte' is Charlotte Bumpus, his girlfriend at the time). A hell of a lot of fun, but it wasn't deemed releasable and finally surfaced 14 years later.

First Release: 'The Killer: 1973-1977' (box-set, 1987)

[9] **ALL THE GOOD IS GONE** (1968)
(Dottie Bruce / Norris 'Norro' Wilson)

Recorded at the same January 1968 session that produced his big Country comeback hit 'Another Place, Another Time', this song is just as memorable, and if anything is even better. Never a concert regular, he did perform it in Chatham in 1972. Joe Stampley covered the song in 1970.

First Release: 'Another Place, Another Time' (1968) + Single B-side (1968)

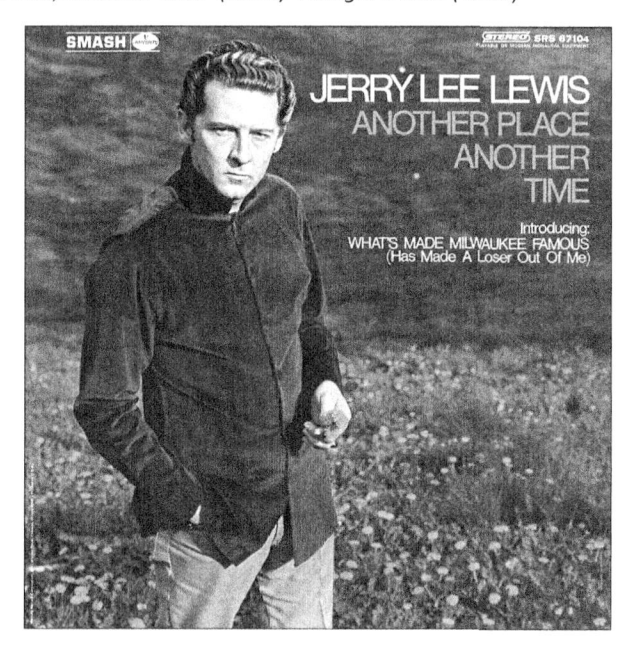

'Another Place, Another Time' (1968)

[10] **ALL-STAR JAM** [with B.B. King, Fats Domino, Little Richard, Ray Charles, Bo Diddley and James Brown] (1988) (L)
(B.B. King / Antoine Domino / Jerry Lee Lewis / Richard Penniman / Ray Charles / Ellas McDaniel / James Brown)

On the 17th November 1988, a charity concert for UNICEF was held at the Sports Palace in Rome, and on the bill were Jerry Lee Lewis, Fats Domino, Little Richard, Bo Diddley, Ray Charles, B.B. King and James Brown (B.B. was brought in as a late replacement for Chuck Berry who cancelled due to illness). For the grand finale, they all got together for a 'Jam', and while it wasn't up to much musically, it was amusing watching Jerry trying to persuade Little Richard to sing Rock 'n' Roll (Richard was still going through one of his Gospel-only phases, though he would thankfully return to the devil's music the following year!). This Jam can be both seen and heard via several official VHS and DVD releases.

First Release: 'Legends of Rock 'n' Roll' (VHS, 1989)

[11] **ALVIN** (1970)
(Jerry Lee Lewis)

A rather slight song, reputedly written by The Killer, 'Alvin' was recorded in March 1970, part of 2 days of sessions that produced everything from a morbid song about a funeral to Coca Cola ads!

First Release: 'The Mercury Sessions' (1985)

[12] **AM I TO BE THE ONE** [with Charlie Rich] (1959)
(Otis Blackwell)

Original recorded by Billy 'Crash' Craddock the previous year, 'Am I To Be The One' is one of two duets Jerry recorded with Charlie Rich at Sun, an experiment that works surprisingly well. 4 takes were taped in June 1959, with the final version being the first to be issued.

First Release: 'A Taste of Country' (1970)

[13] **AMAZING GRACE** (1970) (L)
(Traditional)

In the closing weeks of 1970, two earth-shattering things greatly affected the life of Jerry Lee Lewis: Myra, his wife of 13 years, filed for divorce, and his mother Mamie was diagnosed with terminal cancer. This double-blow prompted him to give up worldly music, and *only* perform Gospel. Thankfully, he reneged on this promise within a matter of weeks, but in December Mercury taped a fascinating "performance" in a Memphis church, where Jerry played 20 Gospel songs, as well as preached. 'Amazing Grace', a song that dates back to around the 1770s, was inevitably amongst these songs. The entire show/sermon was released in 1986, something Jerry was apparently less than pleased about.

First Release: 'The Killer: 1969-1972' (box-set, 1986)

[14] **AND FOR THE FIRST TIME** (1971)
(Charlie Freeman)

Written by Jerry's former guitarist Charlie Freeman (Charlie played on 'By Request'), 'And For The First Time' is a good Country song about a child's reaction to a parent's divorce. Recorded in August 1971 during the sessions for 'Would You Take Another Chance On Me', it was inexplicably overlooked for release.

First Release: '30th Anniversary Album' (1986)

[15] **ANOTHER HAND SHAKIN' GOODBYE** (1971)
(Dallas Frazier)

Following his split from Myra, songs about lost love had an added meaning to Jerry, and 'Another Hand Shakin' Goodbye' is just one of those songs.

First Release: 'Would You Take Another Chance On Me' (1971)

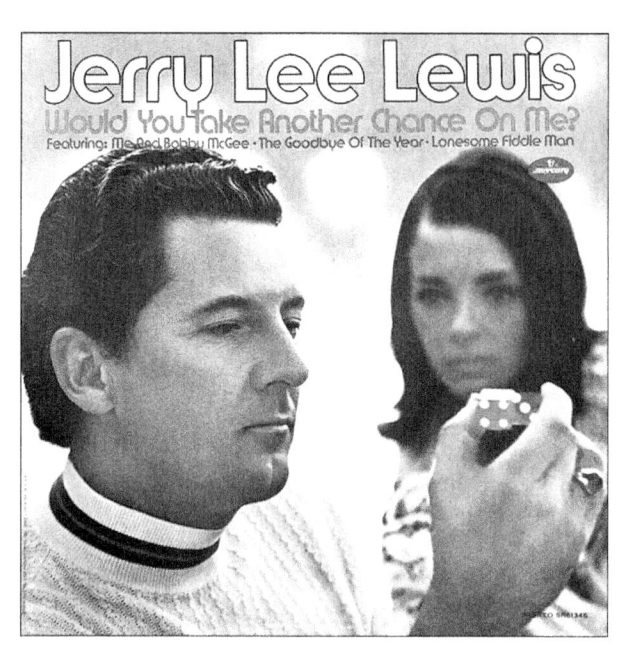

'Would You Take Another Chance On Me' (1971)

[16] **ANOTHER PLACE, ANOTHER TIME** (1968)
(Jerry Chesnut)

Jerry Lee Lewis was *always* a Country music artist, as much as a Rock 'n' Roll one. His pre-Sun Demos were Country songs; almost every Rock 'n' Roll single featured a Country flipside; he'd had a major Country hit in 1957 with 'You Win Again' (the B-side of 'Great Balls Of Fire'); and a couple of more moderate early '60s hits with 'Cold, Cold Heart' and 'Pen and Paper'. Heck, he'd even already released a very fine Country album, 1965's 'Country Songs For City Folks'. Yet, 1968 would be the year of his 'Country comeback', and it was all down to one song, 'Another Place, Another Time'. First recorded by Del Reeves in June 1967 (though released *after* Jerry's version), Jerry's January 1968 recording of this excellent modern Country song made it an almost instant success, reaching No. 4 in the US Country charts, as well as the lower reaches of the Pop charts. It also got him back on national TV for the first time in a couple of years when he performed the song on 'The Joey Bishop Show', with another performance of the song on 'Hee Haw' the following year. Most pointedly, when Jerry finally made his debut on The Grand Ole Opry in 1973, he opened the show with it. The song was still performed very occasionally well into the New Millennium, while significant covers include Arthur Alexander in 1969 and Hank Williams Jr. in 1971.

First Release: 'Another Place, Another Time' (1968) + Single A-side (1968)

Another Place, Another Time / Walking The Floor Over You
(No. 4 Country)

'Hee Haw' (1969)

[17] **ARKANSAS** (1980) *
(Traditional)

More commonly known as 'State Of Arkansas' or 'Old Arkansas', 'Arkansas' is a song whose origins are lost in the mists of time, and those who've recorded it include The Almanac Singers in 1941, Jack Elliott in 1958 and The Weavers in 1959. A bluesy song performed in a minor key, his fascinating run-through was recorded at the famed Elektra 'Caribou' sessions in November 1980, and has since surfaced on bootlegs.

First Release: 'The Caribou Ranch Sessions, 1980-1986' (2012) (bootleg)

[18] **ARKANSAS SEESAW** (1977)
(Michael Bacon / Thomas Cain)

A mid-tempo song with very little piano, 'Arkansas Seesaw' is more Pop than Country. Recorded at Jerry's final Mercury session on 15th December 1977, it is the low-light of 1978's 'Keeps Rockin''. There were far superior songs from his last few Mercury sessions that stayed in the can for nearly a decade.

First Release: 'Keeps Rockin'' (1978)

'Keeps Rockin'' (1978)

[19] **AS LONG AS I LIVE** (1960)
(Dorsey Burnette)

In late January 1960, Jerry spent several days of recording at Sam Phillips new Phillips studio in Memphis. Although he'd often be distracted by other material, the main purpose of the sessions was to record three Pop-Rockers, 'Baby, Baby Bye Bye', 'Bonnie B.' and 'As Long As I Live'. The best of the 3 songs was 'As Long As I Live', an up-tempo number that is notable for its fine piano solo and crisp drumming.

First Release: Single B-side (1961) + 'Jerry Lee's Greatest!' (1961)

[20] **AS LONG AS WE LIVE** (1977)
(Bob McDill)

Not to be confused with 'As Long As *I* Live', 'As Long As *We* Live' is an indifferent modern Country-Pop song from 'Country Memories, with piano that is almost certainly played by session man Hargus 'Pig' Robbins rather than The Killer himself.

First Release: 'Country Memories' (1977)

[21] AUTUMN LEAVES (1980) *
(Joseph Kosma / Johnny Mercer)

In June 1971, Jerry Lee Lewis - along with Linda Gail Lewis, Carl Perkins, Jackie Wilson, Bill Strom, The Rust College Quintet and The Sound Generation - taped a pilot episode for a proposed TV series. One of the more unusual things on it was Jerry performing the old standard 'Autumn Leaves', standing away from the piano, vocally superb, and backed by an orchestra. A TV series never materialized, but thankfully the Pilot survives, and was much later released on VHS and DVD. At the November 1980 'Caribou' sessions, Jerry finally tackled the song in the studio, and whilst his voice sounds nowhere near as good as it did in 1971, he more than makes up for it by contributing some amazing piano. Jerry performed lengthy versions twice on a 1987 European Tour, in Zwolle and Newport, leading to unconfirmed rumors that he'd recorded the song at a recent session. He also dusted it off one last time for his epic 3 hour 66th Birthday Show in 2001.

First Release: 'The Caribou Ranch Sessions, 1980-1986' (2012) (bootleg)

[22] BABY (YOU'VE GOT WHAT IT TAKES) [with Linda Gail Lewis] (1965)
(Murray Stein / Clyde Otis)

First recorded by Dorothy Pay in 1958, it was probably Dinah Washington and Brook Benton's 1960 hit that influenced Jerry and Linda, though George Jones and Margie Singleton's 1962 cover is another possibility. Recorded in September 1965 during the 'Country Songs For City Folks' sessions, this storming Rhythm 'n' Blues performance wasn't included on the album but instead was issued as the B-side of 'Green, Green Grass Of Home'. In 2000, Linda Gail Lewis re-recorded the song, this time duetting with Van Morrison.

First Release: Single B-side (1965)

[23] BABY WHAT YOU WANT ME TO DO (1973)
(Jimmy Reed)

In January 1973, Jerry Lee Lewis, accompanied by guitarist/fiddle player Kenny Lovelace, his son Jerry Lee Lewis junior and manager Jud Phillips, flew over to London to record an 'all-star' album. With such luminaries as Rory Gallagher, Albert Lee, Peter Frampton, Klaus Voorman, Alvin Lee and Kenny Jones in attendance, Jerry wanted to prove who's boss, and he wasn't about to embarrass himself by playing too many songs he was unfamiliar with. First recorded by Jimmy Reed in 1959, and later covered by The Everly Brothers (1960), Etta James (1963), Little Richard (1966), Elvis Presley (1968) and Carl Perkins (1969) amongst others, 'Baby What You Want Me To Do' is a powerful Blues-Rock performance that fitted nicely onto the resulting double album.

First Release: 'The Session' (1973)

[24] BABY, BABY BYE BYE (1960)
(Jerry Lee Lewis / Huey 'Piano' Smith)

A rather light-weight Pop-Rocker, 'Baby, Baby Bye Bye' would've made a pleasant enough B-side or album track. Instead, complete with an overdubbed vocal group that made it sound even weaker, it was released as a single A-side. A complete flop stateside, it did at least reach No. 47 in the UK.

First Release: Single A-side (1960)

Baby, Baby Bye Bye / Old Black Joe
(Not a hit)

[25] BABY, HOLD ME CLOSE (1965)
(Bob Tubert / Jerry Lee Lewis)

What was Jerry's greatest studio album? His 1958 debut is a fabulous collection of songs in a wide variety of styles (Sam Phillips knew exactly what he was doing when he put it together); Those 'Country Comeback' albums are magical, with the pick of 'em all probably being 'She Even Woke Me Up To Say Goodbye'; The All-Star 'The Session' and 'Southern Roots' from 1973 often inspired Jerry to new heights by taking him out of his comfort zones; That 1st Elektra album in 1979 was a sparkling return to form; and 2006's 'Last Man Standing' gave his career a major revival, becoming Jerry's highest selling album ever. But at or near the top *must* be 1965's 'The Return Of Rock'! The Beatles, The Rolling Stones, Bob Dylan and The Beach Boys may all have been exploring new horizons, but Jerry Lee Lewis was back to doing what he does best, albeit with an occasional more contemporary influence. Largely taped over three consecutive days in January 1965, the A-side of the single from the album was 'Baby, Hold Me Close'. A mid-tempo R&B song with soulful female backing vocals that was probably largely written in the studio, from the opening drum intro and Jerry's *"Now listen here baby, to what ole Jerry Lee has to say!"* you know you're in for something a bit special. Memorably performed on 'Shindig!' as well as on 'The Clay Cole Show', it sadly stalled at No. 129 in the US Pop charts. Australian group Billy Thorpe and The Aztecs covered the song later the same year.

First Release: 'The Return of Rock' (1965)

Baby, Hold Me Close / I Believe In You
(No. 129 Pop)

'Shindig!' (1965)

[26] **BAD, BAD LEROY BROWN** (1973/1974)
(Jim Croce)

Despite being signed to Mercury, Jerry cut a number of private sessions for Knox Phillips during 1973-1974. The main purpose of these seemed to be simply to have some fun, with little or no regard to commercial potential. Such is the case with Jim Croce's 1973 hit 'Bad, Bad Leroy Brown'. Clocking in at 7 minutes, and with lyrics like *"If you don't like that you can kiss my ass, and don't give me no sass!"*, it clearly wasn't something that was going to be hit material. The song finally surfaced some 4 decades later, via the fascinating 'The Knox Phillips Sessions: The Unreleased Recordings' CD.

First Release: 'The Knox Phillips Sessions: The Unreleased Recordings' (2014)

[27a] **BAD MOON RISING** [with Chas Hodges] (1973)
(John Fogerty)

The Creedence Clearwater Revival classic from 1969, this is as a duet with Chas Hodges, someone whose voice blended perfectly with Jerry's. They had known each other for years: a fan since the '50s, he'd backed Jerry on bass for a European Tour in 1963 as part of The Outlaws; he reprised the role for a 1968 concert and (aborted) TV show; was invited on stage to play during a show at London's Rainbow Theatre in 1977; and stepped in at the last moment when Jerry needed a bass player for the 1990 Wembley Country Festival. Finding major fame himself from the late '70s onwards as the singer and pianist in Chas 'n' Dave, he remained a JLL fanatic until the end - sadly passing away in 2018, this writer witnessed him a few years earlier performing several Jerry Lee Lewis songs at a Margate show, and inevitably we chatted about The Killer afterwards.

First Release: 'The Session' (1973)

Peter Checksfield with Chas Hodges (1992)

[27b] **BAD MOON RISING** [with John Fogerty] (2008-2010)

Played in a lower key than the 1973 version, this features some nice harmonies and great guitar from John Fogerty, the man who wrote it 40 years earlier.

First Release: 'Mean Old Man' (2010)

[28] **BALLAD OF FORTY DOLLARS** (1970) (L)
(Tom T. Hall)

Originally released by Tom T. Hall in 1968 and covered by Conway Twitty the following year, in Jerry's hands it is an up-tempo country-rocker with amusing lyrics.

First Release: 'Live at The International, Las Vegas' (1970)

'Live at The International, Las Vegas' (1970)

[29a] BEAUTIFUL DREAMER (1973/1974)
(Stephen Foster)

A song that dates back to 1864, this performance features somewhat bizarre spoken intros and outros by ace song-writer and drinking buddy Mack Vickery, and a half-sung half-spoken vocal by Jerry, with improvised lyrics in tribute to writer Stephen Foster. It may or may not have been meant in all sincerely, but everyone sounds far too stoned for listeners to take things seriously.

First Release: 'The Knox Phillips Sessions: The Unreleased Recordings' (2014)

[29b] BEAUTIFUL DREAMER (1986)

In September 1986, Jerry's bassist Bob Moore produced a session in Nashville, accompanied by drummer Murrey 'Buddy' Harman and guitarist/fiddler Kenny Lovelace, while on backing vocals were the legendary Jordanaires. Without a contract at the time, the 12 songs surfaced as 'Rocket' in 1988. The sprightly version of 'Beautiful Dreamer' is just fine, with The Killer in good voice and with inspired piano, despite the somewhat thin production.

First Release: 'Rocket' (1988)

[29c] BEAUTIFUL DREAMER (1987)

A rocked-up version performed alone at the piano, this re-make of 'Beautiful Dreamer' from the December 1987 Hank Cochran session would be even better if it wasn't so short.

First Release: 'At Hank Cochran's' (1995)

[30a] BE-BOP-A-LULA (1962)
(Sheriff Tex Davis / Gene Vincent)

Original recorded by Gene Vincent and His Blue Caps in 1956 and covered by The Everly Brothers in 1957, whereas the original is edgy and wild, in Jerry's hands it is cool and relaxed, albeit not without its charms. It was performed live with a similar arrangement at 'The London Rock 'n Roll Show' in Wembley Stadium in 1972.

First Release: 'Monsters' (1971)

[30b] BE-BOP-A-LULA (1973)

Gene Vincent's song is used as the basis for a *very* bluesy and *very* long jam, an experiment that is only partially successful, despite some top musicianship by all involved.

First Release: 'The Complete Session Volume Two' (1986)

[31] BECAUSE OF YOU (1987)
(Arthur Hammerstein / Dudley Wilkinson)

In December 1987, Jerry dropped by at Country legend Hank Cochran's home studio in Memphis, for a long night of cutting studio Demos. Unfortunately, for most of these, he used a very cheap-sounding electronic keyboard. 'Because Of You' is a good example: a 1951 hit for Tony Bennett, the perfunctory drumming (which sounds suspiciously like an electronic effect) can't hide just how bad that Casio keyboard sounds. The best of this session was released on a semi-official CD in 1995. One dreads to think what the worst sounds like.

First Release: 'At Hank Cochran's' (1995)

[32] BEFORE THE NEXT TEARDROP FALLS (1968)
(Venna Keith / Ben Peters)

Original recorded by Duane Dee in 1967, and quickly covered by David Houston, Dottie West and Charley Pride, 'Before The Next Teardrop Falls' is typical of many of Jerry's Country recordings from 1968-1969: sober-sounding, voice and piano as clear as a bell, and with increasingly formulaic backing. For his first London show in 6 years, Jerry shocked the audience at a London Palladium concert by opening with a subdued low-key version, while other live performances include Chatham 1972, Chase Park 1980 and Kelseyville 1994. In 1975, Freddy Fender would have a huge hit with the song produced by Huey P. Meaux, also Jerry's producer on 1973's 'Southern Roots' album.

First Release: 'Another Place, Another Time' (1968)

[33a] **BEFORE THE NIGHT IS OVER** (1977)
(Ben Peters)

An interesting pop-rocker, with a very contemporary 'Disco' beat and electric piano that is almost certainly played by Hargus 'Pig' Robbins, 'Before The Night Is Over' was a song that divided fans on first release. It was semi-forgotten until Jerry unexpectedly revived it for a show in Greenville, North Carolina in October 1983, and even more unexpectedly, it remained a concert regular for the rest of Jerry's career.

First Release: 'Keeps Rockin'' (1978)

[33b] **BEFORE THE NIGHT IS OVER** [with B. B. King] (2003-2006)

With its up-front piano, this time definitely played by The Killer, and stinging bluesy guitar licks by B.B. King, this is infinitively superior to the 1977 cut. B.B. King was one of only a handful of artists that Jerry regularly praised, and one can imagine him being genuinely thrilled with this recording.

First Release: 'Last Man Standing' (2006)

[33c] **BEFORE THE NIGHT IS OVER** (2006)

A rough 'n' ready live-in-the-studio recording, this was issued as one of several 'Last Man Standing'-era download-only tracks. Until an enterprising bootlegger collected them all together, that is.

First Release: Rhapsody (exclusive download) + 'Rock 'n' Roll Resurrection' (2007) (bootleg)

'Rock 'n' Roll Resurrection' (2007)

[34] **BEFORE THE SNOW FLIES** [with Linda Gail Lewis] (1970)
(Venda Holliday)

Although ostensibly a Linda Gail Lewis solo recording, Jerry contributes occasional harmonies as well as acoustic guitar to this 1970 single A-side. On some later compilations the song is incorrectly called 'Before The Snow *Falls*'.

First Release: Single A-side (1970)

'Before The Snow Flies' (1970)

[35] **BETTER NOT LOOK DOWN** (1982)
(Will Jennings / Joe Sample)

Original a hit for B.B. King in 1979, 'Better Not Look Down' is a Blues-Funk number that is ill-suited to Jerry. That said, the lyrics where Jerry meets The Queen and says *"Well, I'll tell you Queenie, my advice from Jerry Lee Lewis to you honey, hang it in like Gunga Din!"* are quite amusing. An alternate take is on 1991's 'Honky Tonk Rock & Roll Piano Man' CD.

First Release: 'My Fingers Do The Talkin'' (1982)

'My Fingers Do The Talkin'' (1982)

[36a] BIG BLON' BABY (1959)

(Kenny Jacobson / Rhoda Roberts)

First recorded by Ronnie Self in 1958, 'Big Blon' Baby' was clearly an attempt at recreating the magic of 'Great Balls Of Fire'. It's not a bad song, with an interesting rhythm, and made a great B-side to 'Lovin' Up A Storm'. Live performances over the years include Toronto 1967, Atlantic City 1988, Las Vegas 1989, Reno 1990, Dusseldorf 1991, Munich 1991 and Sarpsborg 1993. It was covered by Johnny Kidd and The Pirates in 1960 and Vince Taylor and the Play-Boys in 1962.

First Release: Single B-side (1959)

[36b] BIG BLON' BABY (1971)

The 1971 re-make of 'Big Blon' Baby' is faster, wilder, and totally lacking the charm of the Sun cut. Released on the 'Would You Take Another Chance On Me' album, it would've better suited the following year's 'The Killer Rocks On''.

First Release: 'Would You Take Another Chance On Me' (1971)

[37] BIG BLUE DIAMONDS (1973)
(Earl 'Kit' Carson)

Originally released by Red Perkins in 1950 and covered by Tex Ritter (1951), Earl King (1956), Little Willie John (1962) and Gene Summers (1963), Jerry's version is given a Dixieland treatment with sometimes over-intrusive brass. A rehearsal is available on the 1987 'The Killer: 1973-1977' box-set, while the only known live performance was in Oslo in 1985.

First Release: 'Southern Roots' (1973)

[38a] BIG BOSS MAN (1965)
(Luther Dixon / Al Smith)

Although not generally as highly regarded as 'The Return Of Rock', 1966's 'Memphis Beat' is still very good, and was his last studio album of mostly Rock 'n' Roll until 1972's over-blown 'The Killer Rocks On'. First recorded by Jimmy Reed in 1960 and covered by Frank Frost (1962), Conway Twitty (1963), Charlie Rich (1963) and Eddie Bond (1964), 'Big Boss Man' was cut at the May 1965 session that produced the 'Rocking Pneumonia and Boogie Woogie Flu' / 'This Must Be The Place' single. A fun vocal and loud, slightly distorted piano make it an essential listen.

First Release: 'Memphis Beat' (1966)

'Memphis Beat' (1966)

[38b] **BIG BOSS MAN** (1973)

Lacking the loose and playful vocal of the 1965 version, Jerry's 1973 re-cut is a straight-ahead Chicago Blues, complete with suitably robust-sounding harmonica. Not a song generally played live, he did perform it as part of a medley with 'High Heel Sneakers' in Zurich in 1977.

First Release: 'The Session' (1973)

[39] **BIG LEGGED WOMAN** (1958)
(Traditional)

Sam Phillips wasn't like other record Producers. Instead of just sticking to a planned 2 or 3 songs for musicians to diligently work on, he would keep the tapes rollin' whatever happened, with little or no regard to commerciality of the material. As a prime example, 'Big Legged Woman' is a slow and dirty gut-bucket blues, from its opening verses right up to the closing *"When I start drilling on you baby, you're gonna lose your night gown!"*. The song's origins are lost, but Johnny Temple's 1938 recording seems to be the earliest release, and Booker T. Laury did an authentic-sounding version for 1989's 'Great Balls Of Fire' soundtrack. Following its 1970 release, Jerry performed the song many times right into the 21st Century, but in more later years seemed embarrassed about it and declined any requests.

First Release: Single B-side (1970)

[40] **BIG TRAIN (FROM MEMPHIS)** [with Johnny Cash, Carl Perkins, Roy Orbison and Others] (1985)
(John Fogerty)

Original recorded in 1984 by John Fogerty, 'Big Train (From Memphis)' is the over-long finale to the disappointing and incorrectly-named 'Class of '55' (Jerry didn't arrive at Sun until the tail-end of 1956!). Recorded with Johnny Cash, Carl Perkins and Roy Orbison plus a host of guests that include Sam Phillips, Jack Clement, June Carter-Cash, John Fogerty, Dave Edmunds, Rick Nelson, Wynonna Judd, Naomi Judd and Marty Stuart, it's a shame they couldn't have all got together for a better song. Jerry performed the song on 1985's 'The Johnny Cash Christmas Show', alongside Johnny Cash and his son John Carter-Cash.

'The Johnny Cash Christmas Show' (1985)

[41] BILLY BOY (CHARMING BILLY) (1960)
(Johnny Preston)

For the Sun recordings in this book, recording dates for sessions have been taken from 2015's 'The Collected Works' box-set. However, there is an exception: the 'Probably early 1960' date for the session that produced 'The Wild Side Of Life', 'Billy Boy' and 'My Bonnie' has been changed to 'Probably late 1960'. The reason for this is that 'Billy Boy' was very obviously, both lyrically and musically, influenced by Johnny Preston's 'Charming Billy' - recorded by Mr. Preston on 21st June 1960, and not released until August 1960 as the B-side to 'Up In The Air' (a very minor US hit at No. 105). One of Jerry's earliest stereo recordings, for what is basically a rocked-up nursery rhyme, Jerry does a fair enough job, with some fine piano and saxophone.

First Release: 'Rural Route #1' (1972)

[42] BIRDS AND THE BEES (BOY MEETS GIRL) (1979) *
(unknown)

During Jerry Lee Lewis' brief but prolific period with Elektra for which he released the excellent albums 'Jerry Lee Lewis', 'When Two Worlds Collide' and 'Killer Country' in 1979-1980, there was much additional material recorded. His final sessions for the label in Caribou in November 1980 are well-documented thanks to bootleg releases, but for others the details are far sketchier. 'Birds and The Bees' is a good example: No-one seems completely sure who produced it, who wrote it or even what the correct title is, and it only surfaced via a bootlegged cassette shortly after it was recorded. As for the music, it's an interesting Pop song with a Mexican feel thanks to its mariachi horns, though one couldn't imagine Jerry particularly liking it.

First Release: 'Honky Tonk Stuff - A Collection Of Rare and Unreleased Recordings' (2007) (bootleg)

[43] BLACK BOTTOM STOMP [INSTRUMENTAL] (1956)
(Morton)

After jamming with Elvis Presley and Carl Perkins (but clearly *not* Johnny Cash) at the infamous 'Million Dollar Quartet' session on 4th December 1956, Jerry ran through a handful of songs unaccompanied. Amongst these was an all-too-brief instrumental, loosely based on Jelly Roll Morton's 1926 recording 'Black Bottom Stomp'.

First Release: 'The Complete Million Dollar Session' (1987)

[44] BLACK MAMA (1970)
(Jimmy Wolford)

At his best, Jerry Lee Lewis was *good*. So good in fact, that he could take something as bad as 'Black Mama', and make it sound like a masterpiece.

First Release: '30th Anniversary Album' (1986)

[45] **BLUE CHRISTMAS** (1993) (L)
(Billy Hayes / Jay W. Johnson)

In March 1993, Jerry Lee Lewis, wife Kerrie and son Lee (aka Jerry Lee Lewis III), all relocated to Dublin, Ireland, where they remained for a year. Whilst there, Jerry guested on a Christmas Special called 'In Your Eyes', where he performed 'Great Balls Of Fire' and a great version of 'Blue Christmas'. Backed by an orchestra, these two songs were officially released on a CD single by the RTE label. 'Blue Christmas' was first recorded by Doye O'Dell in 1948, and popularized by Elvis Presley in 1957. However, Jerry introduces the song by saying that he learnt it from Jim Reeves, someone who didn't release the song until 1963. He performed the song numerous times over the years, including London 1978, Wheeling 1979, Dalton 1979, Nashville 1981, Manchester 1992, Skien 1993, Bucharest 1993, Dublin 1993 and Sao Paulo 1993. Mickey Gilley recorded the song in 1981, and The Lewis 3 (Linda Gail Lewis with her daughters Annie Marie Lewis and Mary Jean Lewis) recorded it in 2006.

First Release: Blue Christmas (1993)

'In Your Eyes' (1993)

Peter Checksfield with The Lewis 3: Annie Marie, Mary Jean and Linda Gail (2004)

[46] **BLUE SUEDE SHOES** (1977)
(Carl Perkins)

Original recorded by Carl Perkins in 1955 and covered by Elvis Presley (1956), Eddie Cochran (1956), Buddy Holly (1956), Cliff Richard and The Shadows (1959), Bill Haley and His Comets (1960), Freddy Cannon (1960) and Conway Twitty (1961) amongst others, 'Blue Suede Shoes' is a song Jerry had previously recorded live in 1966 and 1970. Sadly, these fine versions were kept in the can until much later, so most fans would hear it first on 1978's patchy 'Keeps Rockin'' album. It's not terrible, but it's not particularly exciting either. The song was still occasionally performed live well into the New Millennium.

First Release: 'Keeps Rockin'' (1978)

[47] **BLUEBERRY HILL** (1973)
(Al Lewis / Vincent Rose / Larry Stock)

First recorded by Sammy Kaye in 1940 and more famously by Louis Armstrong in 1949, 'Blueberry Hill' would forever be associated with Fats Domino following his 1956 cover, and it was *his* version that influenced Elvis Presley (1957), Conway Twitty (1959), Bill Haley and His Comets (1960), Brenda Lee (1960), Chubby Checker (1961), Cliff Richard with The Shadows (1962), Little Richard (1964), The Everly Brothers (1967) and Clarence 'Frogman' Henry (1969). Jerry's version is quite interesting, with some different chord changes thrown in and Dixieland backing, but because Fats' version is so embedded in everyone's DNA, it inevitably comes off sounding 2nd best.

First Release: 'Southern Roots' (1973)

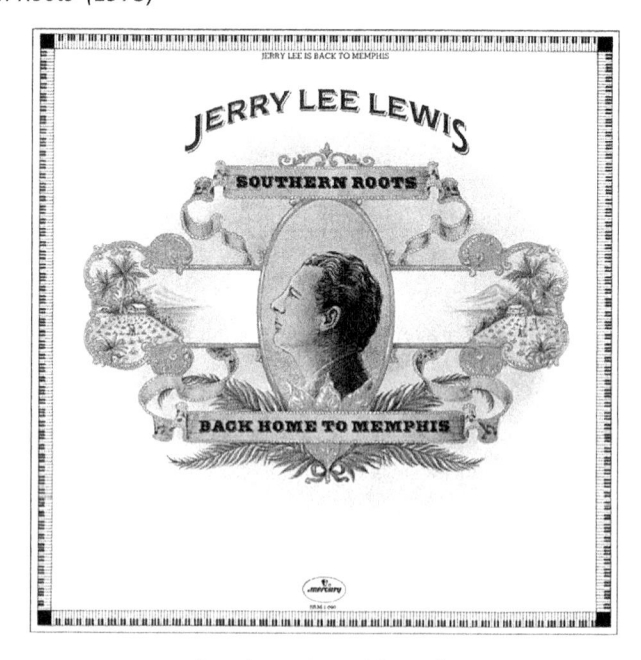

'Southern Roots' (1973)

[48] **BLUER WORDS** (1973)
(Cile Davis / Clyde Pitts)

With his usual producer Jerry Kennedy otherwise engaged, Stan Kesler was brought in for lengthy Country-orientated sessions in July 1973. A Sun luminary (he co-wrote early Elvis hits 'I'm Left, You're Right, She's Gone' and 'I Forgot To Remember To Forget'), one would've hoped he'd bring a bit of subtlety to the sessions: Instead, he used more guitarists, more backing vocalists and more string players than ever before. It was also largely a matter of quantity over quality, with the entire 'Sometimes A Memory Ain't Enough' album and all but 2 tracks for 1974's 'I-40 Country' taped over those 3 days, two albums that would never be on most fans' list of favorites. The best thing about 'Bluer Words' is a clever overdubbed 2nd vocal, where Jerry answers himself during the chorus.

First Release: 'I-40 Country' (1974)

[49] **BLUES LIKE MIDNIGHT** (2008-2010)
(Jimmie Rodgers)

'Blues Like Midnight' was first written and released as 'Blue Yodel No. 6' by Jimmie Rodgers in 1930, and later revived by Lefty Frizzell (1951), Wanda Jackson (1966) and Merle Haggard (1969). Jerry performed the song dozens of times over the years, with the earliest known performance being in Chatham in 1972, and the most recent in Mountain View, California in 2007. The excellent studio recording would be even better if guest guitarist Robbie Robertson was lower in the mix.

First Release: 'Rock & Roll Time' (2014)

[50] **BONNIE B.** (1960)
(Charles Underwood)

A slight song, known more for its 'Honky Tonk' styled guitar riff than piano, a number of rehearsal/alternate takes survive (yet there are none for such legendary songs as 'Mean Woman Blues' and 'Ubangi Stomp'!). When released in Sweden in 1964 it topped the charts there, becoming one of Jerry's best known songs in that country. *Not* that this ever persuaded Jerry to perform it whenever he played there.

First Release: Single B-side (1961)

[51] **BOOGIE WOOGIE COUNTRY MAN** (1974)
(T.J. Seals / Troy Seals)

The title track to his 1975 album of the same name, on 'Boogie Woogie Country Man' Jerry plays some excellent boogie woogie piano that's only slightly marred by the hoarse vocals and the annoying backing singers. The song remained a live favorite for the rest of his career, though after dropping the distinctive stops and starts sometime in the late '80s, it became just another 12-bar Rock 'n' Roll song. Released as a single, 'Boogie Woogie Country Man' got to a respectable No. 24 in the Country charts.

First Release: 'Boogie Woogie Country Man' (1975) + Single A-side (1975)

Boogie Woogie Country Man / I'm Still Jealous Of You
(No. 24 Country)

[52] **BORN TO BE A LOSER** (1973)
(Charles Carpenter)

'Born To Be A Loser' is a nice Country-Blues with some great ad-libs *("If I can't be your lover you good lookin' wench, let me be your friend!")*, despite the odd backing of steel guitar, horns and superfluous tambourine. Jerry performed the song at a hotel jam session in Stockholm in 1985.

First Release: 'Southern Roots' (1973)

[53a] **BORN TO LOSE** (1956)
(Frankie Brown)

A song first released by Ted Daffan's Texans in 1943, 'Born To Lose' was 1 of 4 songs he tackled at his Sun debut session on 15th November 1956. Unusually for this era, it kicks off with a Roland Janes guitar intro, while Jerry already sounds completely at ease with the musicians.

First Release: 'Rockin' and Free' (1987)

[53b] **BORN TO LOSE** (1969)

Like most late '60s re-cuts of songs Jerry first recorded at Sun's 706 Union Avenue in the '50s, this is played as a slower and straighter pure Country song, albeit beautifully sung. 'Born To Lose' got a rare live outing at a 1996 show in Indianapolis.

First Release: 'Sings The Country Music Hall of Fame Hits, Vol. One' (1969)

'Sings The Country Music Hall of Fame Hits, Vol. One' (1969)

[54] **BOTTLES AND BARSTOOLS** (1970)
(Glenn Sutton)

A classic honky tonk drinkin' song, 'Bottles and Barstools' was something Jerry liked enough to perform very occasionally, including in Hollywood 1979, San Francisco 1979, Chicago 1979, Slough 1980 and Cambridge 1987.

First Release: 'There Must Be More To Love Than This' (1970)

[55] **BOTTOM DOLLAR** (1972)
(Doug Finley / Billy Joe Shaver)

The summer of 1972 saw Jerry Lee Lewis at a bit of a musical crossroads. He'd just had major success with a return to Rock 'n' Roll with the album 'The Killer Rocks On' and the single 'Chantilly Lace'; he was continuing to have giant hits in the Country charts; and his Gospel recordings sold poorly. For the next couple years, he would continue pursuing both Rock and Country directions (and all-but-ignore Gospel), with Mercury largely keeping the two genres' releases entirely separate: It wasn't until 1975's 'Boogie Woogie Country Man' and 'Odd Man In' that the company came up with the brilliant idea of putting all of Jerry's musical ideas on one album, something Sam Phillips did in 1958! 'Bottom Dollar' is a mid-tempo song with old-time chord changes, complete with Dixieland backing and a rockin' piano solo. Songwriter Billy Joe Shaver released his own version the following year, while Jerry performed it live in Atlantic City in 1988.

First Release: 'Who's Gonna Play This Old Piano' (1972)

[56] BREAD AND BUTTER MAN (1964)
(Jimmie Loden / Richard Hollingsworth)

An excellent bluesy rocker, complete with harmonica, 'Bread and Butter Man' was released as the B-side to 'I'm On Fire'. The Nashville Teens covered the song in a much faster style in late 1964, and as they were Jerry's backing band earlier in the year when this was the flipside of his latest single, it is easy to imagine that Jerry may have performed the song live in a similar arrangement.

First Release: Single B-side (1964)

[57] BREAK MY MIND (1968)
(John D. Loudermilk)

First recorded by George Hamilton IV the previous year, 'Break My Mind' is about the closest Jerry comes to rockin' on his 1968 "comeback" album 'Another Place, Another Time', though in reality it is no more than mid-tempo Country with a heavy drum beat. Occasional performances include Attica (Indiana) 1971, Nashville 1973, Stockholm 1977, London 1977, Berlin 1977 and Houston 1987.

First Release: 'Another Place, Another Time' (1968)

[58a] BREAK UP (1958)
(Charlie Rich)

Jerry Lee Lewis always liked to give the impression that his classic Sun singles were recorded in just 1 or 2 takes, but in reality nothing can be further from the truth. 'Break Up' took more work than most, as it was taped across at least 3 (possibly 4) sessions in a variety of different arrangements, both with and without a band. The end-result was worth the effort though, becoming one of Jerry's best-loved recordings, even if it didn't do as well as hoped sales-wise. Not a song usually performed beyond the Sun era, a rare exception was during the closing show of the 1983 European Tour in Farnworth, UK, by special request of Jerry's drummer Ronnie Norwood! Ronnie happened to be hanging around at a hotel bar where long-time fan Terry Adams was playing the song on the piano, and after asking him to run-through it a couple of times, decided to try to get Jerry to play it. The song was also recorded by Ray Smith in 1958, while the song's composer Charlie Rich cut his own version in 1960.

First Release: Single A-side (1958) + 'Jerry Lee's Greatest!' (1961)

Break Up / I'll Make It All Up To You
(No. 52 US Pop / No. 85 Pop, No. 19 Country)

[58b] **BREAK UP** (1963)

When Jerry Lee Lewis signed to Smash (a subsidiary of Mercury) in September 1963 after 7 years at Sun, they quickly got him in the studio for 2 days of intense recording sessions. The main aim was to get him to re-cut his '50s hits, though around 10 other songs were recorded, and these were issued on various singles and albums from 1963 to 1967. 'Break Up' is one of the better re-cuts, and may well be the definitive version if it weren't for the annoying backing singers and tinny guitar.

First Release: 'The Golden Hits of Jerry Lee Lewis' (1964)

[59a] **BREATHLESS** (1958)

(Otis Blackwell)

A very worthy 'Great Balls Of Fire' follow-up, 'Breathless' was only slightly easier to record, with at least 9 takes over two January '58 sessions. The song inspired several covers, including Cliff Richard's 1st Demo record (1958) and Tom Jones' 1st Single B-side (1964), as well as fine versions by Mickey Gilley (1965), Chas 'n' Dave (1979), Wanda Jackson (1982) and Mike Berry (1998). As one of his of his top 3 biggest hits, casual fans might've expected the song at every concert, eh? *Wrong!* Perhaps it was the stop-start rhythm, or maybe it was a challenge to sing. Possibly Jerry just didn't like it. *Whatever* the reason, after promoting it on a handful of 1958 TV and radio shows (including 'The Dick Clark Show', 'The Phillip Morris Show' and 'American Bandstand') shortly after the record's release, live performances were few and far between, and included 'Shindig!' (1965), 'Bruce Morrow's Go-Go Show' (1965), Paris (1966), Toronto (1967), 'The Midnight Special' (1973), Sacramento (1976), Copenhagen (1977), 'Salute to Jerry Lee Lewis' (1983), Dartford (1985), Augusta, Maine (1985), Vancouver (1986), Toronto (1987) and Las Vegas (1989).

First Release: Single A-side (1958)

Breathless / Down The Line
(No. 7 Pop, No. 4 Country, No. 3 R&B)

'The Dick Clark Show' (1958)

[59b] **BREATHLESS** (1963)

Probably the best of the 1963 'Golden Hits' re-cuts, 'Breathless' has more drive than any of the Sun versions, with The Killer spitting out the lyrics like a machine gun. The over-production inevitably renders it 2nd best though. In early 1989, this writer somehow found himself sitting at a table with Jerry Lee Lewis in a London hotel, where he was doing a series of press interviews to (supposedly) promote the forthcoming 'Great Balls of Fire!' movie. Asking him a few questions, our conversation went something like this: PC: *"You recently re-recorded some of your hits for the movie, are you pleased with them?"* JLL: *"Yeah, better than the originals!"* PC: *"That's good. You previously re-recorded your hits for Smash in 1963, did you like them?"* JLL: *"Better than the originals!"* PC: *"Well, maybe 'Breathless'..."* JLL: *"'Whole Lotta Shakin'' is better too!"* PC: *"I disagree..."* JLL: *"I don't give a damn what you think, boy!"*... (I got off lighter than some: a couple of young European fans brought along Myra's book for Jerry to sign, and after writing several rather rude words on a couple of pages, he ripped them out and threw them on the floor. The book was then handed back to the fans, minus a few pages and minus any autograph!).

First Release: 'The Golden Hits of Jerry Lee Lewis' (1964)

[59c] **BREATHLESS** (1988)

A musician himself, when Dennis Quaid was cast as Jerry Lee Lewis in 'Great Balls Of Fire', he also wanted to sing and play on the movie soundtrack. Jerry was adamant that *he* should do it though, so was sent to the studio to give it his best shot - and astounded everyone with the results. 'Breathless' was never a song he was keen on and he rarely performed it live, but the re-make turned out far better than anyone had dared hope.

First Release: 'Great Balls Of Fire!' (1989) + Single B-side (1989)

[60] **BRIGHT LIGHTS, BIG CITY** (2006)
(Jimmy Reed)

First released by Jimmy Reed in 1961, Jerry's version of 'Bright Lights, Big City' is a no-nonsense mid-tempo Rhythm 'n' Blues song, with suitably gritty guitar courtesy of Neil Young. Initially a 'Last Man Standing' era download-only track, it was also included in edited form on 2014's 'Rock & Roll Time'. Jerry performed the song live at a televised 'Farm Aid' event in 2006.

First Release: Walmart (exclusive download) + 'Rock 'n' Roll Resurrection' (2007) (bootleg)

[61] **BROWN EYED HANDSOME MAN** (1969)
(Chuck Berry)

For the first time since 'The Return Of Rock' in 1965, Jerry finally cut a convincing Rock 'n' Roll performance in the studio. Originally released by Chuck Berry in 1956, and playfully ran-through at the 'Million Dollar Quartet' session, it is a song that was performed occasionally well into the '90s.

First Release: 'She Even Woke Me Up To Say Goodbye' (1970)

[62] **BURNING MEMORIES** (1969)
(Mel Tillis / Wayne Walker)

Original recorded by Ray Price in 1964 and covered by Waylon Jennings (1964), Kitty Wells (1965) and Mel Tillis (1966), 'Burning Memories' is a great Country song with a memorable chorus. It was performed in Sacramento in 1976 and Las Vegas in 1977.

First Release: 'Sings The Country Music Hall of Fame Hits, Vol. Two' (1969)

[63a] **C.C. RIDER** (1960)
(Chuck Willis / Ma Rainey / Lena Arent)

First recorded by Ma Rainey as 'See See Rider Blues' in 1925, Jerry Lee Lewis probably learnt the song via Chuck Willis' 1957 update. Clearly a favorite of his, this earliest version is performed at a sprightly pace, with Jerry's piano and slightly hoarse voice competing against some fine saxophone. From 1972 onwards, 'C.C. Rider' became a concert regular, though it was very occasional performed much earlier.

First Release: 'Rockin' Rhythm & Blues' (1969)

[63b] **C.C. RIDER** (1961)

A nice, polished take, this is marred a little by the background vocalists and handclaps.

First Release: 'The Sun Years' (Box-Set, 1983)

[63c] **C.C. RIDER** (1972)

Arguably the ultimate studio cut, complete with a memorable fiddle solo by Kenny Lovelace, something he regularly recreated on stage during the '70s and '80s. It is also one of the less over-produced tracks from 1972, despite the female backing vocalists.

First Release: 'The Killer Rocks On' (1972)

[63d] **C.C. RIDER** (1979) *

A very slow and over-long version that lasts nearly 5 minutes, this Elektra outtake was perhaps better left in the can.

First Release: 'Honky Tonk Stuff - A Collection Of Rare and Unreleased Recordings' (2007) (bootleg)

[63e] **C.C. RIDER** (1987) *

A week or so before the April 1987 European Tour, Jerry cut at least 7 songs in a session for Eddie Kilroy. These include a fine mid-tempo re-cut of 'C.C. Rider', where instead of Kenny's expected fiddle break, an unknown player contributes a nice bluesy guitar solo. Like other songs on this session, it is officially unreleased but circulates unofficially.

First Release: 'The Caribou Ranch Sessions, 1980-1986' (2012) (bootleg)

[63f] **C.C. RIDER** (2008-2010) *

With very good vocals, great piano, bluesy harmonica, and a prominent (and unknown) soulful female co-vocalist, Jerry proved that he was still more than capable of revisiting old songs and coming up with worthwhile versions.

First Release: 'Come Sundown' (2014) (bootleg)

[64] **CANDY KISSES** (1983)

(George Morgan)

Original recorded by George Morgan in 1949, this performance from Jerry's 2nd MCA album is nice but unexceptional.

First Release: 'I Am What I Am' (1984)

[65] CARELESS HANDS (1983)
(Carl Sigman / Bob Hilliard)

First recorded by Sammy Kaye in 1949 and covered by Tex Ritter the same year, 'Careless Hands' is a worthy album track, featuring some great piano plus a Kenny Lovelace guitar solo. It was performed live very occasionally during the '80s, including Toronto 1984, Worcester (Massachusetts) 1984, Zurich 1985, Hollywood 1985, Oslo 1989 and Las Vegas 1989.

First Release: 'I Am What I Am' (1984)

[66] CARRY ME BACK TO OLD VIRGINIA (1963)
(Traditional)

The last song to be recorded at his final Sun session on 28th August 1963, this rocked up and modernized interpretation of an ancient song was a perfect way to end his 7 year association with the company. Written in 1878 and first recorded by S. H. Dudley as 'Carry Me Back to Old Virginny' in 1900, it was probably Ray Charles' 1960 version that inspired Jerry. In 1965 the song was released as the A-side of his final single on the original Sun label, 2 years after he'd signed with Smash records, and was performed live at the 66th birthday show in Memphis in 2001.

First Release: Single A-side (1965)

Carry Me Back To Old Virginia / I Know What It Means
(Not a hit)

[67] CHANGE PLACES WITH ME (1980)
(David Wilkins / Maria A. Kilroy)

A superior mid-tempo Country song with excellent lyrics *("You think I've got it made friend, well let me show you where you're wrong!")*, Jerry clearly sings and plays from the heart, which makes it all the more surprising that the song never made it to the concert stage.

First Release: 'Killer Country' (1980) + Single B-side (1981)

[68] CHANGING MOUNTAINS (1986)
(Bob Moore)

Producer and bassist Bob Moore isn't someone who was known for his songwriting skills, but he contributed a nice Gospel ballad to the September 1986 sessions. Jerry sings and plays well, the bass and drums are unobtrusive, and the Jordanaires sound as good as they did on Elvis Presley's '50s ballads.

First Release: 'Rocket' (1988)

[69] CHANTILLY LACE (1972)
(Jiles Perry Richardson)

After 3 years of huge Country hits, by 1972 it was time for Jerry Lee Lewis to get back to Rock 'n' Roll. He'd been dabbling with the genre on record with 'Brown Eyed Handsome Man' and re-cuts of 'Let's Talk About Us' and 'Big Blon' Baby', and of course he'd never ever stopped performing Rock 'n' Roll live, his brief commitment to Gospel aside. The problem is, Jerry Kennedy was still at the helm, and his approach was the same as on Jerry Lee's more recent Country hits, cramming in as many musicians and backing singers as possible. Recorded complete with a string section live in the studio (none of the usual overdubs), a half-remembered version of The Big Bopper's 1958 classic didn't seem like the best way of getting Jerry back in the Pop charts. Yet it somehow worked despite of everything, getting to No. 43 in the US Pop charts, topping the US Country charts, and giving him his first UK hit in 9 years. He performed the song many times well into the 21st Century, but probably the most memorable was for the UK's 'Old Grey Whistle Test' TV show in 1972, where he even used a telephone as a prop.

First Release: 'The Killer Rocks On' (1972) + Double-A-side Single (1972)

Chantilly Lace / Think About It Darlin'
(No. 43 Pop, No. 1 Country / No. 1 Country)

'The Old Grey Whistle Test' (1972)

[70] **CHEATER PRETEND** [with Linda Gail Lewis] (1970)
(Thomas LaVerne / Bill Taylor)

A nice duet, 'Cheater Pretend' is as good as most tracks on the previous year's 'Together'. The probable reason for its lack of release though is a quite audible mistake on the piano, something *extremely* unusual for Jerry (this can be heard a few seconds after the one minute mark).

First Release: 'The Mercury Sessions' (1985)

[71] **CHILDREN GO WHERE I SEND THEE** [with Johnny Cash, June Carter-Cash, Carl Perkins and Roy Orbison] (1977) (L)
(Traditional)

For 1977's 'The Johnny Cash Christmas Show' taped just 2 months after Elvis' death, Johnny invited his old Sun colleagues Jerry Lee Lewis, Carl Perkins and Roy Orbison onto the show, where they got together to perform a few Gospel numbers. First recorded by Dennis Crumpton and Robert Summers in 1936, 'Children Go Where I Send Thee' is a song where they're clearly having a ball. The quartet would get together again in 1985 to record the 'Class of '55' album, something that is generally far less fun.

First Release: 'Johnny Cash - Christmas Special 1977' (DVD, 2008)

[72] **CIRCUMSTANTIAL EVIDENCE** (1982)
(Fred Koller)

A slightly silly Pop-Rock song with vaguely amusing lyrics, Jerry liked the song enough to perform it live a few times, including New York in 1983, Worcester in 1984 and Skien in 1989. An alternate take was released on the 1991 'Honky Tonk Rock & Roll Piano Man' CD.

First Release: 'My Fingers Do The Talkin'' (1982) + Single B-side (1983)

[73] **CITY LIGHTS** (1965)
(Bill Anderson)

Just as Jerry had been releasing Country singles long before his much-heralded 'Country Comeback' in 1968, he also released a Country album earlier, with 1965's excellent 'Country Songs For City Folks'. The only real difference is that he kept away from 'hillbilly' instrumentation like fiddle and steel guitar in 1965, something he would fully embrace in 1968. Recorded during 3 days of sessions from 30th August to 1st September, Bill Anderson's 1958 hit 'City Lights' is a highlight, with Jerry in excellent voice. He performed a powerful version in Lausanne (Switzerland) in 1966, with other live performances including Toronto 1967, Paris 1977 and Las Vegas 1989.

First Release: 'Country Songs For City Folks' (1965)

'Country Songs for City Folks' (1965)

[74a] **COLD, COLD HEART** (1958)
(Hank Williams)

A much-covered song first recorded by Hank Williams in 1951, Jerry first attempted 'Cold, Cold Heart' in the studio during a January 1958 session where he also recorded 'Breathless'. With a very slow tempo, it was probably an attempt to recreate the magic of 'You Win Again', but whereas that sounds majestic, this just sounds like its dragging.

First Release: 'The Sun Years' (Box-Set, 1983)

[74b] **COLD, COLD HEART** (1961)

Recorded in Nashville with the city's finest session men, this time the tempo is just right, and the musicians know exactly what they're doing - and check out that piano solo! It got to No. 22 in the Country charts, quite an achievement during the 1959-1967 'wilderness years'.

First Release: Single A-side (1961) + 'Jerry Lee's Greatest!' (1961)

Cold, Cold Heart / It Won't Happen With Me
(No. 22 Country)

[74c] **COLD, COLD HEART** (1969)

Recorded 8 years after the previous version, albeit with some of the same session men, this version has a looser, almost Jazzy vocal, but the 1961 single has a far superior mix. Not the easiest of songs to sing, he occasionally performed it live well into the '90s.

First Release: 'Sings The Country Music Hall of Fame Hits, Vol. Two' (1969)

[75] **COLD, COLD MORNING LIGHT** (1973)

(Thomas LaVerne / Bill Taylor)

'Cold, Cold Morning Light' kicks off with an intro that sounds very much like 'What's Made Milwaukee Famous', but this is as good as it gets. File under 'mediocre'.

First Release: 'I-40 Country' (1974) + Single B-side (1974)

[76] **COME AS YOU WERE** (1982)

(Paul Craft)

First recorded by Joe Stampley in 1980 and covered by Johnny Lee in 1982, 'Come As You Were' is a melodic Country-Pop song with electric piano, almost certainly played by session man Shane Keister. Released as a single, it deserved better than its No. 66 chart placing.

First Release: 'My Fingers Do The Talkin'' (1982) + Single A-side (1983)

Come As You Were / Circumstantial Evidence
(No. 66 Country)

[77] **COME ON IN** (1977)
(Bobby Braddock)

A superb Country-Pop song with a dramatic minor key bridge and electric piano played by Hargus 'Pig' Robbins, it got to No. 10 in the Country charts. 'Come On In' was performed live occasionally into the early '80s, most notably several times on the 1983 European Tour.

First Release: 'Country Memories' (1977) + Single A-side (1977)

Come On In / Who's Sorry Now
(No. 10 Country)

[78] **COME SUNDOWN** (2008-2010) *
(Kris Kristofferson)

Original recorded by Bobby Bare in 1970, 'Come Sundown' was also covered by Bill Anderson (1971), Roy Drusky (1971) and George Jones (1974), while Kris Kristofferson released his own version in 1979. Jerry's relaxed mid-pace version hasn't been officially released (yet), but is the title track of a popular bootleg.

First Release: 'Come Sundown' (2014) (bootleg)

[79] **COME WHAT MAY** (1958)
(Franklin Tableporter)

First recorded by Al Casey in 1957 and covered by Etta James in 1957 and Clyde McPhatter in 1958, Jerry's solo (without a band) performance is a delight. He often told the story about how Elvis Presley requested him to run through the song several times on an unnamed date, only for Elvis to record it himself - something he did indeed do in 1966. Jerry went on to play the song at a couple of private 'hotel sessions' in Stockholm in 1985, and Cambridge in 1987.

First Release: 'Rockin' and Free' (1974)

[80a] **COMIN' BACK FOR MORE** (1971)
(Ray Griff)

A beautifully-sung Country song, it was clearly a favorite of Jerry's, as he performed the song fairly often right into the New Millennium, even opening a show in Hull with it in 1972.

First Release: 'Touching Home' (1971)

[80b] **COMIN' BACK FOR MORE** (1979) *

Longer and slower, this slightly pointless re-make is nowhere near as good as the earlier version.

First Release: 'Honky Tonk Stuff - A Collection Of Rare and Unreleased Recordings' (2007) (bootleg)

[81a] **CORRINE, CORRINA** (1965)
(Bo Chatmon / Mitchell Parish / J. Mayo Williams)

A song whose origins date back to at least Charlie McCoy and Bo Chatman in 1929, amongst those who recorded it later are Big Joe Turner (1956), Johnny Carroll (1956), Bill Haley and His Comets (1958), Ray Peterson (1960) and Lloyd Price (1961). A fast rocker with impressive piano and expressive vocals, it is one of several superb tracks on 1965's 'The Return Of Rock'. Live performances include Memphis 1974, Bergen 1978, Dendermonde 1987 and Pasadena 1987.

First Release: 'The Return of Rock' (1965)

'The Return of Rock' (1965)

[81b] **CORRINE, CORRINA** (1977)

Faster, and with backing that includes fiddle, this would've made a great addition to the 'Keeps Rockin'' album. It's certainly superior to 'Arkansas Seesaw'!

First Release: 'The Mercury Sessions' (1985)

[82] **COUNTRY MEMORIES** (1977)
(Jerry Foster / Bill Rice)

A wonderful up-tempo Country song with old-time chord changes, 'Country Memories' is enhanced even further by some lovely Dixieland backing. It is a song that was played live occasionally until around 1989, and was a show highlight whenever it was performed.

First Release: 'Country Memories' (1977)

[83] **COUPLE MORE YEARS** [with Willie Nelson] (2003-2006)
(Dennis Locorriere / Shel Silverstein)

Originally released by Dr. Hook in 1976 and covered by both Waylon Jennings and Willie Nelson soon afterwards, 'Couple More Years' is a duet with the latter. Jerry and Willie duet with feeling and sensitivity, even if their 'harmonies' are a bit out! They performed the song together at the 'Last Man Standing Live' taping, but this ended up on the cutting room floor, while Jerry played the song solo for 2006's 'IMUS In The Morning' TV show, as well as in both Anaheim and Durant later in the year.

First Release: 'Last Man Standing' (2006)

[84a] CRAZY ARMS (1956)

(Ralph Mooney / Chuck Seals)

By 1956, Jerry Lee Lewis had already cut a couple of solo Demos alone at the piano. Now, for the A-side of his first single proper, he added just one musician, magical drummer Jimmy Van Eaton (well, almost: Billy Lee Riley returned from the bathroom towards the end of the take, and thinking it was just a rehearsal, picked up a guitar and strummed just one off-key chord right at the very end of the song). Yet the sound is full, with both musicians fully complimenting each other, knowing instinctively what to play and what to leave out. Originally released by Kenny Brown and Marilyn Kaye earlier in the year, it was Ray Price's cover that Jerry would've been familiar with, but just like Elvis Presley with his ground-breaking Sun recordings 2 years earlier, he created something new and exciting. Recorded on the 14th November and released as a single 2 weeks later, the record was not a hit, but it got him noticed, and Jerry always spoke fondly of the song. Never a concert regular, it was performed very occasionally well into the New Millennium.

First Release: Single A-side (1956) + 'Jerry Lee Lewis' (1958)

Crazy Arms / End Of The Road
(Not a hit)

[84b] CRAZY ARMS (1958)

During a mid-1958 solo session without a band, Jerry included a playful version of his debut A-side, probably just for his own amusement.

First Release: 'The Sun Years' (box-set, 1983)

[84c] CRAZY ARMS (1963)

On this 1963 Smash re-cut, Jerry's voice and playing sound just fine. It's a shame about the "ooh-ing" backing singers, the horns, and the thin, tinny guitar though!

First Release: 'The Golden Hits of Jerry Lee Lewis' (1964)

[84d] **CRAZY ARMS** (1965)

For his very first Country album, Jerry did the unexpected: a fast Rock 'n' Roll version, complete with honking saxophone. It somehow works too!

First Release: 'Country Songs For City Folks' (1965)

[84e] **CRAZY ARMS** [with Dennis Quaid] (1988)

For the 'Great Balls of Fire' Movie Soundtrack album (though *not* the actual movie), Dennis Quaid overdubbed 'Crazy Arms', making it an ill-fitting duet. The un-dubbed version is on 1991's intriguing 'The Killer's Private Stash' bootleg.

First Release: 'Great Balls Of Fire!' (1989)

'Great Balls of Fire!' (1989)

[85] **CRAZY HEART** (1958)
(Maurice Murray / Fred Rose)

At the March 1958 session that produced the classic single cut of 'High School Confidential', Jerry and the band attempted 5 takes of Hank Williams' 1951 song 'Crazy Heart'. While all are more than listenable, Jerry sounds a tad uncomfortable singing in a key that is a perhaps a little too high for him. When cutting a 'solo' version at a session a few months later, he took the song down a couple of notches, and sounds far more at ease.

First Release: 'Rockin' and Free' (1974)

[86] CRAZY LIKE ME (2008-2010) *
(Dennis Morgan / Shawn Camp / Billy Burnette)

A fast Country-Rock song with interesting lyrics, Jerry's lengthy version sounds like a rehearsal, and doesn't feature piano. It clearly needed more work to make it releasable, but can be found on the 'Come Sundown' bootleg. The song was later recorded by Willie Nelson in 2014 and by the song's co-composer Billy Burnette in 2017.

First Release: 'Come Sundown' (2014) (bootleg)

[87] CROWN VICTORIA CUSTOM '51 (1994)
(Andy Paley / Jerry Lee Lewis / James Burton / Kenny Lovelace)

Although still touring to wide acclaim and often appearing on TV, by the mid-'90s Jerry's career as a recording artist was considered by most to be over: It had been 10 years since he'd last had a long-term contract, and his last new studio recording ('It Was The Whiskey Talkin' (Not Me)') had been buried on a soundtrack album for a Madonna movie in 1990. Still, the producer of that session Andy Paley persevered, eventually recording Jerry in 1994 for what turned out to be 1995's 'Young Blood' album. On paper at least, the album had everything: A dream mixture of songs from Jerry's youth combined with a couple of excellent new songs, sympathetic backing from top session men without over-doing things (the string players and backing vocalists stayed at home), and Jerry on fine musical form, both vocally and in his playing. Yet, it is now strangely overlooked. Perhaps it was the odd-sounding Mono-only mixing? Or maybe it was the fact that Jerry himself gave it very little promotion, not bothering to perform the songs live? For listeners though, despite some reservations about the sound quality, 'Young Blood' was Jerry Lee Lewis' last consistently great album from start to finish. Written in the studio, 'Crown Victoria Custom '51' is a fine nostalgic Rock 'n' Roll song, with everyone playing well. That murky mix is *horrible* though!

First Release: 'Young Blood' (1995) + Single B-side (1995)

[88] CRY (1973)
(Churchill Kohlman)

Original recorded by Ruth Casey in 1951, and more successfully covered by Johnnie Ray the same year, others who recorded the song include Sam Cooke (1960), Roy Orbison (1960), Brenda Lee (1961), Timi Yuro (1961), Jackie Wilson (1961) and Ray Charles (1964). Jerry's version is fine, and thankfully features more restrained backing than some of the songs from the 'Southern Roots' sessions. It was finally released in 1987, as was an instrumental rehearsal of the song. Rumored to have been re-cut for 'Last Man Standing', at the 'Last Man Standing Live' filming, Jerry performed 4 takes of the song as a duet with Chris Isaak, with one of them ending up on the essential DVD of the event.

First Release: 'The Killer: 1973-1977' (box-set, 1987)

[89a] **CRYIN' TIME** (1966) (L)
(Buck Owens)

On the 'By Request (More of The Greatest Live Show on Earth)' album, taped in Fort Worth in 1966, one of the highlights is a performance of 'Cryin' Time', a Buck Owens song from 1964 that was popularized by Ray Charles the following year. The album itself, though thinly recorded and poorly edited, is far better than its usually given credit for, even if it doesn't quite match the excitement of 1964's 'Live at The Star Club, Hamburg' and 'The Greatest Live Show on Earth'.

First Release: 'By Request (More of The Greatest Live Show on Earth)' (1966)

'By Request (More of The Greatest Live Show on Earth)' (1966)

[89b] **CRYIN' TIME** [with Linda Gail Lewis] (1969)

A relaxed but enjoyable duet, Jerry and Linda had been performing the song together since at least a Toronto concert in October 1967. The song was performed live (without Linda) in Connecticut in 1994.

First Release: 'Together' (1969)

[90] **DANNY BOY** (1965)
(Frederick Edward Weatherly)

First recorded by Ernestine Schumann-Heink in 1918, later covers include Sam Cooke (1958), Frankie Ford (1959), Conway Twitty (1959), Johnny Preston (1960), Jim Reeves (1961), Johnny Cash (1965) and Jackie Wilson (1965). Jerry's superb version was only available on an early '70's bootleg for many years, finally getting an official release in 1986. He very occasionally performed the song live, including Toronto (1967), 'The Many Sounds of Jerry Lee' (1969), Hull (slow and fast, 1972), Coventry (ditto, 1972) and Birmingham, Alabama in 1974. He also backed Conway Twitty on the song, for the 'Conway Twitty On The Mississippi' TV special in 1982.

First Release: 'The Killer: 1963-1968' (box-set, 1986)

[91] **DAUGHTERS OF DIXIE** (1982)
(Clark / Zerface)

When songs from the patchy 1982-1984 MCA albums 'My Fingers Do The Talkin'' and 'I Am What I Am' were reissued (and sometimes remixed) along with bonus material for a couple of CDs in 1991/1992, one of the very highlights were two takes of a previously unknown song called 'Daughters Of Dixie'. A mid-tempo Country-Rocker with lyrics like *"There's something extra special in the kisses of the Daughters of Dixie!"*, one could easily imagine the song going down a storm in the Southern states, but sadly Jerry quickly forgot the song and almost certainly never performed it live.

First Release: 'Honky Tonk Rock & Roll Piano Man' (1991)

[92] **DEAD FLOWERS** [with Mick Jagger] (2008-2010)
(Mick Jagger / Keith Richards)

A druggy Country Rock song, first recorded by The Rolling Stones in 1971, Jerry's laid-back version features otherwise fine overdubbed Mick Jagger harmonies that don't quite gel. An interesting experiment that is only partially a success.

First Release: 'Mean Old Man' (2010)

[93] **DEEP ELEM BLUES** (1956)
(Traditional)

Original released by The Lone Star Cowboys in 1933 (and possibly influenced by The Wilburn Brothers' 1956 single), two storming takes were recorded at an undated late 1956 session. Unusually featuring Roland playing his guitar solo *before* Jerry's piano solo, take 2 was issued in 1970. Occasional performances include Paris 1977, Long Beach 1978, Paris 1992 and Jerry's 66th Birthday concert in Memphis in 2001.

First Release: First Release: 'Ole Tyme Country Music' (1970)

[94] DETROIT CITY (1965)
(Danny Dill / Mel Tillis)

First recorded by Billy Grammer (as 'I Wanna Go Home') in 1962, Bobby Bare's 1963 cover was probably Jerry's inspiration. With its classic guitar riff and heartfelt vocals about loneliness in the big city, 'Detroit City' is one of the outstanding songs on his first Country-orientated album. JLL fanatic Tom Jones thought so too, covering the song, as well as 'Green, Green Grass Of Home', and having a big hit with it in 1967 - the same year that both Carl Perkins and Solomon Burke also did worthy covers. Jerry performed the song in Ipswich, Peterborough (the show's opening number), Brussels and Slough in 1972, in Berlin, Vienna, Munich, Hamburg, Bremen, Essen and Munich in 1977, and in Nashville in 1979.

First Release: 'Country Songs For City Folks' (1965)

[95] DIXIE [INSTRUMENTAL] (1956)
(Traditional)

Written in 1859, and first recorded by Geo J. Gaskin in 1896, 'Dixie' has long been *the* Southern anthem, and much loved by '70s British Rock 'n' Roll / Rockabilly fans who also took the Confederate flag to its collective heart. Jerry's instrumental is *almost* up there with Duane Eddy 1961 cut as the definitive version of the song.

First Release: 'Jerry Lee Lewis and His Pumping Piano' (1974)

[96] DON'T BE ASHAMED OF YOUR AGE [with George Jones] (2003-2006)
(Cindy Walker / Bob Wills)

Originally released by Cindy Walker in 1947 and covered by Bob Wills and His Texas Playboys (1949) and Ernest Tubb and Red Foley (1949), 'Don't Be Ashamed Of Your Age' is great fun! This author got an "exclusive" on this, during a time when the 'Last Man Standing' sessions were cloaked in extreme secrecy: having the great honor of chatting to Jerry's original Sun guitarist Roland Janes at the Phillips Studio in Memphis in 2005, he mentioned that he'd last seen Jerry just a couple of nights previously, when he dropped by with George Jones to do a vocal overdub. The Killer had previously performed the song live with Mickey Gilley for a couple of TV shows in 1978 and 1980.

First Release: 'Last Man Standing' (2006)

[97a] DON'T BE CRUEL (1958)
(Otis Blackwell / Elvis Presley)

In February 1958, Jerry got together at 706 Union Avenue with just a bassist and a drummer to record a session that mostly consisted of songs associated with Elvis Presley - including 'Don't Be Cruel', arguably the finest *ever* cover of an Elvis song. Sam Phillips was so impressed he chose it as the opening track on Jerry's debut album.

First Release: 'Jerry Lee Lewis' (1958)

'Jerry Lee Lewis' (1958)

[97b] DON'T BE CRUEL (1972)

From the sublime to the ridiculous. Whereas Jerry's Sun cut is remarkable for working so well because he didn't *need* many musicians, the Mercury cut fails thanks to having *four* guitarists, *six* backing singers and a cast of *dozens* on strings! A real shame, because underneath it all it's not bad at all, if a bit on the fast side. Only rarely performed during the '60s (Keanesburg 1962, Toronto 1967 and Toronto 1969 are 3 examples), it was played most nights on the 1972 European Tour, and much more occasionally until around 2001.

First Release: 'The Killer Rocks On' (1972)

[98] DON'T BOOGIE WOOGIE (WHEN YOU SAY YOUR PRAYERS TONIGHT) (1974)
(Layng Martine Jr.)

Originally released by Ray Stevens in 1974, this quasi-boogie-woogie with humorous lyrics almost certainly features Hargus 'Pig' Robbins playing piano instead of The Killer. Consequently, Jerry never bothered learning it properly, despite it being a minor Country hit, though he did struggle through part of it in Hamburg in 1977.

First Release: 'Odd Man In' (1975) + Single A-side (1975)

Don't Boogie Woogie / That Kind Of Fool
(No. 58 Country)

[99] DON'T DROP IT (1960)
(Terry Fell)

First recorded by Terry Fell and The Fellers in 1954, it is almost certainly Wilbert Harrison's superior cover that influenced Jerry's version. Even *he* couldn't do a great deal with such a mediocre song though.

First Release: 'Don't Drop It!' (1988)

[100a] DON'T LET GO (1965)
(Jesse Stone)

Originally released by Roy Hamilton in 1957 and covered by Clyde McPhatter (1962), Dorsey Burnette (1962) and Gene Simmons (1964), Jerry's playful version of 'Don't Let Go' is marred by the insistent guitar and the relative lack of piano. Consequently, it is one of the weaker tracks on 'The Return Of Rock'.

First Release: 'The Return of Rock' (1965)

[100b] DON'T LET GO (1979)

After years of increasingly bland and formulaic production, for Jerry 1st album on Elektra, it was all change: a new producer, Bones Howe; top session players such as James Burton on guitar and Hal Blaine on drums; and a new location, Filmways-Heider Recording, in Hollywood. The end result was a crisp, tight album, where nearly every song mattered. The opening number was a re-cut of 'Don't Let Go', which benefits greatly from the new approach, even if, as with the 1965 version, there are no piano or guitar solos. Jerry performed the song at least once, at a 1979 show in Nashville.

First Release: 'Jerry Lee Lewis' (1979)

[101] **DON'T LET ME CROSS OVER** [with Linda Gail Lewis] (1969)
(Joe Penny)

Originally released by Carl Butler in 1962, other covers include Skeeter Davis (1963), Jim Reeves (1963), Wanda Jackson (1964), Carl Smith (1965), Roy Drusky and Priscilla Mitchell (1965) and George Jones (1966). Performed in waltz-time, Jerry and Linda do a wonderful job, and it deservedly became their most successful duet, peaking at No. 9 in the Country charts. They did a great live version for 'The Mike Douglas Show' in 1969, but otherwise Jerry largely avoided the song: In Newport (Wales) in 1987, this author requested the song, only for Jerry to respond by saying *"'Don't Let Me Cross Over' is a hillbilly piece of crap!"*, and performed 'Roll Over Beethoven' instead! Jerry (and Linda) did later relent though, playing the song at a hotel 'jam session' in Sarpsborg, Norway in 1993.

First Release: 'Together' (1969) + Single A-side (1969)

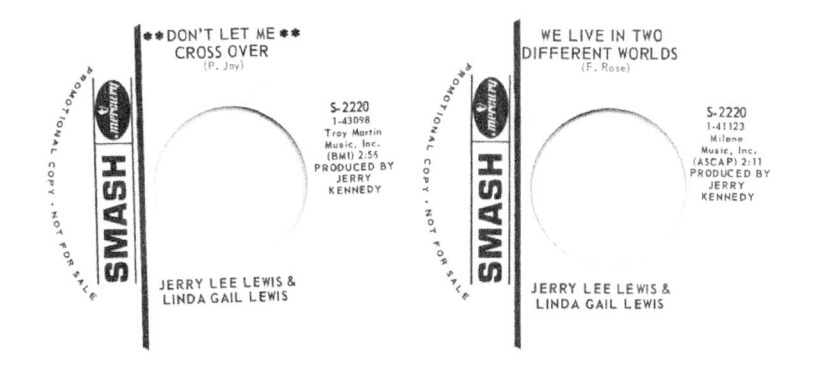

Don't Let Me Cross Over / We Live In Two Different Worlds
(No. 9 Country)

'The Mike Douglas Show' (1969)

[102] DON'T LET THE STARS GET IN YOUR EYES (1977)
(Slim Willet)

Originally released by Slim Willett with The Brush Cutters in 1952 and a hit for Perry Como the same year, other artists who recorded it are Carl Mann (recorded 1960, released 1977), George Jones (1962) and Conway Twitty (1969). Jerry's very fast version features some great fiddle, and is only slightly spoilt by the very straight-sounding backing singers.

First Release: 'Keeps Rockin'' (1978) + Single B-side (1978)

[103] DON'T STAY AWAY (TILL LOVE GROWS COLD) (1952)
(Lefty Frizzell)

Sometime during the summer of 1952, 16-year-old Jerry Lee Lewis and his best friend (and future manager / brother-in-law) Cecil Harrelson visited New Orleans in search of work for Jerry in the city's clubs. They were largely unsuccessful in this quest owing to his youthful age and appearance, but while they were there they visited Cosimo Matassa's J&M Recording Studios, a place where Fats Domino, Smiley Lewis and Lloyd Price had already cut several ground-breaking discs. They also learnt that it was possible to make a Demo (demonstration disc) for $2.50, and after persuading Cecil to pay the fee, Jerry got to work. For the A-side, he decided on Lefty Frizzell's 'Don't Stay Away (Till Love Grows Cold)', perhaps not the wisest of choices given Lefty's notoriously idiosyncratic vocal style. He gives it his best shot though, and can be forgiven for sounding a little inexperienced and nervous, particularly as his piano-playing is already adventurous, unique and quite brilliant. It is the B-side though, 'Jerry Lee's Boogie (New Orleans Boogie)' that really show's off Jerry Lee's prowess. After being thought lost for many years, Cecil rediscovered the Demo, and both sides were finally issued in 2006.

First Release: 'A Half Century Of Hits' (2006)

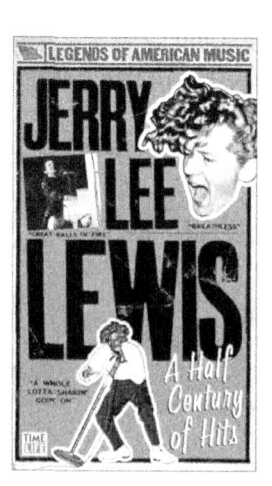

Jerry's 1951 Demo, and the box-set it was eventually released on in 2006

[104] **DON'T TAKE IT OUT ON ME** [with Linda Gail Lewis] (1969)
(Linda Gail Lewis / Kenneth Lovelace)

One of the lesser songs on 'Together', this unison-sung number was performed on 1969's 'The Many Sounds of Jerry Lee', where Jerry makes up for being unsure of the lyrics by playing a wild Rock 'n' Roll piano solo.

First Release: 'Together' (1969)

'The Many Sounds of Jerry Lee' (1969)

Peter Checksfield with Linda Gail Lewis (1987)

[105] DON'T TOUCH ME (1986)
(Hank Cochran)

A popular Country song, 'Don't Touch Me' was first recorded by Hank Cochran's wife Jeannie Seely in 1966, with covers quickly following by Wilma Burgess, Ray Price, Don Gibson and Tammy Wynette. Jerry's excellent version from September 1986 features him sympathetically backed just by bass, drums and the Jordanaires.

First Release: 'Rocket' (1988)

[105] DON'T TOUCH ME (1987)

With a guitar intro and an (albeit low-mixed) real piano, this is one of the better recordings from the 1987 Hank Cochran sessions.

First Release: 'At Hank Cochran's' (1995)

[106a] DOWN THE LINE (1958)
(Roy Orbison)

'Down The Line' was originally released in 1956 by Roy Orbison and Teen Kings as 'Go! Go! Go!', an up-tempo but slightly awkward-sounding Rockabilly song. Jerry slowed it down but at the same time made it tougher and more menacing, and after at least 8 earlier takes, came up with the perfect B-side for 'Breathless'. He even performed the song live on US TV, on 'The Today Show' in April 1958, notable for being the only 1957/1958 TV appearance to feature a guitarist. It was on stage where the song would *really* come to life though, with Jerry often opening shows with it, while playing at twice the speed and 20 times the power of the studio cut. This was never captured better than for the taping of the legendary 'Live at The Star Club, Hamburg' on 5th April 1964. Regarded by anyone with ears as THE wildest Rock 'n' Roll album of all time, it is also one of the few to have a whole book written about it, namely Joe Bonomo's 'Lost and Found'. As for the live 'Down The Line', due to a sound fault during the opening seconds, it wasn't included on the original album, and instead popped up on a German various artists compilation. Those who've covered the song include Ricky Nelson (1958), Cliff Richard and The Drifters (1959), Marty Wilde (1959), The Hollies (1965), Mickey Gilley (1965) and Billy Lee Riley (1978), while Roy Orbison re-recorded the song JLL-style in 1969. But, no-one, *no-one*, can surpass Jerry's live cut.

First Release: Single B-side (1958)

[106b] DOWN THE LINE (1963)

The 'Golden Hits' re-cut of 'Down The Line' owes more to Roy Orbison's 'Go! Go! Go!' original than it does to the SUN cuts, with a very fast but awkward rhythm. This arrangement was performed live just the *once*, on the '33 & a 3rd Revolutions Per Monkee' TV special in 1969.

First Release: 'The Golden Hits of Jerry Lee Lewis' (1964)

[106c] **DOWN THE LINE** (1973)

This otherwise strong run-through from the January 1973 recordings for 'The Session' is marred a little by Jerry's slightly worn-out voice, particularly at around the 3 minute mark. A '60s regular, from the '70s onwards 'Down The Line' was only performed occasionally. However, around the summer of 2006 Jerry revived it, starting a great many shows with the song in later years, including his final concert ever in 2019.

First Release: 'The Session' (1973)

[107] **DOWN THE ROAD APIECE** (1994)
(Don Raye)

Original recorded by The Will Bradley Trio in 1940 and later recorded by Amos Milburn (1947), Ella Mae Morse (1947), Merrill Moore (1956) and Chuck Berry (1960), perhaps surprisingly it is Chuck's version that seems to be the main inspiration for Jerry's 1994 revival. Kicking off with a James Burton guitar lick, he is almost as prominent as Jerry on this fine but murkily-mixed performance.

First Release: 'Young Blood' (1995)

[108] **DOWN THE SAWDUST TRAIL** (1980) *
(Millie Lou Pace)

Amongst the many songs Jerry recorded at the November 1980 'Caribou' sessions, there were enough Gospel songs to fill an album, no doubt much to Elektra executives' horror. Amongst these was a nice relaxed version of 'Down The Sawdust Trail'. Originally released by the duo Mary Jayne and Polly in 1965, it was also recorded by Jimmie Davis in 1968 and Jimmy Swaggart in 1972, while Jerry had previously performed the song live at the Memphis Church recording in 1970, on the 1971 'The Jerry Lee Lewis Show' pilot with Carl Perkins and Jackie Wilson, and in Copenhagen in 1977.

First Release: 'The Caribou Ranch Sessions, 1980-1986' (2012) (bootleg)

'The Jerry Lee Lewis Show' (1971)

[109] **DOWN YONDER [INSTRUMENTAL]** [with Del Wood] (1973) (L) *
(Louis Wolfe Gilbert)

Prior to recording for Sun, Jerry tried his luck in Nashville, and like Elvis before him, he was ridiculed and rejected. One person who *did* treat him with respect and kindness however was Country pianist Del Wood, something Jerry would never forget. So when he finally appeared on The Grand Ole Opry in 1973, he made sure that Del Wood was invited on stage, where they both played a spirited version of her 1951 instrumental hit 'Down Yonder'. The entire show survives as a pristine quality radio broadcast, and circulates widely on bootlegs.

First Release: bootleg only

[110] **DREAM BABY (HOW LONG MUST I DREAM)** (1967)
(Cindy Walker)

With none of his releases selling anywhere like the numbers they were hoping for, in 1967 Smash came up with a rather drastic measure for Jerry Lee Lewis: Take away his piano! The very idea horrified many fans, but with Jerry at his very peak vocally and some strong material, the missing piano isn't missed as much one might fear. That said, he doesn't really add much to Roy Orbison's 1962 hit 'Dream Baby', good though it is. At a show in Skien, Norway in 1993, an ill-tempered Jerry took out his aggression on a remarkable Rock 'n' Roll version of 'Dream Baby', the only known live performance of the song.

First Release: Soul My Way (1967)

'Soul My Way' (1967)

[111] DRINKIN' CHAMPAGNE (1970) (L)
(Bill Mack Smith)

Originally released by Bill Mack in 1967 and covered by Billy Walker (1968), Cal Smith (1968), Faron Young (1969) and Ray Price (1969), 'Drinkin' Champagne' is a fine Country song that Jerry never recorded in the studio. Live performances include San Francisco 1975, 'Pop Goes The Country' with Mickey Gilley in 1978, Margate 1978, Oslo 1978, London 1978, Chicago 1979 and Oslo 1989.

First Release: 'Live at The International, Las Vegas' (1970)

[112a] DRINKIN' WINE SPO-DEE-O-DEE (1957)
(Sticks McGhee / J. Mayo Williams)

Originally released by 'Stick' McGhee and His Buddies in 1947 (who re-recorded it more successfully in 1949 when changing the scene from Petersburg to New Orleans), cover versions include Wynonie Harris (1949), Malcolm Yelvington (1954), Glenn Reeves (1956) and Johnny Burnette and The Rock 'n Roll Trio (1956). Jerry's 1st and best Sun cut features a unique descending piano intro and an animated vocal.

First Release: 'Monsters' (1971)

[112b] DRINKIN' WINE SPO-DEE-O-DEE (1958)

During a lengthy and sometimes frustrating November 1958 session where the main purpose was to perfect 'I'll Sail My Ship Alone' and 'It Hurt Me So', Jerry knocked off a couple of wild takes of 'Drinkin' Wine Spo-Dee-O-Dee'.

First Release: 'The Sun Years' (Box-Set, 1983)

[112c] DRINKIN' WINE SPO-DEE-O-DEE (1963)

Like many of Jerry's mid-'60s recordings, his 1963 take of 'Drinkin' Wine Spo-Dee-O-Dee' has a loose, almost jazzy vocal, as well as the usual excellent piano. When released 3 years later, it fit perfectly onto the 'Memphis Beat' album.

First Release: 'Memphis Beat' (1966)

[112d] DRINKIN' WINE SPO-DEE-O-DEE (1973)

By lowering the tempo and key a little and upping the amplifiers and drums, this version from the January 1973 London sessions has more of a *Rock* feel with less of the *Roll*. It very much fit in with the times though, and effortlessly got to No. 41 US Pop and No. 20 US Country, perhaps helped by major TV promotion on 'In Concert' and 'The Midnight Special'. Although rarely played live prior to 1973, from here on it remained a concert regular for the rest of Jerry's career.

First Release: 'The Session' (1973) + Single A-side (1973)

Drinkin' Wine Spo-Dee O-Dee / Rock & Roll Medley

(No. 41 Pop, No. 20 Country)

[113] **DUNGAREE DOLL** (1973)

(Ben Raleigh / Sherman Edwards)

A 1955 hit for Eddie Fisher, a short impromptu version of the song was recorded in January 1973.

First Release: 'The Complete Session Volume One' (1986)

[114] **EARLY MORNING RAIN** (1973)

(Gordon Lightfoot)

A Gordon Lightfoot up-tempo Folk song from 1964, others who recorded it include Billy Lee Riley (1966), Ronnie Hawkins (1968), Buddy Knox (1969), Jerry Reed (1971) and Elvis Presley (1972). Kenny Lovelace was largely surplus to requirements at the January 1973 recordings for 'The Session', but he got his one chance to shine on 'Early Morning Rain', where the fiddle is almost as impressive as Jerry's excellent piano work. An instrumental rehearsal circulates unofficially. The only known live performance was a more subdued version at a Las Vegas show in 2001.

First Release: 'The Session' (1973)

[115] **EARTH UP ABOVE** [with Linda Gail Lewis] (1969)

(Donald Murray)

A fast Country number with a fine combined piano/fiddle solo, 'Earth Up Above' is amongst the most enjoyable of the duets on 'Together'. It had previously been recorded the previous year without Linda Gail as '(Grand Old) Moon Up Above', though this unreleased version has sadly been lost. As the song was released shortly after the Apollo 11 moon landings, perhaps it was renamed to give it a more topical "out-of-this-world" title? Linda re-recorded it with Norwegian Country-Rocker Stephen Ackles in 1992.

First Release: 'Together' (1969)

'Together' (1969)

[116] **EASTER PARADE** (1980) *
(Irving Berlin)

Originally released by Meyer Davis and His Orchestra in 1933, 'Easter Parade' was also covered by Bing Crosby (1942), Judy Garland and Fred Astaire (1949) and Fats Domino (1961). Jerry's swinging mid-tempo version is excellent. He performed it live in Sacramento, Nashville 1979, Stockholm 1981 and Oslo 1985.

First Release: 'The Caribou Ranch Sessions, 1980-1986' (2012) (bootleg)

[117] **ECHOES** (1968)
(Cecil Harrelson / Linda Gail Lewis)

Although well-played, 'Echoes' is a somewhat average Country song, played in ¾ time. So why was it the closing track on the albums 'She Still Comes Around' *and* 'She Even Woke Me Up To Say Goodbye'?!

First Release: 'She Still Comes Around' (1969) + Single B-side (1969) + 'She Even Woke Me Up To Say Goodbye' (1970)

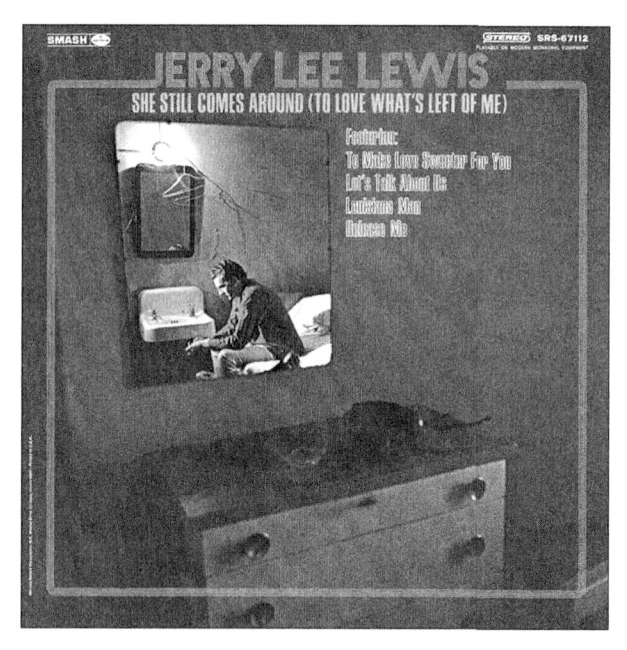

'She Still Comes Around' (1969)

[118] **EIGHT BY TEN** (1980) *
(unknown)

A drinkin' song, 'Eight By Ten' is one of the more commercial new songs from the Caribou sessions, and would've fit nicely on any of his '80s Elektra/MCA albums.

First Release: 'The Caribou Ranch Sessions, 1980-1986' (2012) (bootleg)

[119a] **END OF THE ROAD** (1956)
(Jerry Lee Lewis)

Recorded at the same debut Sun session on 14th November 1956 as 'Crazy Arms', for his first single's flip, Jerry Lee Lewis recorded a self-composed song - or was it? Lyrically at least, the song bears more than a passing resemblance to 'Waiting At The End Of The Road', an Irving Berlin song first released by Daniel Haynes and the Dixie Jubilee Singers in 1929, though if it is more probable that Jerry first heard it via Frankie Laine's 1949 version. Whatever and wherever the song's origins, 'End Of The Road' pretty much set the template for 'Whole Lotta Shakin' Goin' On', right down to the piano intro and the Roland Janes guitar solo. Later live performances were few and far between, but he did perform the song on 3 TV shows: 1969's 'The Many Sounds of Jerry Lee' (for which the song ended up on the cutting room floor), 1981's 'Knott's Berry Farm' and 1992's French 'Dorothée show'. Later covers include those by Ray Smith (recorded 1962 - released 1981), Larry Donn (recorded 1964 - released 1995), Dick Curless (1968), Brenda Patterson (1973), Linda Gail Lewis and The Firebirds (2001) and Tom Jones and Jools Holland (2004).

First Release: Single B-side (1956)

[119b] **END OF THE ROAD** (1963)

This otherwise very good 1963 re-make is spoilt by some rather intrusive horns.

First Release: 'The Golden Hits of Jerry Lee Lewis' (1964)

[119c] **END OF THE ROAD** (1980) *

A lengthy and very wild version complete with piano lid-banging, this could be a candidate for one of Jerry's best ever re-makes if it weren't for the over-the-top "heavy" guitar licks.

First Release: 'The Caribou Ranch Sessions, 1980-1986' (2012) (bootleg)

[120] **EVENING GOWN** [with Mick Jagger and Ron Wood] (2002-2006)
(Mick Jagger)

First released by Mick Jagger in 1993, he claimed at the time that he wrote it as a Jerry Lee Lewis-styled Country song. So, when former Mick Jagger sideman Jimmy Rip started the recording sessions for 'Last Man Standing', this was the first song he thought of. Jerry does a fabulous job on what is a fine song, and Mick Jagger's duet vocal compliments him nicely. Definitely an album highlight.

First Release: 'Last Man Standing' (2006)

'Last Man Standing' (2006)

[121] **EVERY DAY I HAVE TO CRY** (1979)
(Arthur Alexander)

Originally released by Steve Alaimo in 1962, it was later covered by Dusty Springfield (1964), Johnny Rivers (1966), Ike and Tina Turner (1966) and Bob Luman (1969), while the song's composer Arthur Alexander finally recorded it himself in 1975. A Pop song without piano, Jerry sounds far more committed that one might expect, and even ad-libs a verse on his former wives and current girlfriend Charlotte Bumpus: *"Once there was Dorothy and then came Jane, look out Myra you look insane, c'mon Jaren you're struttin' your stuff, I think I'll take Bumpus cause I can't get enough!"*.

First Release: 'Jerry Lee Lewis' (1979)

[122] **FADED LOVE** (2008-2010) *
(Billy Burnette / Shawn Camp)

Not to be confused with the much-covered Bob Wills song from 1950, *this* 'Faded Love' was first released by Billy Burnette in 2006, and later covered by Lauren Mascitti. Jerry's mid-paced Country-Rock recording is more than worthwhile, with some nice Kenny Lovelace fiddle.

First Release: 'Come Sundown' (2014) (bootleg)

[123] **FALLING TO THE BOTTOM** (1973)
(Carmen Holland / S. Lenard)

Although not the greatest of songs, Jerry sounds good vocally. That is until the strings and backing singers come in, almost drowning him out.

First Release: 'Sometimes A Memory Ain't Enough' (1973) + Single B-side (1973)

[124] **FEVER** (1980) *
(Eddie Cooley / Otis Blackwell)

Originally released by Little Willie John in 1956, and famously covered by Peggy Lee in 1958 and Elvis Presley in 1960, other covers include Ann-Margret (1962), Conway Twitty (1963), Dion (1963), James Brown (1967), Wanda Jackson (1968) and Link Wray (1979). Little more than a ragged jam *("It sounds like Sixteen Tons!")*, with a bit more work Jerry could've come up with a very worthwhile version.

First Release: 'The Caribou Ranch Sessions, 1980-1986' (2012) (bootleg)

[125] **FILIPINO BABY** (1979) *
(Clarke Van Ness / Bill Cox)

Originally released by Bill Cox and Cliff Hobbs in 1938 though based on a much older song, Jerry recorded a great Rock 'n' Roll version for Elektra in 1979 which circulates unofficially. He performed it live in Copenhagen 1977, New York 1996, Memphis 2000 and Las Vegas 2001.

First Release: bootleg only

[126] **FIVE FOOT TWO, EYES OF BLUE (HAS ANYBODY SEEN MY GIRL)** [with Mickey Gilley] (1978) (L)
(Ray Henderson / Joe Young / Sam Lewis)

Originally released by Sam Lanin and His Orchestra in 1925, the song was covered by Louis Prima (1949), Merrill Moore (1955), Freddy Cannon (1960), Lloyd Price (1960) and Mickey Gilley (1977). Jerry performed it with Mickey Gilley on the 'Pop Goes The Country' TV show in 1978.

First Release: Greatest Live Performances of the '50s, '60s and '70s (DVD, 2007)

'Pop Goes The Country' (1978)

[127] **FLIP, FLOP AND FLY** (1965)
(Charles E. Calhoun / Chuck Calhoun / Lou Willie Turner)

Originally released by Big Joe Turner in 1955, and revived in 1961 by both Billy Lee Riley and Bill Haley and His Comets, Jerry's expressive vocals and playful extra chords make this another stand-out track on 'The Return Of Rock'. Live performances include 'The Many Sounds of Jerry Lee' 1969, Las Vegas 1970 (the only Rock 'n' Roll song released on the original 'Live at The International, Las Vegas' album), Memphis 1972, Manchester 1980, Tulsa 1980, Zurich 1985 and Hamburg 1991.

First Release: 'The Return of Rock' (1965)

[128a] **FOLSOM PRISON BLUES** (1980)
(Johnny Cash)

Originally released by Johnny Cash and The Tennessee Two in 1955 (though based on an older song called 'Crescent City Blues'), other covers include Thumper Jones (aka George Jones, 1956), Gene Simmons (1965), Merle Haggard (1968), Conway Twitty (1968), Waylon Jennings (1968), Carl Perkins (1969), Hank Williams Jr. (1970), Jerry Reed (1973), Charlie Feathers (1974) and Ray Campi (1977). Jerry's 1980 version can best be described as 'Rock-Funk', an idea that works surprisingly well. He largely recreated this arrangement at a London concert in 1981 to great effect, but most later performances stuck to a slightly more straight-forward approach.

First Release: 'Killer Country' (1980) + Single B-side (1980)

[128b] **FOLSOM PRISON BLUES** (2008-2010)

Very occasionally from the late '60s until well into the '90s, Jerry would borrow Kenny Lovelace's guitar, and perform either 'Mystery Train' or 'Folsom Prison Blues' (and more rarely, a medley of the two). He plays lead guitar on this version... very raggedly. Overdubbed with other instrumentation, the results are, erm, "interesting", but it would've been preferable if one of the many other unreleased songs from these sessions was released on 'Rock & Roll Time' instead. The un-dubbed solo version is on the 'Come Sundown' bootleg.

First Release: 'Rock & Roll Time' (2014)

[129] **FOOLAID** (1970)
(Cecil Harrelson / Carmen Holland)

A pretty average Country song, albeit with some clever lyrics *("It will numb your brain and ease your pain from your head down to your toes!")*. One of the more lighter recordings from the October 1970 sessions that produced the 'In Loving Memories' Gospel album.

First Release: 'There Must Be More To Love Than This' (1970)

[130] **FOOLISH KIND OF MAN** (1971)
(Linda Gail Lewis / Kenneth Lovelace)

When this writer asked Kenny Lovelace about the songs he'd written for Jerry, one he spoke about with some pride was 'Foolish Kind Of Man', with some justification. Unfortunately, it is not a song known to have been performed live.

First Release: 'Touching Home' (1971) + Single B-side (1971)

[131a] FOOLS LIKE ME (1958)
(Jack Clement / Pee Wee Maddux)

An excellent Country song in the Hank Williams mold, even the overdubbed backing vocals by Roy Orbison, Jack Clement and Roland Janes don't distract too much. Released as the B-side of 'High School Confidential', it (oddly) got to No. 11 in the Rhythm 'n' Blues charts in its own right. Artists who covered the song include Connie Hall (1961), Moon Mullican (1963) and The Merseybeats (1964). Jerry performed the song live at a 1974 show in Birmingham, Alabama.

First Release: Single B-side (1958) + 'Jerry Lee Lewis' (1958)

[131b] FOOLS LIKE ME (1963)

Generally it was the Country material that came off best at the Smash 'Golden Hits' sessions, and 'Fools Like Me' is a good example. With subtle strings and female backing vocals, it may even have the edge over the Sun version.

First Release: 'The Golden Hits of Jerry Lee Lewis' (1964)

'The Golden Hits of Jerry Lee Lewis' (1964)

[132] **FOR THE GOOD TIMES** (1971)
(Kris Kristofferson)

A strangely popular Kris Kristofferson song which was first recorded by Bill Nash in 1968, this is as close as Jerry ever came to cutting an Easy Listening recording. Live performances include Gothenburg 1972, Long Beach 1978, '25 Years of Jerry Lee Lewis' 1982, 'Salute To Jerry Lee Lewis' 1983 and Oslo 1985.

First Release: 'Would You Take Another Chance On Me' (1971)

[133a] **FOREVER FORGIVING** (1974)
(Mack Vickery)

Although not as memorable as some of Mack Vickery's songs, 'Forever Forgiving' is a nice enough Country ballad, with good piano and fiddle. Very occasionally performed live well into the '90s, the song owes a resemblance to both 'Pledging My Love and 'What Am I Living For', and has indeed been played as medley with those songs.

First Release: 'Boogie Woogie Country Man' (1975)

[133b] **FOREVER FORGIVING** (1982)

Slower and lengthier, the earlier cut has superior production, but on this his voice is in better shape. An alternate take is on 1991's 'Honky Tonk Rock & Roll Piano Man' CD.

First Release: 'My Fingers Do The Talkin'' (1982) + Single B-side (1982)

[134] **FOUR WALLS** (1969)
(George Campbell / Marvin Moore)

First recorded by Jim Reeves in 1957, Jerry's heartfelt version conveys the sense of loneliness and loss even more than the original. Rarely performed live, exceptions were Ipswich in 1972 and Belfast in 1985.

First Release: 'Sings The Country Music Hall of Fame Hits, Vol. One' (1969)

[135] **FRANKIE AND JOHNNY** (1959)
(Traditional)

A very old song that first appeared on record by Paul Biese Trio in 1921, later covers include Gene Autry (1930), Lead Belly ('Frankie and Albert', 1939), Josh White (1946), Pete Seeger (1957), Big Bill Broonzy (1957) and Gene Vincent (1958). Recorded in 1959, Jerry's fun version was released two years later on his 2nd album. It was performed live in Westbury in 1986, and again at his epic 2002 67th Birthday Concert in Memphis.

Released: 'Jerry Lee's Greatest!' (1961)

'Jerry Lee's Greatest!' (1961)

[136] **FRAULEIN** (1969)
(Lawton Williams)

First recorded by Bobby Helms in 1957, and later covered by Hank Snow (1961), Mickey Gilley (1962), Chuck Berry (1964), Willie Nelson (1966) and Conway Twitty (1966), 'Fraulein' is typical of the 1969 'Country Music Hall of Fame' recordings: Beautifully sung and played, but with highly predictable and formulaic production (why do those darn backing singers come in on the 2nd verse of *every* song?!). Jerry performed the song live fairly often well into the '90s.

First Release: 'Sings The Country Music Hall of Fame Hits, Vol. Two' (1969)

[137] **FRIDAY NIGHT** (1958)
(Jerry Lee Lewis)

An interesting rocker that would be even better if it was longer, this may or may not have been written by The Killer himself.

First Release: 'Rockin' and Free' (1974)

[138] FROM A JACK TO A KING (1975)
(Ned Miller)

Original recorded by Ned Miller in 1957, and later covered by Bobby Darin (1963), Jim Reeves (1963) and Elvis Presley (1969), Jerry cut 5 acceptable takes at a late 1975 session, of which only 2 have been released to date. The song was performed live in Dartford in 1985.

First Release: 'The Killer: 1973-1977' (box-set, 1987)

[139] FUNNY HOW TIME SLIPS AWAY (1965)
(Willie Nelson)

A much-covered Willie Nelson song from 1961, Jerry's involved vocal is excellent, but for once the guitar picking is more impressive than the piano (can that *really* be Jerry playing something so repetitive and unadventurous?). It was performed live in Tulsa 1979, St. Louis 1980, Las Vegas 1985 and Las Vegas 1996, but perhaps the most memorable version was on the 'This Is Tom Jones' TV show in 1969: Sung by Tom, Jerry complete upstages him just by playing piano. The two played the song again 37 years later at the 'Last Man Standing Live' taping, but this time it ended up on the cutting room floor.

First Release: 'Country Songs For City Folks' (1965)

[140] GAMES PEOPLE PLAY (1972)
(Joe South)

Perhaps more impressive than the over-produced Rock 'n' Roll revivals, on 'The Killer Rocks On' Jerry recorded a couple of Joe South songs, 'Walk A Mile In My Shoes' and this one, 'Games People Play'. The orchestration is still there, but Jerry's inspired renditions almost overcome that. Joe South recorded his own version in 1968, and amongst those who got there before Jerry are Petula Clark (1969), Conway Twitty (1969), Hank Williams Jr. (1969), Dolly Parton (1969), Wanda Jackson (1969), Brenda Lee (1970), Jeannie C. Riley (1970), Mack Vickery (1970) and even Bill Haley and The Comets (1971).

First Release: 'The Killer Rocks On' (1972)

[141] GATHER 'ROUND CHILDREN (1970)
(Cecil Harrelson / Linda Gail Lewis)

Cecil Harrelson and Linda Gail Lewis were great songwriters, who wrote from the heart. There is no doubting that. They also wrote some of the most somber songs Jerry ever recorded, and 'Gather 'Round Children', with its lyrics about attending a mother's funeral is probably the most downbeat of 'em all - and very poignantly, actually features Jerry's mother Mamie on backing vocals. Linda Gail Lewis released a solo version as a single B-side around the same time as this session.

First Release: 'In Loving Memories: The Jerry Lee Lewis Gospel Album' (1970)

'In Loving Memories: The Jerry Lee Lewis Gospel Album' (1970)

[142a] **GEORGIA ON MY MIND** (1977)

(Hoagy Carmichael / Stuart Gorrell)

Originally released by Hoagy Carmichael in 1930, it was almost certainly Ray Charles' 1960 hit that inspired Jerry - indeed, he was performing it live as early as the 1962 concerts in Keanesburg, New Jersey. Jerry's 1977 cut is very nicely sung and played, but marred a little by an organ solo instead of a piano break. Following its release on 'Country Memories', the song became a concert regular for the rest of his career.

First Release: 'Country Memories' (1977) + Single B-side (1977)

[142b] **GEORGIA ON MY MIND** (1980) *

Although not quite as good vocally, the 1980 re-cut has the added bonuses of a fabulous piano solo, an equally good fiddle solo, and lighter production.

First Release: 'The Caribou Ranch Sessions, 1980-1986' (2012) (bootleg)

[143] **GET OUT YOUR BIG ROLL DADDY** (1983)
(Troy Seals / Roger Chapman)

Originally released by Roger Chapman and The Shortlist in 1982 and covered by Levon Helm the same year, 'Get Out Your Big Roll Daddy' is the closest Jerry came to Rock 'n' Roll on the 'I Am What I Am' album. It is also a *horrible* song, that doesn't suit him at all. Never performed live, an alternate version was belatedly issued as a single 2 years later.

First Release: 'I Am What I Am' (1984) + Single A-side (1986)

Get Out Your Big Roll Daddy / Honky Tonkin' Rock 'n' Rollin' Piano Man
(Not a hit)

[144] **GIVE ME SOME ACTION** (1968) (L) *
(Ray Pohlman / Emil Dean Zoghby)

Jerry Lee Lewis has always been unpredictable. As long-time fan and friend Graham Knight always said *"With Jerry Lee Lewis, expect the unexpected!"*. But few would've predicted that Jerry Lee Lewis would be cast in a Shakespearean play, much less that he'd *excel* in the role! In the early months of 1968, he played the character Iago in 'Catch My Soul', a musical based on 'Othello', where for about six weeks in a Los Angeles theatre, he could be seen uttering lines like *"O, beware, my lord, of jealousy! It is the green-eyed monster which doth mock!"*, as well as performing a few specially-written songs. Sadly, there has never been a soundtrack recording, and not even a bootleg tape of a performance. However, polished rehearsals of a couple of songs *do* circulate, 'Let A Soldier Drink' and 'Lust Of The Blood' (see separate entries for those songs). Later in 1968, Jerry went to the UK to perform on a TV show called 'Innocence, Anarchy and Soul'; however, there was a technicians' strike, so it was never actually filmed. Despite this, Jerry went ahead and performed a few songs, and one of these was 'Give Me Some Action'. Basically a wild Rock 'n' Roll song with Shakespeare-inspired lyrics, thankfully a tape survives of this short but unique performance.

First Release: bootleg only

[145] GOLDMINE IN THE SKY (1973)
(Charles Kenny / Nick Kenny)

A song first recorded by Will Osborne and His Orchestra in 1937, as well as by Bing Crosby (1937), Gene Autry (1938), Pat Boone (1957), Nat 'King' Cole (1957) and Slim Whitman (1962). Beautifully played, this slow Gospel ballad from January 1973 would've sounded very out of place on 'The Session', and consequently wasn't issued until much later.

First Release: 'The Complete Session Volume Two' (1986)

[146a] GOOD GOLLY MISS MOLLY (1962)
(Robert 'Bumps' Blackwell / John Marascalco)

Originally recorded by Little Richard in 1956 (though first *released* by The Valiants in 1957), Jerry's September 1962 studio recording sounds strangely stilted, with voice and piano fighting against tinny guitars, riffing saxes, and ooh-ing and ahh-ing backing vocalists. It is on stage where the song really came alive though, as anyone who's heard the 1964 'Live at The Star Club, Hamburg' album will testify! In 2008, a bootleg CD called 'The Real Thing: Rare and Unreleased' surfaced, and amongst other material, on it were 'You Win Again', 'Your Cheatin' Heart' and 'Good Golly Miss Molly' - all from a live radio broadcast of a concert in Paris in 1963. It was running a bit slow, but after a little pitch-correction, sounds almost as good as the Star Club version, and is just as frenzied. It was confirmed around this time that tapes for Jerry's Paris radio broadcasts from 1963, 1966 and 1972 *still survive in the archives, in pristine quality!* Alas, any efforts to get them released were (allegedly) thwarted by Jerry's management at the time. Hopefully, someone will try again soon. The song remained a show regular well into the '90s, albeit usually as part of a medley with other Little Richard songs.

First Release: Single A-side (1962)

Good Golly Miss Molly / I Can't Trust Me (In Your Arms Anymore)
(Not a hit)

[146b] **GOOD GOLLY MISS MOLLY** (2008-2010) *

Although a little on the short side, this re-cut of the song is surprisingly good, with Jerry still reaching the notes and some pretty nifty piano work.

First Release: 'Come Sundown' (2014) (bootleg)

[147] **GOOD LOVE (SHOULDN'T FEEL SO BAD)** (2008-2010) *
(Kris Kristofferson)

Originally released by Kris Kristofferson in 1995, 'Good Love (Shouldn't Feel So Bad)' is a good old fashioned and melodic Country song, with backing that includes steel guitar and fiddle. The one thing that lets it down though is the lack of piano.

First Release: 'Come Sundown' (2014) (bootleg)

[148] **GOOD NEWS TRAVELS FAST** (1979)
(Rick Klang)

A modern-sounding Rock 'n' Roll song, Jerry sounds inspired, both vocally and on piano. Unfortunately, the female backing singers are very upfront and annoying, all but ruining proceedings. A rougher alternate take without those dreaded singers circulates unofficially. The song popped up occasionally in concert up until around 1989.

First Release: 'When Two Worlds Collide' (1980) + Single B-side (1980)

[149a] **GOOD ROCKIN' TONIGHT** (1958)
(Roy James Brown)

Originally released by Roy Brown in 1947, the song was covered by Wynonie Harris in 1948, and more famously, Elvis Presley in 1954. Not released until the '80s, Jerry's 1958 cut is a piano playing tour-de-force.

First Release: 'The Sun Years' (Box-Set, 1983)

[149b] **GOOD ROCKIN' TONIGHT** (1962)

Whereas the '50s cut is wild and frantic, the 1962 version is cool and sexy, with very different but equally expressive vocals and inspired piano. Jerry later performed the song (usually as part of a medley) a handful of times, including East Rutherford (1985), Paris (1992), Wolfen (1992) and Sao Paulo (1993).

First Release: 'Rockin' Rhythm & Blues' (1969)

[150] **GOOD TIME CHARLIE'S GOT THE BLUES** (1979)
(Danny O'Keefe)

First released by The Bards in 1969, with later versions by the song's composer Danny O'Keefe (1970), Waylon Jennings (1973), Elvis Presley (1974), B.J. Thomas (1975) and Conway Twitty (1977), 'Good Time Charlie's Got The Blues' is a superior mid-tempo Country-Pop song. Jerry does a fine job on it, with pumpin' piano and bluesy fiddle, even though the backing singers are over-loud. He performed the song live a handful of times, including in St. Louis (1979), Slough (1980) and London (1985). Interestingly, for the 1985 London performance, Jerry played the song JLL style, while guitarist James Burton played it Elvis Presley style, and it worked, too! Long rumored, singer Moetta Hill confirmed to this author in 1987 that Jerry and her cut a duet of the song in 1973, at the same session as 'Why Me Lord'. If so, it appears to have been lost.

First Release: 'When Two Worlds Collide' (1980)

[151a] **GOODNIGHT IRENE** (1956)
(Huddie Ledbetter / John A. Lomax)

First recorded by Leadbelly in 1933, it was probably The Weavers' 1950 cut which influenced Jerry, though Moon Mullican's version from the same year is another possibility. Jerry taped 4 complete takes at a late 1956 session including one that is part-rockin', but it's a slower and more majestic version that Sam Phillips selected for his debut album, albeit overdubbed with an unnecessary vocal group. He performed the song very occasionally up until the mid-'90s, with a London 1989 duet with Van Morrison being particularly outstanding.

First Release: 'Jerry Lee Lewis' (1958)

[151b] **GOODNIGHT IRENE** (1975)

Perhaps remembering his attempt to rock up the song in the '50s, the 1975 version has an up-tempo 'Memphis, Tennessee'-type beat, with prominent pounding piano, fiddle and harmonica. Only Jerry's hoarse vocals and an over-bearing vocal chorus mar things slightly.

First Release: 'Odd Man In' (1975)

[152] **GOOSEBUMPS** (1994)
(Al Anderson / Andy Paley)

A sort of modern update of 'Breathless', at least lyrically, 'Goosebumps' was released on 1995's 'Young Blood', as well as on a single. Jerry even performed the song live, on 'Jay Leno's Tonight Show' in 1995, albeit whilst reading the words from a studio monitor. A little-shown Promo Video was also made.

First Release: 'Young Blood' (1995) + Single A-side (1995)

Goosebumps / Crown Victoria Custom '51
(Not a hit)

'Goosebumps' Promo Video (1995)

[153] **GOT YOU ON MY MIND** (1965)
(Howard Biggs / Joe 'Cornbread' Thomas)

Originally released by John Greer and The Rhythm Rockers in 1951 and covered by Piano Red in 1956 and Big Joe Turner in 1959, Jerry Lee Lewis very likely learnt the song via Cookie and His Cupcakes' 1963 version. A bluesy Swamp-Rocker, Jerry's reverberating voice is particularly effective following the piano solo, and it made a fitting climax to arguably his finest studio Rock 'n' Roll album.

First Release: 'The Return of Rock' (1965)

[154] GOT YOU ON MY MIND AGAIN [with Linda Gail Lewis] (1970) (L)
(Buck Owens)

For the shows that were later edited down for the 'Live at The International, Las Vegas', Jerry chose a few new songs that he'd never recorded or performed before. One of these was Buck Owens' 1968 song 'Got You On My Mind Again', recorded by Buck as *'I've* Got You on My Mind Again'. Jerry had to read the lyrics *("She learnt it, I didn't!")*, but it's a lovely duet that didn't deserve to be kept in the can for 15 years.

First Release: 'The Killer: 1969-1972' (box-set, 1986)

[155a] GOTTA TRAVEL ON [with Linda Gail Lewis] (1969)
(Paul Clayton / Larry Ehrlich / Lee Hays / Fred Hellerman / Dave Lazar / Pete Seeger)

Originally released by The Weavers (as 'Done Laid Around') in 1958, other covers include Billy Grammer (1958), Bill Monroe and His Blue Grass Boys (1959), Solomon Burke (1962), Sonny James (1962), Bobby Bare (1963) and The Kingston Trio (1964). Jerry and Linda's fine duet is one of several highlights of the 'Together' album. They performed the song on 'The Many Sounds of Jerry Lee' in 1969.

First Release: 'Together' (1969)

[155b] GOTTA TRAVEL ON (1994)

A little faster and with a drum intro, this could almost be a solo outtake from 1969. Jerry's voice is *that* good!

First Release: 'Young Blood' (1995)

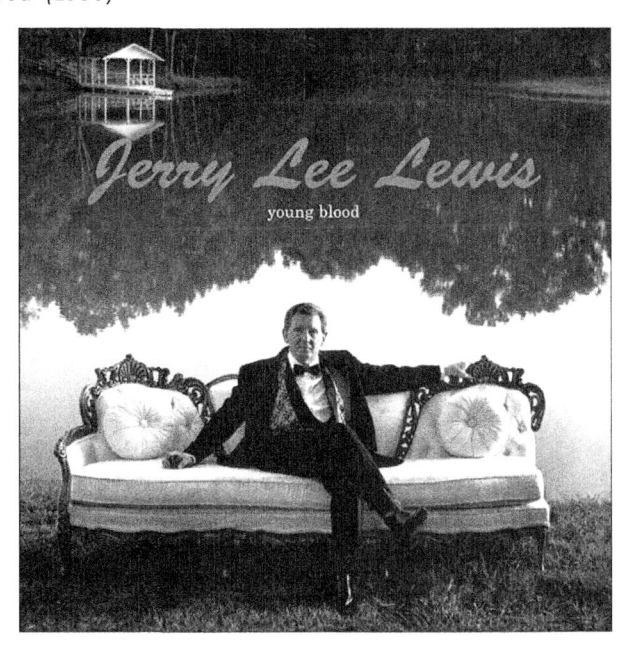

'Young Blood' (1995)

[156a] GREAT BALLS OF FIRE (1957)
(Otis Blackwell / Jack Hammer)

'Great Balls Of Fire' is Jerry's best-known recording, even more so than 'Whole Lotta Shakin' Goin' On'. Yet, if it wasn't for a decision by Carl Perkins, it would be considered *his* song instead. Around the early summer of 1957, Warner Brothers invited Carl and the then-up-and-coming Jerry Lee Lewis to make cameos in their forthcoming low-budget movie, 'Jamboree'. For this, they sent demos of 2 songs to Sun, and those songs were 'Great Balls Of Fire' and 'Glad All Over'. Because Carl was the most senior and the most successful, he had first choice, and chose 'Glad All Over'! The version of 'Great Balls Of Fire' in 'Jamboree' is very different and vastly inferior to the Sun single, and for a long time it was assumed that the two were recorded no more than days apart, around October 1957. However, research for the 2015 'The Collected Works' box-set revealed that the 'Jamboree' taping was almost certainly taped *prior* to Jerry's first trip to New York in late July/early August, when he made his TV debut on 'The Steve Allen Show' (28th July 1957), also appearing on 'Alan Freed's Big Beat Party' (2nd August 1957), and that his 'Jamboree' cameo was taped on that same trip. In other words, *he first recorded 'Great Balls Of Fire' before he'd even found major success!* Of course, it is the famous single we should focus on, recorded in one take, and featuring just Jerry live in the studio with a drummer, without any overdubs. Correct? Wrong on three accounts: It took at least 6 takes at the October 1957 to get things right (and at least 9 more takes at the earlier July session); a bassist can be heard on the issued cut, largely during the 2nd part of the solo; and, as made clear on 'The Collected Works', the distinctive echoing 'rim-shot' was an overdub! There have been many cover versions, including Georgia Gibbs (1957), The Crickets (1960), Conway Twitty (1961), Billy J. Kramer with The Dakotas (1963), Larry Donn (1970, released 1995), Otis Blackwell (1977), Billy Lee Riley (1978), Dr. Feelgood (1979) and Brian Setzer (2012). Best avoided though are versions by Tiny Tim (1968), Mae West (1972), Dolly Parton (1979), The Flying Lizards (1984) and Rolf Harris (1983). Jerry's Sun single got to No. 2 in the US Pop charts, and No. 1 in both Country and R&B, as well as No. 1 in the UK.

First Release: Single A-side (1957) + 'Jerry Lee's Greatest!' (1961)

Great Balls Of Fire / You Win Again
(No. 2 Pop, No. 1 Country, No. 1 R&B / No. 95 Pop, No. 4 Country)

'Jamboree' (1957)

[156b] **GREAT BALLS OF FIRE** (1963)

The Smash 'Golden Hits' version of 'Great Balls Of Fire' is amongst the weakest of the 1963 re-cuts, though it would be quite acceptable if it didn't have all that over-production.

First Release: 'The Golden Hits of Jerry Lee Lewis' (1964)

[156c] **GREAT BALLS OF FIRE** (1975)

Completely re-working the song, the 1975 cut has bizarre old-time 'Ragtime' chord changes. Jerry even performed this arrangement live occasionally during the '70s and '80s, *usually* proceeding or following the usual Rock 'n' Roll arrangement. However, at one shambolic gig in Birmingham (UK) in 1978, he *only* performed this arrangement.

First Release: '30th Anniversary Album' (1986)

[156d] **GREAT BALLS OF FIRE** (1988)

Around 1986 (and, very occasionally, much earlier) Jerry started to perform extended versions of 'Great Balls Of Fire' on stage, much to the obvious delight of the audiences. When in late 1988 it came time to re-record the song for the movie of the same name, he decided to utilize this arrangement, resulting in one of the best ever re-cuts of a big hit. The one downside for many fans though is that, following the publicity and relative success of the movie, he started closing shows with the song instead of 'Whole Lotta Shakin' Goin' On'. This wasn't *quite* set in stone (Jerry never became *that* predictable!), but more often than not it was the case well into the New Millennium.

First Release: 'Great Balls Of Fire!' (1989) + Single B-side (1989)

[157] GREAT SPECKLED BIRD (1960)
(Guy Smith / Guy Massey)

Originally released by Roy Acuff in 1937 and later covered by Kitty Wells (1959) and Johnny Cash (1959), Jerry played both slow and fast versions at a January 1960 session. It's an experiment that mostly works too, even if the slow/fast 'Mexicali Rose' from around the same time is far better known.

First Release: 'Don't Drop It!' (1988)

[158] GREEN, GREEN GRASS OF HOME (1965)
(Curly Putman)

Originally released by Johnny Darrell and covered by Porter Wagoner, both in 1965, Jerry's version of 'Green, Green Grass Of Home', with its tasteful backing including harmonica, is one of the highlights of 'Country Songs For City Folks'. JLL-fanatic Tom Jones so too, and after recording it himself had a gigantic world-wide hit with the song. Performed live occasionally into the New Millennium, including on 1969's 'The Many Sounds of Jerry Lee' where he played it on guitar, Jerry and Tom finally sang the song together for 2006's 'Last Man Standing Live'.

First Release: 'Country Songs For City Folks' (1965)

Green, Green Grass Of Home / Baby You've Got What It Takes
(Not a hit)

'The Many Sounds of Jerry Lee' (1969)

[159] **HADACOL BOOGIE** [with Buddy Guy] (2003-2006)
(Bill Nettles)

In the summer of 1981, Jerry's wild lifestyle caught up with him, and he was hospitalized for a couple of months with a perforated stomach. Afterwards, in those slower-communication, pre-internet days, fans wondered what he'd be like. Would he be too frail to play? Had he given up Rock 'n' Roll to concentrate on Gospel? In December of that year, he performed a concert in Nashville, and broadcast on radio, tapes quickly started circulating amongst fans. We needn't have worried, as apart from a marginally thinner voice (something that would be a permanent legacy of his 1981 near-death experience), he was performing with great enthusiasm and power. The highlight of this tape was a Rock 'n' Roll song with weird lyrics entitled 'Hadacol Boogie'. Originally released by Bill Nettles and His Dixie Blue Boys in 1949, the song popped up occasionally after that throughout the '80s and '90s, including Las Vegas and London in 1985, South Amboy in 1987, Hamburg in 1990, and Memphis in 1991. By the turn of the 21st Century it was performed more often, so it wasn't a great surprise to learn that it had finally been recorded in the studio for the 'Last Man Standing' album. Duetting both vocally and instrumentally with Blues giant Buddy Guy, it is a definite album highlight, and when they reprised the duet for 'Last Man Standing Live' it was a highlight of that too.

First Release: 'Last Man Standing' (2006)

[160] **HALLELUJAH, I LOVE HER SO** (1963)
(Ray Charles)

Originally released by Ray Charles in 1956, covers include Conway Twitty (1959), Peggy Lee (1959), Eddie Cochran (1959), Brenda Lee (1960), Bobby Darin (1962) and Little Stevie Wonder (1962). Jerry rarely disappoints with Ray Charles songs, and this is no exception. Held over for release until 1966, it is up to the general high standard of the other songs on the 'Memphis Beat' album.

First Release: 'Memphis Beat' (1966)

[161] **HAND ME DOWN MY WALKIN' CANE** (1957)
(James A. Bland)

A very old song, with the earliest known recording being Kelly Harrell's in 1926, this is a typical rocked-up oldie from his early days at Sun, with Jerry, guitarist Roland Janes and drummer Jimmy Van Eaton playing like one musician with six arms. He later performed the song at an after-show jam session in Stockholm in 1985.

First Release: 'Ole Tyme Country Music' (1970)

[162] **HANDWRITING ON THE WALL** [with Linda Gail Lewis] (1970)
(Nadine Hopson)

Also recorded by The Hopson Family around the same time, 'Handwriting On The Wall' is an unusual Gospel song, and one of Jerry and Linda's most passionately-sung duets. The guitar introduction is played by the late Buck Hutcheson - it was Jerry's idea to copy the intro on 'Maybelline'.

First Release: Single B-side (1972)

[163a] **HANG UP MY ROCK 'N' ROLL SHOES** (1960)
(Chuck Willis)

The Chuck Willis classic from 1958, Jerry's cover from 1960 starts with a repeated descending piano riff, and although he sounds a little hoarse, it's a good version with excellent saxophone. Although never a concert regular, there have been a number of live performances over the years, including Keanesburg 1962, 'In Concert', Los Angeles 1974, Slough 1980, Dendermonde, Cambridge, Northampton and Rome 1987, London 1989, Zurich 1990, Paris and Manchester 1992, Hamburg 1993, Indianapolis 1996 (the show's opener!) and Anaheim 2006.

First Release: Single A-side (1960)

Hang Up My Rock 'n' Roll Shoes / John Henry
(Not a hit)

[163b] **HANG UP MY ROCK 'N' ROLL SHOES (1987)** *

A couple of weeks before the April 1987 European Tour, Jerry re-recorded the song. Longer, more laid-back vocally, and without the stop-starts, it has prominent, pounding piano work, with some nice slide guitar playing. It's a shame these sessions didn't develop into a full album, as it could've been his strongest since at least the 1979 Elektra debut.

First Release: 'The Caribou Ranch Sessions, 1980-1986' (2012) (bootleg)

[164a] **HARBOR LIGHTS (1973/1974)**
(Gordon Kennedy / Hugh Williams)

Originally released by Roy Fox and His Orchestra in 1937 and revived by The Platters in 1959, Jerry gives 'Harbor Lights' the full Rock 'n' Roll treatment. It mostly works too, despite the key being a little too high, with lots of pounding piano and a surprise saxophone solo.

First Release: 'The Knox Phillips Sessions: The Unreleased Recordings' (2014)

[164b] **HARBOR LIGHTS (1976)**

Played as a straight ballad, this would've fit nicely on the back-to-form 'Country Class' album, perhaps instead of the contrived 'Jerry Lee's Rock 'n' Roll Revival Show'. Live performances include Memphis 1972, Reno 1976, Sacramento 1976, Tulsa 1979, Hollywood 1979, Pasadena 1981 and Ringstedt 1997.

First Release: 'From The Vaults' (1986)

[165] **HAVE I GOT A SONG FOR YOU (1983)**
(Ed Penney / Jerry McBee)

Featuring piano that almost certainly is *not* played by Jerry, 'Have I Got A Song For You' is an OK Country-Pop song that doesn't particularly suit him.

First Release: 'I Am What I Am' (1984)

[166] **HAVE I TOLD YOU LATELY THAT I LOVE YOU (1980)** *
(Scotty Wiseman)

Originally released by Gene Autry in 1946, later covers include Marty Robbins (1957), Elvis Presley (1957), Eddie Cochran (1957), Ricky Nelson (1957), Willie Nelson (1967) and Ringo Starr (1970). Jerry's 1980 revival has a nice mid-tempo 'Swing' feel to it, with some great piano. He performed it a handful of times, including in Newport 1993, Sarpsborg 1993 and Pistoia 2005.

First Release: 'The Caribou Ranch Sessions, 1980-1986' (2012) (bootleg)

[167] HE CAN'T FILL MY SHOES (1973)
(Frank Dycus / Larry Kingston)

Originally released by Landon Williams in 1972, 'He Can't Fill My Shoes' is a pretty good Country song that is burdened by over-production. Despite it being a Top 10 Country hit, the song wasn't played live much, though Jerry did perform it at a 1974 show in Memphis.

First Release: 'I-40 Country' (1974) + Single A-side (1974)

He Can't Fill My Shoes / Tomorrow's Takin' My Baby Away
(No. 8 Country)

[168] HE LOOKED BEYOND MY FAULT (1970)
(Dottie Rambo)

Originally released by The Singing Rambos in 1968, 'He Looked Beyond My Fault' is one of Jerry's most heartfelt Gospel ballad recordings, even though the song's melody is strongly based on 'Danny Boy'. He performed it live several times on the 1972 European Tour, including in Ipswich, Peterborough, Coventry and Amsterdam. A great later cover was by Jerry Lee's niece/Linda Gail's daughter Mary Jean - and it was all thanks to this author! In 2004, I had the pleasure of spending an evening with Mary, when she sang and played piano for a hour or two. The highlight of the evening was a lovely version of 'He Looked Beyond My Fault'. Two years later, when recording her debut solo album, she asked me for song ideas. I immediately replied, 'He Looked Beyond My Fault'!

First Release: 'In Loving Memories: The Jerry Lee Lewis Gospel Album' (1970)

Mary Jean's solo debut 'It's About Me' (2006)

Peter Checksfield with Mary Jean Lewis (2006)

[169] **HE SET ME FREE - I SAW THE LIGHT** (1980) *
(Albert E. Brumley) - (Hank Williams)

Originally record by The Statesmen with Hovie Lister in 1959 and Hank Williams in 1948, respectively, this lively medley of two sound-a-like songs includes some inspired piano, fiddle and guitar solos. Jerry would record a live version of 'I Saw The Light' with Johnny Cash and Carl Perkins for 'The Survivors' album in 1981 (see separate entry), as well as perform it on various TV shows and in concerts.

First Release: 'The Caribou Ranch Sessions, 1980-1986' (2012) (bootleg)

[170] HE TOOK IT LIKE A MAN (1963)
(Jerry Lee Lewis)

A Jerry Lee Lewis original, with light-hearted lyrics about such Biblical figures as Samson and Delilah, John the Baptist and King David, it's surprising that he was comfortable even *singing* it, let alone *writing* it! A catchy Pop-Rock song that features some nifty piano work, it's perhaps not the greatest song ever written, though it's not the worst either.

First Release: Soul My Way (1967)

[171] HE'LL HAVE TO GO (1969)
(Audrey Allison / Joe Allison)

Originally released by Billy Brown in 1959 and made famous by Jim Reeves the same year, covers include Connie Francis (1962), Nat 'King' Cole (1962), Solomon Burke (1964), Faron Young (1966) and Tom Jones (1967). Originally recorded during 1965's 'Country Songs For City Folks' sessions - a recording that is unissued and lost - his 1969 released version is sung with both feeling and respect. Jerry performed the song on guitar on 'The Many Sounds of Jerry Lee' in 1969, while other live performances include London 1972 and Gloucester 1972.

First Release: 'Sings The Country Music Hall of Fame Hits, Vol. Two' (1969)

'Sings The Country Music Hall of Fame Hits, Vol. Two' (1969)

[172] **HEARTACHES BY THE NUMBER** (1969)
(Harlan Howard)

Originally released by Ray Price in 1959 and covered by Guy Mitchell (1959), George Jones (1961), Buck Owens (1961), Webb Pierce (1962), Willie Nelson (1966) and Waylon Jennings (1967), Jerry's version of 'Heartaches By The Number' is like many tracks on the 'Country Music Hall of Fame' albums: Sober and professional, but a tad formulaic and predictable.

First Release: 'Sings The Country Music Hall of Fame Hits, Vol. One' (1969)

[173] **HEARTS WERE MADE FOR BEATING** (1971)
(Lamar Morris)

First recorded by the song's composer Lamar Morris the previous year, 'Hearts Were Made For Beating' is one of those slightly corny Country songs with a play-on-words punch-line *("Hearts were made for beating, and what a beating my heart's had!")*. It's nicely sung and played, but there's really little to distinguish it from several other songs Jerry recorded around this time.

First Release: 'Touching Home' (1971)

'Touching Home' (1970)

[174] **HELLO HELLO BABY** (1958)
(Jerry Lee Lewis)

Basically a cleaned-up version of 'Big Legged Woman', even the fairly innocuous lyrics can't hide Jerry's lasciviousness! He performed this 12-bar Blues in Keansburg in 1962.

Released: 'Jerry Lee's Greatest!' (1961)

[175a] **HELLO JOSEPHINE (MY GIRL JOSEPHINE)** (1961)
(Dave Bartholomew / Fats Domino)

Originally released by Fats Domino as 'My Girl Josephine' in 1960, Jerry's 1st and best-known version of the song features some great honking saxophone courtesy of legendary player Johnny 'Ace' Cannon. Released on his 2nd album, it was played live around this time quite often, including Memphis 1961 and Keansburg 1962, as well as later in Coventry in 1972. Incidentally, during the 1963-1966 'British Invasion', a host of UK bands covered the song, including Wayne Fontana and The Mindbenders, The Applejacks, King Size Taylor and The Dominoes, Lee Curtis and The All-Stars and Them. Every one of them were clearly influenced by Jerry Lee Lewis' 1961 version rather than Fats' original, even using his song title.

Released: 'Jerry Lee's Greatest!' (1961)

[175b] **HELLO JOSEPHINE (MY GIRL JOSEPHINE)** (1962)

Despite already cutting a version in June 1961 that was deemed good enough for release, in January 1962 he recorded it again. With guitar instead of saxophone, and a very different, almost Jazzy vocal, it first popped up on a 1969 compilation. Then, in June 1962, he recorded it again, but this time it wasn't particularly interesting (it was probably just a warm up song for the session), and stayed in the can until 1989.

First Release: 'Rockin' Rhythm & Blues' (1969)

[176] **HELP ME MAKE IT THROUGH THE NIGHT** (1971)
(Fred Foster / Kris Kristofferson)

First recorded by the song's composer Kris Kristofferson in 1970 and covered by just about everyone afterwards, it is to Jerry's credit that his version is one of the most memorable. It was performed live occasionally well into the '90s, and again at his 67th Birthday Show in Memphis in 2002. Then in 2009, at a show in Tilburg, Holland, Jerry played it one last time, dedicating the song to Els Versteijnen, a long-time fan who had recently very sadly passed away.

First Release: 'Touching Home' (1971)

[177] HERE COMES THAT RAINBOW AGAIN [with Shelby Lynne] (2008-2010)
(Kris Kristofferson)

Recorded by Kris Kristofferson in 1981 and covered by Johnny Cash in 1985, Jerry's mellow duet with Shelby Lynne first appeared as a 'Mean Old Man'-era bonus track with very limited availability. It was then issued on a bootleg single, and more widely heard when released on 2014's 'Rock & Roll Time'. An un-dubbed solo version is available unofficially.

First Release: Single B-side (2012) (bootleg) + Rock & Roll Time (2014)

[178] HERMAN THE HERMIT (1965)
(Rink Hardin / Marion Turner)

Nothing to do with Peter Noone, 'Herman The Hermit' is a Chuck Berry-styled rocker, though Chuck would have come up with better rhymes than "hermit" and "permit"! Slightly dodgy lyrics aside, it is a powerful performance.

First Release: 'The Return of Rock' (1965)

[179] HEY BABY (1967)
(Bruce Channel / Margaret Cobb)

First recorded by Bruce Channel in 1961, 'Hey Baby' was covered by The Marvelettes (1962), Arthur Alexander (1962), Del Shannon (1963), Paul Revere and The Raiders (1963), The Shirelles (1964), Chris Montez (1966) and Delbert McClinton (1966). Jerry's version, without piano but with harmonica and saxophones, is fine, albeit without adding much to the original. The song was performed live, with piano, in Las Vegas 1985, Vancouver 1986, Rome 1987, Bourges 1987, Bremen 1991, Wallingford 1994 and Las Vegas 1996.

First Release: Soul My Way (1967)

[180] HEY GOOD LOOKIN' (1979) (L)
(Hank Williams)

A Hank Williams classic from 1951, 'Hey Good Lookin'' was also covered by Johnny Cash (1958), Gene Vincent (1958), Carl Perkins (1958), George Jones (1960), Ronnie Hawkins (1960), Marvin Rainwater (1961), Ray Charles (1962), Hank Williams Jr. (1964), Del Shannon (1964), Charlie Rich (1967), Linda Gail Lewis (1969) and Roy Orbison (1970), amongst many others. Recorded live at The Palomino in Hollywood in 1979, unfortunately Jerry's only officially-released version is dreadful, with Jerry and the drummer playing very out of time with each other. The song was performed live many times up until around 1997… almost always sounding better than the record.

First Release: 'Six Of One, Half Dozen Of The Other' (1985)

[181] **HIGH BLOOD PRESSURE** (1994)
(Huey 'Piano' Smith)

Originally released by Huey 'Piano' Smith and The Clowns in 1958 and covered by Maurice Williams and The Zodiacs (1961), Gene Vincent (1963) and Ronnie Hawkins (1964), 'High Blood Pressure' is one of several songs on 1995's 'Young Blood' that could've been tailor-made for Jerry. If only he'd performed it live!

First Release: 'Young Blood' (1995)

[182a] **HIGH HEEL SNEAKERS** (1964) (L)
(Tommy Tucker)

Originally released by Tommy Tucker earlier the same year, the most significant new (to Jerry) song on 'The Greatest Live Show on Earth' live album from Birmingham, Alabama, was 'High Heel Sneakers'. With its pounding Rhythm 'n' Blues intro and stomping beat, and enhanced by 5,000 audience members clapping along in unison, when edited down a bit, it made a very exciting single. The song got more TV promotion in 1964-1965 than any single before or since, including appearances on 'American Bandstand', 'Shindig!', 'Hollywood A Go Go' and 'The Lloyd Thaxton Show', while in the UK it was plugged on 'Ready, Steady, Go!', as well as live-in-the-studio performances on the 'Saturday Club' and 'Top Gear' radio shows. Despite all this, it scraped to just No. 91 in the US Pop charts, and flopped all together in the UK. The song remained a very occasional inclusion on stage for much of Jerry's career, with him opening a California show with the song as late as 2005. Incidentally, Tommy Tucker's real name was Robert Higginbotham, hence the different writing credit on some releases.

First Release: 'The Greatest Live Show on Earth' (1964) + Single A-side (1964)

High Heel Sneakers / You Went Back On Your Word
(No. 91 Pop)

'Ready, Steady, Go!' (1964)

[182b] **HIGH HEEL SNEAKERS** (1980) *

An inspired version of his 1964 minor hit, as there had never been a proper studio recording (apart from on British radio), this would've made a very worthy release.

First Release: 'The Caribou Ranch Sessions, 1980-1986' (2012) (bootleg)

[183a] **HIGH POWERED WOMAN** (1961)
(unknown)

A Rock 'n' Roll song with interested lyrics and chord changes, the song's origins are unknown (Blues man Sonny Terry recorded an album track of with title in 1960, but it's a completely different song). This lesser-known version sneaked out on a US compilation in the late '70s, and features an Ace Cannon saxophone solo.

First Release: 'Golden Rock & Roll' (1977)

[183b] **HIGH POWERED WOMAN** (1962)

Kicking off with a 'What'd I Say'-type intro, the 1962 version includes a piano solo. It's no better and no worse than the earlier cut, just very different. Perhaps the reason why it wasn't released is because of the *"You're the monkey on my back!"* lyric; it is also slang for drug addiction.

First Release: '16 Songs Never Issued Before 1' (1975)

[184a] HIGH SCHOOL CONFIDENTIAL (1958)
(Ron Hargrave / Jerry Lee Lewis)

As with 'Great Balls Of Fire', 'High School Confidential' was performed in a movie in very different form, and also like that former hit, it took a *lot* of work to perfect, with at least 20 takes cut over two separate sessions in February and March 1958 (slightly beyond the scope of this book, devotees should check out ALL of the rejected takes out - some are arguably superior to the released version!). Curiously, a master tape of the 'Movie' version without guitar has never been found in the Sun archives, leading to some speculation that it was cut somewhere else, or at least at an undated 3rd session. The single cut of course is one of the most exciting Rock 'n' Roll records ever made, despite it actually being an edit of two recordings (the last few seconds being from a different take). It got to No. 21 Pop, No. 9 Country and No. 5 R&B. There have been many cover versions, but perhaps the most significant were by Adam Faith, Cliff Richard and Marty Wilde in 1958-1959: Britain's biggest stars, this is proof that Jerry's influence amongst musicians did not diminish post 'scandal'. The song was played fairly regularly for decades afterwards, but certainly not at every show, and appeared less and less frequently in later years. It finally disappeared altogether following one last performance at a festival in Bobital, France, in 2006, but those who want the *ultimate* live version should listen to 1964's 'Live at The Star Club, Hamburg'!

First Release: Single A-side (1958) + 'Jerry Lee Lewis' (1958)

High School Confidential / Fools Like Me
(No. 21 Pop, No. 9 Country, No. 5 R&B / No. 11 R&B)

'High School Confidential' (1958)

[184b] **HIGH SCHOOL CONFIDENTIAL** (1963)

Although the enthusiastic tambourine-bashing and weak-sounding guitar doesn't do the song any favors, the 1963 re-cut is still more than OK.

First Release: 'The Golden Hits of Jerry Lee Lewis' (1964)

[184c] **HIGH SCHOOL CONFIDENTIAL** (1988)

One of the best re-makes from the 'Great Balls Of Fire' movie soundtrack, the piano solo on this probably surpasses all previous versions. Incidentally, the song also appeared on 1973's 'The Session' in instrumental form: however, this does *not* feature Jerry Lee Lewis, and is merely a studio jam made by musicians waiting for him to show up (he did, eventually!).

First Release: 'Great Balls Of Fire!' (1989)

[185] **HILLBILLY MUSIC (FEVER)** (1959)
(George Vaughn)

Alternatively called 'Hillbilly Music', 'Hillbilly Fever' or, more oddly, 'Country Music Is Here To Stay', the earliest recording appears to be by Kenny Roberts in 1950. Whatever it's called, it is a great track, from Jimmy Van Eaton's fabulous drum intro onwards, with growling vocals from The Killer, wild piano, and a fine guitar solo, played by Brad Suggs instead of the usual Roland Janes.

Released: 'Jerry Lee's Greatest!' (1961)

[186] **HIS HANDS** (1987)
(Stuart Hamblen)

Original recorded by Stuart Hamblen in 1955, this semi-instrumental performance is rendered largely unlistenable by the Casio keyboard Jerry's playing.

First Release: 'At Hank Cochran's' (1995)

[187] **HIT THE ROAD, JACK** (1963)
(Percy Mayfield)

Hoping to replicate the success of 'What'd I Say', for Smash's first Jerry Lee Lewis single they cut another Ray Charles song, this time his 1961 hit 'Hit The Road, Jack'. Cut on 22nd September 1963 and released the following month, it was released on the flipside of minor Country hit 'Pen and Paper'. Perhaps dissatisfied with the take from two days earlier, Jerry recorded a slower and superior version on the 24th September 1963. It first appeared, possibly accidentally, on the 'All Time Smash Hits' various artists compilation the following year. Never a concert regular, rare exceptions were performances on 'The Many Sounds of Jerry Lee' in 1969 and in Gothenburg in 1972.

First Release: Single B-side (1963)

[188] **HOLD ON I'M COMING** (1973)
(Isaac Hayes / David Porter)

Originally released by Soul duo Sam and Dave (as 'Hold On! I'm A Comin'') in 1966, other covers include Cliff Bennett and The Rebel Rousers (1966), Joey Dee and The Starliters (1966), Chuck Jackson (1966), The Righteous Brothers (1967), The Walker Brothers (1968) and Jackie Wilson (1969). With a Funky guitar intro, a plodding beat and intrusive (if soulful) backing vocalists, Jerry's version isn't the best, and a too fast alternate take that wasn't released until 1987 only marginally improves it. He performed a far superior live version on 'The Midnight Special', where both Jerry and the young, mixed-race audience really got into it.

First Release: 'Southern Roots' (1973)

'The Midnight Special' (1973)

[189] HOLD YOU IN MY HEART [with Shelby Lynne] (2008-2010)
(Eddy Arnold / Tommy Dilbeck / Howard Horton)

Originally released by Eddy Arnold as 'I'll Hold You in My Heart (Till I Can Hold You in My Arms)' in 1947, the song was covered by Eddie Fisher (1951), Glen Campbell (1963), Slim Whitman (1964), Dean Martin (1965), Al Martino (1966), Elvis Presley (1969) and Dottie West (1969). As with her other duet with Jerry 'Here Comes That Rainbow Again', this duet with Shelby Lynne is relaxed, mellow and sweet. The song wasn't new to Jerry, as he'd previously performed it at a concert in Phoenix, Arizona way back in 1983.

First Release: 'Mean Old Man' (2010)

[190] HOLDIN' ON (1967)
(Marjorie Barton / Bobby Dyson)

A superb ballad that deserves wider fame, 'Holdin' On' features one of Jerry's most heartfelt and believable vocal performances. Although not everything is great, the best of 'Soul My Way' is vastly superior to his other 'Soul' album, 1973's 'Southern Roots'. Soul *Jerry's* way!

First Release: Soul My Way (1967) + Single B-side (1967)

[191] HOME (1959)
(Roger Miller)

First recorded by Jim Reeves in 1959, 'Home' is a mid-tempo Country-Pop song with a catchy guitar-riff and jolly lyrics (one can just imagine his mama saying *"Get it on home Jerry, I'm missing you so!"*). Released on Jerry's 2nd album, composer Roger Miller recorded his own version in 1966.

Released: 'Jerry Lee's Greatest!' (1961)

Peter Checksfield outside Jerry Lee Lewis' home (2005)

[192] HOME AWAY FROM HOME (1970)
(Jerry Chesnut)

Sung in a higher register than usual, this is one of the more memorable tracks on the 'There Must Be More To Love Than This' album.

First Release: 'There Must Be More To Love Than This' (1970) + Single B-side (1970)

[193] HOMECOMING (1970) (L)
(Tom T. Hall)

Originally released by Tom T. Hall the previous year, 'Homecoming' is an amusing semi-spoken song, played quite fast. Taped live at The International Hotel in Las Vegas, it is a bit *too* similar to 'Ballad Of 40 Dollars' for them both to be included on the live album from the venue.

First Release: 'The Killer: 1969-1972' (box-set, 1986)

[194a] HONEY HUSH (1956)
(Big Joe Turner)

Originally released by Big Joe Turner in 1953 and covered by The Johnny Burnette Trio in 1956, lines like *"Gonna knock you down with a baseball bat!"* rendered it un-releasable at the time. Despite the numerous studio recordings by Jerry over the years (none of which were originally released), it is a song that has only been performed occasionally, most notably during the 1972 European Tour.

First Release: 'Monsters' (1971)

[194b] HONEY HUSH (1973)

A loud, drunken and slightly messy version from the September 1973 'Southern Roots' sessions, this was first released in 1987.

First Release: 'The Killer: 1973-1977' (box-set, 1987)

[194c] HONEY HUSH (1974)

Despite the over-dominant harmonica and the fade out after a little over 2 minutes, this take from the October 1974 'Boogie Woogie Country Man' sessions is largely more palatable than the '73 cut.

First Release: 'The Mercury Sessions' (1985)

[194d] HONEY HUSH (1980) *

During the fascinating 'Caribou' sessions for Elektra in November 1980, Jerry cut arguably the wildest version of 'Honey Hush' to date. Sadly, this still awaits official release, though it does circulate widely unofficially.

First Release: 'The Caribou Ranch Sessions, 1980-1986' (2012) (bootleg)

[195] **HONG KONG BLUES** (1963)
(Hoagy Carmichael)

Originally released by Hoagy Carmichael in 1938, this *"Story about a very unfortunate colored man!"* is one of Jerry's most unique recordings. Up-tempo and minor-keyed, it stood little chance of release at the time, but the great thing about so many songs cut during the 1960-1967 era is that they tried *everything* and *anything* in order to get a hit. Once success returned in 1968, any such musical adventurism largely disappeared, at least for a few years. Jerry performed it live, after an audience member requested it, in Atlantic City in 1988, but the band weren't familiar with it.

First Release: 'Jerry Lee Lewis and His Pumping Piano' (1974)

[196] **HONKY TONK HEART** (1983)
(Bob Morrison / Johnny McKay / Wanda Mallotte)

'Honky Tonk Heart' is a fairly typical but more than acceptable mid-tempo Country song that is far more interesting lyrically than it is musically.

First Release: 'I Am What I Am' (1984)

'I Am What I Am' (1984)

[197] **HONKY TONK HEAVEN** (1982)
(Larry Henley / Bill Burnett)

A tough and contemporary sounding Country song with an 'Outlaw' beat, this probably would've suited Waylon Jennings more than it did Jerry.

First Release: 'My Fingers Do The Talkin'' (1982)

[198] **HONKY TONK ROCK 'N' ROLL PIANO MAN** (1982)
(Steve Collom)

Many of the songs from the 1982-1984 MCA albums were remixed for a couple of compilation CDs in 1991-1992, a largely very pointless exercise. However, there is one notable exception, and that is 'Honky Tonk Rock 'n' Roll Piano Man'. The piano is largely buried on the original release, but when remixed it becomes clear just how fabulous Jerry's playing really is, even if it can't disguise the mediocrity of the song. An alternate take is on 1992's 'Pretty Much Country' CD.

First Release: 'My Fingers Do The Talkin'' (1982)

[199] **HONKY TONK SONG** [with Webb Pierce, Mel Tillis and Faron Young] (1984)
(Mel Tillis)

First recorded by Mel Tillis in 1957, and later covered by Webb Pierce and Faron Young, Jerry Lee Lewis performs this Country classic with all 3 of them for 1985's highly enjoyable 'Four Legends' album.

First Release: 'Four Legends' (1985)

[200] **HONKY TONK STUFF** (1979)
(Jerry Chesnut)

Probably the best traditional Country song on Jerry's 2nd Elektra album, a superior alternate take was issued as a single, getting to No. 28 in the Country charts. It was performed in St. Louis and Nashville in 1980.

First Release: 'When Two Worlds Collide' (1980) + Single A-side (1980)

Honky Tonk Stuff / Rockin' Jerry Lee
(No. 28 Country)

[201] **HONKY TONK WINE** (1973)
(Mack Vickery)

Originally released by Doug Kershaw in 1972, with its 'High Heel Sneakers' rhythm, 'Honky Tonk Wine' is one of the more interesting songs from the 1973 Stan Kesler sessions that produced the disappointing 'Sometimes A Memory Ain't Enough' and 'I-40 Country' albums. In 1975 Mickey Gilley cut a fast Rock 'n' Roll version, and it is this arrangement that they both performed together on 'Pop Goes The Country' in 1978.

First Release: 'Sometimes A Memory Ain't Enough' (1973)

[202] **HONKY TONK WOMAN** [with Kid Rock] (2003-2006)
(Mick Jagger / Keith Richards)

Originally released by The Rolling Stones as 'Honky Tonk *Women*' in 1969 and much covered since, if one person can be guaranteed to come up with a very different version of a song, then that person is Jerry Lee Lewis. Starting off slowly with just him and his piano, it quickly transforms into a fast modern Rock 'n' Roll song. It's highly debatable whether Kid Rock detracts from or enhances it, but 'Honky Tonk Women' is amongst the more popular tracks on 'Last Man Standing'.

First Release: 'Last Man Standing' (2006)

'Honky Tonk Woman' Promo Video (2006)

[203] **HONKY TONKIN'** [with Kenny Lovelace] (1981)
(Hank Williams)

Originally released by Hank Williams in 1947, The Killer's long-time sideman Kenny Lovelace cut a rockin' update in 1981, with Jerry adding some fabulous Boogie Woogie piano and occasional vocals. It was released 6 years later on his debut solo album.

First Release: 'Twenty Years Overnight' (1987)

Peter Checksfield with Kenny Lovelace (1987)

[204] (HOT DAMN) I'M A ONE WOMAN MAN (1979)
(Michael Dosco / Edward Whiting)

In January 1979, Bones Howe produced Jerry's 1st Elektra album 'Jerry Lee Lewis', to great acclaim from both critics and fans. He cut a few other songs with Jerry that year, but the only one that gained an official release is '(Hot Damn) I'm A One Woman Man'. A storming modern Rock 'n' Roll song with James Burton on guitar and a bass backing singer, it's the kinda song Elvis excelled at in his later years. Jerry does a great job vocally, even though there is no piano. It is heard briefly in the 1980 movie 'Roadie', and was released on the soundtrack album of the same name.

First Release: 'Roadie - Original Motion Picture Sound Track' (1980)

[205a] HOUND DOG (1958)
(Jerry Leiber / Mike Stoller)

Originally released by Willie Mae 'Big Mama' Thornton in 1953 and covered by Freddie Bell and The Bell Boys in 1955 whose version in turn influenced Elvis Presley's 1956 hit, Jerry first recorded the song at a February 1958 session that was largely devoted to covering songs associated with Elvis. It's not the best song from the session or even Jerry's best version of 'Hound Dog', but he certainly doesn't embarrass himself either. He performed it fairly frequently in the '60s, including on both 1964 live albums, as well as at the 1969 Toronto Peace Festival. Later performances tended to be as part of medleys, something he'd occasionally still do right up until the late '90s.

First Release: 'Rockin' and Free' (1974)

[205b] HOUND DOG (1960)

Jerry recorded the song again in 1960, but this type he did it in a more Bluesy Big Mama Thornton style, very different both from the earlier recording and all known live versions.

First Release: 'Don't Drop It!' (1988)

[206] HOW GREAT THOU ART (1984) (L) *
(Carl Boberg / Stuart Hine)

Originally recorded by Bill Carle with the Ralph Carmichael Orchestra and Chorus in 1954, 'How Great Thou Art' is another song strongly associated with Elvis Presley thanks to his memorable 1967 recording and later live performances. Jerry performed the song in Worcester, Massachusetts in 1984, a show that was broadcast on radio and issued on a rare 'Radio Transcription Disc', as well as on a 1986 bootleg.

First Release: 'The Killer Is Back!' (1986) (bootleg)

[207] **HOW'S MY EX TREATING YOU** (1962)
(Vic McAlpin)

One of Jerry's best 'modern' country recordings, 3 takes were recorded at a June 1962 session, though only the originally issued version features the memorable bass guitar intro. It was covered by Mickey Gilley in 1976 and Hank Williams Jr. in 1978, while live performances include Keansburg 1962, Fort Worth 1966 (released on the 'By Request' album), Toronto 1967, Memphis 1972, Columbia, South Carolina 1974, Birmingham, Alabama 1974, San Francisco 1975, Oslo 1985, the 40th Anniversary show in Memphis 1996, Las Vegas 1996 and the 67th Birthday show in Memphis 2002.

First Release: Single B-side (1962)

[208] **I AIN'T LOVED YOU** (1979) *
(unknown)

'I Ain't Loved You' is a contemporary-sounding Pop-Rock song, possibly written by Kenny Lovelace. Produced by Bones Howe in 1979, it is only available unofficially.

First Release: 'Alive and Rockin'' (1986) (bootleg)

[209] **I AM WHAT I AM** (1983)
(Ken Lovelace / Bill Taylor)

A Rock 'n' Roll song with some interesting chord changes and lyrics specially written for Jerry Lee Lewis, it was both the highlight and the title track of 1984's 'I Am What I Am' album. To Kenny's obvious delight, it was performed occasionally for the next 30 years. Incidentally, at a 1977 Las Vegas show, Jerry performed a completely different song of that title. It sounded like it was ad-libbed, but could this have given Kenny the germ of an idea?

First Release: 'I Am What I Am' (1984) + Single A-side (1984)

I Am What I Am / That Was The Way It Was Then
(Not a hit)

[210] **I BELIEVE IN YOU** (1965)
(Frank Brunson)

A fast rocker played with Gospel-like fervor and chord changes, 'I Believe In You' features one of the most impressive piano solos ever put on tape. Released on 'The Return Of Rock' and as the B-side of 'Baby, Hold Me Close', the song was promoted on 'Shindig!', 'The Soupy Sales Show' and 'The Clay Cole Show', all in 1965.

First Release: 'The Return of Rock' (1965)

'Shindig!' (1965)

[211] **I BETCHA GONNA LIKE IT** (1964)
(Buddy Killen / Robert Riley)

First recorded by Jeb Stuart in 1962, Jerry's version of the song storms along at an absolutely frantic pace, with riffing saxophone and excitable drums. Recorded at the February 1964 'I'm On Fire' sessions, it stayed unreleased until 'Soul My Way' over 3 years later.

First Release: Soul My Way (1967)

[212] **I CAN HELP** (1975)
(Billy Swan)

Originally released by Billy Swan in 1974 and covered by Elvis Presley in 1975, Jerry recorded two quite different takes at the same December 1975 session, both of them released in 1986. A loose, low-keyed and laid-back version was issued on the '30th Anniversary Album'; then just months later, a faster version that's a bit closer in style to the original was released on 'From The Vaults'. In 1996, Jerry performed the song with Billy Swan at the 40th Anniversary Show in Memphis.

First Release: '30th Anniversary Album' (1986)

[213] I CAN STILL HEAR THE MUSIC IN THE RESTROOM (1974)
(Tom T. Hall)

A very good drinkin' and druggin' Country song *("I had a snort or two on my way down to the ol' waterhole!")*, Jerry sings like he means it, and with the help of a bizarre marketing campaign featuring a toilet seat, got to No. 13 in the Country charts. It was performed live very occasionally over the next decade or so, including Cincinnati 1975, Sacramento 1976, Owensboro 1978, Pasadena 1982 and New York 1986.

First Release: 'Boogie Woogie Country Man' (1975) + Single A-side (1975)

I Can Still Hear The Music In The Restroom / (Remember Me) I'm The One Who Loves You
(No. 13 Country)

[214] (I CAN'T GET NO) SATISFACTION (1973)
(Mick Jagger / Keith Richards)

A stodgy, over-blown version of The Rolling Stones 1965 classic, this January 1973 recording was quite rightly left off of 'The Session', finally surfacing 13 years later. An alternate take with Rory Gallagher on lead vocals was issued as a limited edition single in 2020.

First Release: 'The Complete Session Volume One' (1986)

[215] I CAN'T GET OVER YOU (1968)
(Ben Peters)

A Bluesy ballad, immaculately sung and played, 'I Can't Get Over You' is fairly typical of the often unadventurous but always professional recordings from 1968-1969.

First Release: 'She Still Comes Around' (1969)

[216] I CAN'T GIVE YOU ANYTHING BUT LOVE (1973)
(Dorothy Fields / Jimmy McHugh)

First recorded by Meyer Davis' Swanee Syncopators in 1928 and later revived by Bob Wills and His Texas Playboys (1936), Fats Waller (1940), Louis Prima (1946), Bobby Darin (1960) and Fats Domino (1961), Jerry ad-libbed a brief version of the song in January 1973.

First Release: 'The Complete Session Volume Two' (1986)

[217] I CAN'T HAVE A MERRY CHRISTMAS, MARY (WITHOUT YOU) (1968)
(Bill Lancaster)

Taped in October 1968 but not released until over 2 years later, the Country ballad 'I Can't Have A Merry Christmas, Mary (Without You)' is one of the very few Christmas songs Jerry recorded over the years. It was performed in Melbourne in 1970, and then largely forgotten… until it was rehearsed and taped for 'The Johnny Cash Christmas Show' in 1985, only to end up on the cutting room floor! This did explain though how Jerry was able to perform such a polished version a year later at a show in Reykjavik, Iceland.

First Release: Single B-side (1970)

[218a] I CAN'T HELP IT (1958)
(Hank Williams)

Originally released by Hank Williams in 1951, Jerry's version of 'I Can't Help It' is up to his usual high standard of Hank covers, and is particularly superb vocally. The song was performed live very occasionally up until the mid '80s.

First Release: 'Nuggets Volume 2: Rare Tracks by Jerry Lee Lewis' (1977)

[218b] I CAN'T HELP IT (YOU CAN'T HELP IT) (1960)

In January 1960, Jerry cut several takes of a rocked up version of the song, but this time with the lyrics reversed, i.e. *"I can't help it (if I'm still in love with you)"* was changed to *"You can't help it (if you're still in love with me!")*. Only Jerry Lee Lewis could do that and somehow get away with it!

First Release: 'Keep Your Hands Off Of It!' (1987)

[219] I CAN'T KEEP MY HANDS OFF OF YOU (1975)
(Bobby Borchers / Mack Vickery)

Originally released by Cal Smith in 1973 and quickly covered by Jerry Wallace (1973), Jeanne Pruett (1974), Waylon Jennings (1974) and Charley Pride (1975), Jerry's otherwise fine version is marred by his tired and lethargic vocals. An overdub could have made it releasable, but instead it stayed in the vaults for over a decade.

First Release: 'From The Vaults' (1986)

[220] **I CAN'T SEEM TO SAY GOODBYE** (1963)
(Don Robertson)

When Shelby Singleton bought the rights to the Sun catalogue in 1969, he found that Jerry had cut some very contemporary-sounding modern Country songs during his final sessions 6 years earlier, with 'Invitation To Your Party', 'One Minute Past Eternity' and the stunning ballad 'I Can't Seem To Say Goodbye' being just as good as anything he was currently charting with at Mercury. Released as singles, these all became Top 10 Country hits, and Jerry seemingly had no qualms about performing them alongside his more recent recordings. Live performances of this song include Las Vegas 1970 and Nashville 1973.

First Release: 'A Taste of Country' (1970) + Single A-side (1970)

I Can't Seem To Say Goodbye / Goodnight Irene
(No. 7 Country)

[221] **I CAN'T STOP LOVING YOU** (1969)
(Don Gibson)

Originally released by Don Gibson in 1957, it is Ray Charles' slower orchestrated recording from 1962 that became far more famous. Jerry's version is up-tempo, albeit not *too* rockin', as he wasn't ready to alienate his new-found Country fans just yet. It was performed live very occasionally until the end of the '90s, sometimes slow and sometimes fast, and was played both ways at his 64th Birthday show in Tunica in 1999.

First Release: 'Sings The Country Music Hall of Fame Hits, Vol. Two' (1969) + Single B-side (1969)

[222] I CAN'T TRUST ME (IN YOUR ARMS ANYMORE) (1962)
(Tommy Certain / Vic McAlpin)

A nice modern Country song, Jerry's mid-paced and saxophone-accompanied recording made a perfect B-side to 'Good Golly Miss Molly'. In 1973, Shelby Singleton stripped away most of the backing, and overdubbed it with something far more contemporary and ornate. Released a single, it flopped, and is rarely heard even by fans today thanks to its general unavailability.

First Release: Single B-side (1962)

[223] I COULD NEVER BE ASHAMED OF YOU (1959)
(Hank Williams)

Originally released by Hank Williams in 1952, Jerry's version was perfected over 2 sessions, and is amongst his very best interpretations of Hank's songs. Strangely rarely heard live, he did perform it in Memphis in 1961 (as heard on a '70s bootleg), and Jerry and Linda sang it as a duet in Attica (Indiana) in 1971.

First Release: Single B-side (1959) + B-side (1969)

[224] I DON'T DO IT NO MORE [with Tim McGraw] (2008-2010) *
(Shel Silverstein)

Original released in 1998 by Old Dogs (a Country Super-group featuring Bobby Bare, Waylon Jennings, Jerry Reed and Mel Tillis), 'I Don't Do It No More' is a fine Country-tinged Rock 'n' Roll song. Duetting with Tim McGraw, who does his best George Jones impression, this is more than worthy of official release.

First Release: 'Come Sundown' (2014) (bootleg)

[225] I DON'T HURT ANYMORE (1954) *
(Don Robertson / Walter E. Rollins)

Over 2 years after cutting his first Demo record in 1952 ('Don't Stay Away (Till Love Grows Cold)' b/w 'Jerry Lee's Boogie (New Orleans Boogie)'), he cut another one, this time at KWKH Radio studios in Shreveport, Louisiana, in November 1954. Again playing without a band, the two songs were 'If I Ever Needed You (I Need You Now)', and this one, Hank Snow's then recent hit 'I Don't Hurt Anymore'. Sung fairly straight, it is the piano playing that stands out the most, though he doesn't embarrass vocally either. Never officially released, both songs surfaced via a very scratchy acetate on a 1991 bootleg. 23 years after making the Demo, Jerry surprised everyone by performing a word-perfect live version at a 1977 concert in Paris, the song's only known performance.

First Release: 'The Killer's Private Stash' (1991) (bootleg)

[226] I DON'T KNOW WHY (I JUST DO) (1971)
(Fred E. Ahlert / Roy Turk)

Originally released by The Aristocrats in 1931 and later covered by Frank Sinatra (1946), The Platters (1956), Moon Mullican (1958), Cliff Richard and The Shadows (1959), Linda Scott (1961), Eden Kane (1962), Ruby and The Romantics (1963) and Marvin Gaye (1964), Jerry's version of this standard doesn't disappoint, and certainly didn't deserve to remain unheard for 14 years.

First Release: 'The Mercury Sessions' (1985)

[227] I DON'T LOVE NOBODY (1957)
(Traditional)

A song whose origins are long lost, the earliest known releases were by Gid Tanner and His Skillet-Lickers and Earl Johnson and His Dixie Entertainers, both in 1927. Kicking off with a 'Whole Lotta Shakin''-styled intro, Jerry's up-tempo version is notable for some nice interplay with guitarist Roland Janes during the solo.

First Release: 'Collectors' Edition' (1974)

[228a] I DON'T WANT TO BE LONELY TONIGHT (1974)
(Baker Knight)

A Country-Rocker distinguished by some nice chord changes, Jerry first attempted the song at the January 1973 London sessions, but that recording wasn't released, and is now sadly lost. Meanwhile, Rick Nelson and The Stone Canyon Band recorded the song in June 1973, and released their version in January 1974. Jerry finally re-cut the song at a October 1974 session for the following year's 'Odd Man In', a version that disappointedly features only a guitar solo, with no piano solo. He then pretty much forgot it until 1983, when he started performing the song fairly often, and it was still played occasionally well into the New Millennium.

First Release: 'Odd Man In' (1975)

[228b] I DON'T WANT TO BE LONELY TONIGHT (2006)

A slightly ragged but enjoyable live-in-the-studio performance marred by a sloppy non-ending, this was one of several 'Last Man Standing' era bonus tracks.

First Release: Urge (exclusive download) + 'Rock 'n' Roll Resurrection' (2007) (bootleg)

'Odd Man In' (1975)

[229] I FORGOT MORE THAN YOU'LL EVER KNOW (1970)
(Cecil A. Null)

Originally released by Sonny James in 1953 and also covered by artists as diverse as The Davis Sisters (1953), Johnny Cash (1962), Little Esther Phillips (1962), Peter and Gordon (1966), The Andrews Sisters (1967) and Bob Dylan (1970), Jerry's beautifully-played version is the definitive one. It was performed in Dalton, Georgia in 1979.

First Release: 'There Must Be More To Love Than This' (1970)

[230a] I FORGOT TO REMEMBER TO FORGET (1957)
(Charlie Feathers / Stan Kesler)

A much-covered song originally released by Elvis Presley in 1955, Jerry recorded several takes of 'I Forgot To Remember To Forget' in the summer of 1957. None are particularly good (at least by 706 Union Avenue standards), and tend to drag. Co-writer Charlie Feathers finally recorded his own version in 1974.

First Release: 'The Sun Years' (Box-Set, 1983)

[230b] **I FORGOT TO REMEMBER TO FORGET** (1961)

Cut at Jerry's first ever Nashville session in February 1961, what this lacks in spontaneity, it gains in polish and professionalism. It was a productive session, as also recorded that day were the hit versions of 'What'd I Say' and 'Cold, Cold Heart', as well as the lesser 'Livin' Lovin' Wreck'.

First Release: '16 Songs Never Issued Before 2' (1975)

[231a] **I GET THE BLUES WHEN IT RAINS [INSTRUMENTAL]** (1960)
(Marcy Klauber / Harry Stoddard)

At a lengthy recording session in January 1960, Jerry cut a couple of piano instrumentals, 'In The Mood', and this one, 'I Get The Blues When It Rains'. Originally released by Carl Haworth in 1928, Sam Phillips decided to issue both songs on his Phillips International imprint under the alias 'The Hawk', in order to get around DJ's reluctance to play Jerry Lee Lewis records. Absolutely no-one fell for the ruse, as his piano style is unmistakable, but it did make an intriguing release.

First Release: Single B-side (1960)

[231b] **I GET THE BLUES WHEN IT RAINS** (1969)

In 1969, Jerry re-cut the song with vocals, though the piano solo is so lengthy, one wonders if he momentarily forgot! It was performed live very occasionally, including in Zwolle 1987, Mannheim 1991, Memphis 1993, Las Vegas 2001 and Eindhoven 2007.

First Release: 'Sings The Country Music Hall of Fame Hits, Vol. Two' (1969)

[232] **I GOT A WOMAN** (1980) (L) *
(Ray Charles)

According to some pressings of 'The Greatest Live Show On Earth' and 'Live At The Star Club, Hamburg', they include a live performance of Ray Charles' 'I Got A Woman': This isn't true, as these are simply 'Mean Woman Blues' with the wrong title and composer credits. However, a live version of 'I Got A Woman' *is* available, albeit as a ropey audience recording from somewhere in the USA circa 1980. It was released in the '90s on the imaginatively-titled 'Live in Concert' CD by on the 'Tring' label.

First Release: 'Live in Concert' (early '90s)

[233] **I HATE GOODBYES** (1973)
(Jerry Foster / Bill Rice)

First released by Bobby Bare in 1973, 'I Hate Goodbyes' is one of the better tracks on 'I-40' Country, with marginally lighter production, as well as a closing yodel.

First Release: 'I-40 Country' (1974)

[234a] I HATE YOU (1973/1974) *
(Lee Daniels / Dan Penn)

First recorded by Patsy Sledd in 1972, and by Ronnie Milsap and Dan Penn, both in 1973, 'I Hate You' is a song that Jerry had been playing around with long before he recorded it for 'Keeps Rockin' in 1977. This earlier version, recorded for Knox Phillips on an unspecified date, is slower and more subdued than the later cut. It circulates unofficially in poor quality.

First Release: bootleg only

[234b] I HATE YOU (1977)

Despite its title, Jerry's final Mercury album 'Keeps Rockin'' was a mixture of Rock 'n' Roll, Pop and Country. 'I Hate You' falls firmly into the 3rd category.

First Release: 'Keeps Rockin'' (1978)

[235] I KNOW THAT JESUS WILL BE THERE [with Linda Gail Lewis] (1970)
(Cecil Harrelson / Linda Gail Lewis)

Although nominally a duet, Linda Gail Lewis sings 'I Know That Jesus Will Be There' largely solo, with Jerry only joining in for the choruses, as well as contributing a short spoken part. Arguably Linda Gail's greatest vocal performance, for those who'd rather not hear her, Jerry performed the song solo at the live Memphis Church recording in December 1970.

First Release: 'In Loving Memories: The Jerry Lee Lewis Gospel Album' (1970)

[236] I KNOW WHAT IT MEANS (1962)
(Stan Kesler)

Originally released by Sun artist Mikki Wilcox in 1961, 'I Know What I Mean' is part Country, part Blues, and part Old Time Pop. The end result is irresistible, and is amongst Jerry's finest and most underrated recordings. Incidentally, it has the strange distinction of being the *only* song from the June 1960 to August 1963 latter Sun era to only exist in Mono.

First Release: Single B-side (1965)

[237] I LIKE IT LIKE THAT (1979)
(Chris Kenner / Allen Toussaint)

Originally released by Chris Kenner in 1961 and covered by Steve Alaimo (1962), The Nashville Teens (1964), The Dave Clark Five (1965) and The Kingsmen (1965), Jerry's version is given a modern and slightly Funky make-over. The male backing vocalists are perhaps a little over-bearing at times, but otherwise this is one of many great tracks on The Killer's acclaimed 1979 Elektra debut.

First Release: 'Jerry Lee Lewis' (1979)

'Jerry Lee Lewis' (1979)

[238a] **I LOVE YOU BECAUSE** (1958)
(Leon Payne)

Originally released by Leon Payne in 1949 and covered by Ernest Tubb (1950), Gene Autry (1950), Elvis Presley (recorded 1954, released 1956) and Ray Price (1957), 'I Love You Because' is a song Jerry returned to several times. This first version, cut at a 1958 session whose main purpose was to record 'Breathless' and 'Down The Line', was probably just a warm-up number. It's not bad, but it is a little bit plodding tempo-wise, as well as over-long.

First Release: 'The Sun Years' (Box-Set, 1983)

[238b] **I LOVE YOU BECAUSE** (1961)

Taken at quite a jaunty pace, this is a nice polished take, even if the organ and the *"I do, I do, I do"* backing singers are both unnecessary.

First Release: 'Original Golden Hits Volume III' (1971)

[238c] **I LOVE YOU BECAUSE** (1969)

Sedate, professional, and perhaps a little sterile, Jerry's 1969 version owes more to Jim Reeves' 1963 release than it does to any previous versions. He performed the song live in Memphis in 1974 and in Oslo in 1985.

First Release: 'Sings The Country Music Hall of Fame Hits, Vol. One' (1969)

[239] I LOVE YOU SO MUCH IT HURTS (1958)
(Floyd Tillman)

Originally released by Floyd Tillman in 1948 and covered by Eddy Arnold (1954) and Charlie Gracie (1957), 'I Love You So Much It Hurts' is played as a slow waltz with some excellent piano. At a Sarpsborg (Norway) concert in 1993, Jerry performed the song as a duet with Kenny Lovelace, something they also did at least once at a US concert in 1974.

First Release: 'A Taste of Country' (1970)

[240] I ONLY WANT A BUDDY, NOT A SWEETHEART (1979)
(Edward H. Jones)

Original recorded by the Stewart Harmony Singers in 1932, 'I Only Want A Buddy, Not A Sweetheart' features full Dixieland backing (something he'd previously tried with Mercury on songs like 'Who's Gonna Play This Old Piano' and 'Country Memories'), as well as some fine, imaginative piano playing. The song was performed live in Hollywood 1983, Las Vegas 1985, Oslo 1985, Montreal 1986, Honefoss 1989, and at the 40th Anniversary Show in Memphis in 1996, where he closed a 4-hour concert with it!

First Release: 'When Two Worlds Collide' (1980)

'When Two Worlds Collide' (1980)

[241] I REALLY DON'T WANT TO KNOW [with Gillian Welch] (2008-2010)
(Howard Barnes / Don Robertson)

Originally released by Eddy Arnold in 1953, this standard has also been covered by Billy Ward and His Dominoes (1954), Johnny Burnette (1960), Chubby Checker and Dee Dee Sharp (1962), Ann-Margret (1963), Loretta Lynn (1967), Elvis Presley (1970), Freddy Fender (1979), Mickey Gilley (1982) and Dolly Parton with Willie Nelson (1983). Jerry's version is a late career highlight, even if Gillian Welch's (probably overdubbed) occasional harmonies don't really add much.

First Release: 'Mean Old Man' (2010)

[242] I SAW HER STANDING THERE [with Little Richard] (2003-2006)
(John Lennon / Paul McCartney)

Originally released by The Beatles in 1963, perhaps surprisingly, this is the first (and last) Lennon-McCartney song ever covered by Jerry. A pretty good Rock 'n' Roll performance, Little Richard harmonizes and does the occasional *"Whoooo!"*, adding greatly to the fun. Richard had previously cut the song himself in 1970, and was of course a major influence on Paul McCartney's vocal style.

First Release: 'Last Man Standing' (2006)

[243] I SAW THE LIGHT [with Johnny Cash and Carl Perkins] (1981) (L)
(Hank Williams)

First recorded by Hank Williams in 1948, this is one of several songs that Jerry performed with Johnny Cash and Carl Perkins in Stuttgart in 1981 for 'The Survivors' album. Gloriously ragged (but right), a slightly more polished solo arrangement was performed in Worcester, Massachusetts in 1984.

First Release: 'The Survivors' (1982)

[244a] I SURE MISS THOSE GOOD OLD TIMES (1973)
(Mack Vickery)

One of Mack Vickery's best songs (and he wrote several great ones), it was first attempted at the September 1973 'Southern Roots' sessions. Jerry sounds a little intoxicated and plays around with the melody a lot, and there are the obligatory horns, but it still could've been an album highlight if released at the time. It was first issued on a box-set in 1987, which also included a rehearsal of the song.

First Release: 'The Killer: 1973-1977' (box-set, 1987)

[244b] I SURE MISS THOSE GOOD OLD TIMES (1976)

More mellow, and with backing that includes steel guitar and fiddle, the 1976 re-cut is also more palatable. Surprisingly for such a memorable song, there is no record of it ever being performed live.

First Release: 'Country Class' (1976)

[245] **I THINK I NEED TO PRAY** (1973)
(Cecil Harrelson / Richard Mohr / Bill Taylor)

Get past the Mantovani strings, and this is a typically deep spiritual song, (partly) written by Cecil Harrelson. *"If you've got time to listen, Lord, I think I need to pray!"*, Amen!

First Release: 'Sometimes A Memory Ain't Enough' (1973) + Single B-side (1973)

[246] **I THREW AWAY THE ROSE** (1967)
(Merle Haggard)

When Jerry appeared on the TV show 'Music City Tonight' in 1994, a special guest was Jeff Cook, from the Country group Alabama. He recalled how in 1967, Jerry Lee Lewis, Linda Gail Lewis and Kenny Lovelace came to his home studio, and recorded a version of Merle Haggard's 'I Threw Away The Rose'. He then surprised a clearly touched Jerry by playing part of the tape. There is no piano, but he is in fabulous voice, with Linda and Kenny contributing some great harmonies. The full tape has never surfaced publicly, but it would be a good candidate for a collection of previously unreleased gems. Two years later, Jerry performed the song with Jeff Cook at the 1996 40th Anniversary Show in Memphis. Sadly, Jeff died in 2022, little more than a week after The Killer.

First Release: bootleg only

[247] **I WALK THE LINE** [with Kid Rock] (2005) *
(Johnny Cash)

The Johnny Cash classic from 1956, in 2005 Jerry guested with Kid Rock on a TV special called 'I Walk The Line: A Tribute To Johnny Cash', and despite his voice sounding a little shaky, it's a spirited performance, with some good piano. Never released officially, not even on DVD, it's a song that would've suited the 'Last Man Standing' or 'Mean Old Man' albums. Curiously, Jerry had previously performed the song several times at US concerts in 1974, including shows in Columbia and Birmingham.

First Release: bootleg only

'I Walk The Line: A Tribute to Johnny Cash' (2005)

[248] I WAS SORTA WONDERIN' (1975)
(Bill Kearns / Moon Mullican / Dusty Ward)

Originally released by early inspiration Moon Mullican in 1950, Jerry's otherwise fine interpretation is marred a little by a semi-spoken vocal, perhaps because his voice was sounding a little shot at the time. Although there were no known previous live performances, Jerry finally played the song several times in 2007, including in Memphis, Tampa Bay, New York and Malmo.

First Release: 'Boogie Woogie Country Man' (1975)

[249] I WISH I WAS EIGHTEEN AGAIN (1979)
(Sonny Throckmorton)

After Jerry reached his 40s, he started occasionally recording age-appropriate material. 'Middle Age Crazy' is one song, and another is 'I Wish I Was Eighteen Again'. Never a show regular, Jerry performed it occasionally well into the 21st Century - indeed, it was probably the highlight of 2011's Jack White produced 'Live At Third Man Records' album. George Burns covered the song in 1979, while composer Sonny Throckmorton released his own version in 1985.

First Release: 'Jerry Lee Lewis' (1979) + Single B-side (1979)

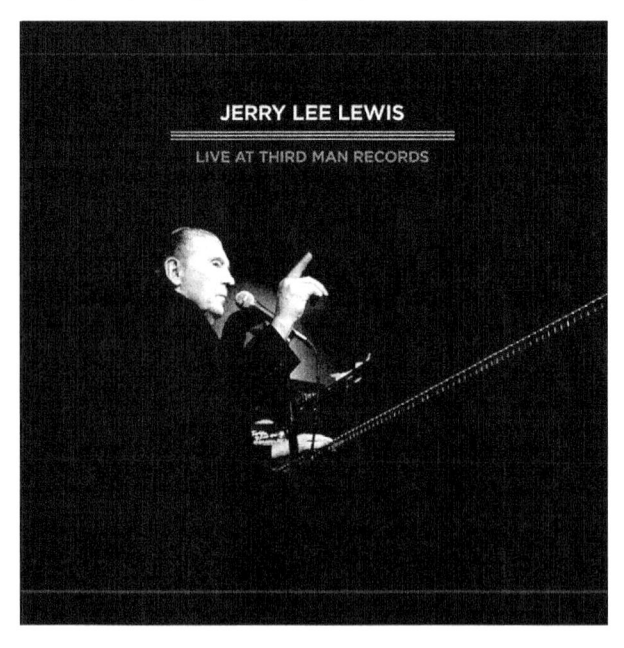

'Live at Third Man Records' (2011)

[250] I WISH YOU LOVE (1980) *
(Leo Chauliac / Albert A. Beach)

Originally released by Keely Smith in 1956, 'I Wish You Love' was also covered by Andy Williams (1960), Dean Martin (1962), Sam Cooke (1963), Judy Garland (1964), Frank Sinatra (1964), The Drifters (1965), Shirley Bassey (1968) and Engelbert Humperdinck (1969), amongst others. As with 'Autumn Leaves' from the same sessions, Jerry plays some incredible piano on a song that's a very unusual choice for him. In 1982, he played the song at a London hotel jam session, and enjoyed it so much he did it on stage in Rotterdam the next night. Linda Gail Lewis performed the song on 'The Many Sounds of Jerry Lee' in 1969.

First Release: 'The Caribou Ranch Sessions, 1980-1986' (2012) (bootleg)

[251] I WON'T HAVE TO CROSS JORDAN ALONE (1970) (L)
(Charles Durham / Thomas Ramsey)

Originally released by The Blackwood Brothers Quartet in 1946 and covered by Jimmie Davis (1951), The Louvin Brothers (1957) and Johnny Cash (1962), Jerry's live version (a congregation request!), is good but short.

First Release: 'The Killer: 1969-1972' (box-set, 1986)

[252] I WONDER WHERE YOU ARE TONIGHT (1969)
(Johnny Bond)

'I Wonder Where You Are Tonight' was originally released by Jimmy Wakely and His Rough Riders in 1941 and covered by Hank Snow (1950), Roy Drusky (1961), Porter Wagoner (1961), Arthur Alexander (1963), Lester Flatt and Earl Scruggs (1963), Bobby Bare (1963) and Bill Monroe (1967). Jerry's version, with its outstanding vocal and piano, and lighter than usual production, is one of the highlights of the 'Country Music Hall of Fame' sessions.

First Release: 'Sings The Country Music Hall of Fame Hits, Vol. One' (1969)

[253] I'D BE TALKIN' ALL THE TIME (1970)
(Chuck Howard / Larry Kingston)

First recorded earlier the same year by Ringo Starr, Jerry's excellent version would've made a great single and deserves to be more well-known.

First Release: 'There Must Be More To Love Than This' (1970)

[254] I'D DO IT ALL AGAIN (1980)
(Jerry Foster / Bill Rice)

One of those great 'middle-aged' songs that Jerry clearly identified with, 'I'd Do It All Again' was a highlight of his 3rd Elektra album 'Killer Country'. For some reason (probably because he had no current single release) it was performed on 'Hee Haw' as late as 1985, while other live performances include Rhode Island 1983, Phoenix 1983, Frankfurt 1983 and Tupelo 1986.

First Release: 'Killer Country' (1980) + Single A-side (1982)

I'd Do It All Again / Who Will Buy The Wine
(No. 52 Country)

'Killer Country' (1980)

[255] I'LL FIND IT WHERE I CAN (1977)
(Michael Clark / Zack Vanasdale)

During the mid '70s, the 'Outlaw' Country music sub-genre developed, which largely rejected the increasingly formulaic and slick productions from Nashville, and took the music in a more Rock-orientated direction. Jerry was never quite part of that movement (despite being the *original* outlaw!), but 'I'll Find It Where I Can' is the closest he ever came to that genre. A Top 10 Country hit, it was a concert regular during the late '70s and early '80s, but had disappeared by the mid '90s. The song was covered by Gary 'Auf Wiedersehen, Pet' Holton in 1981, and by the king of Outlaw himself Waylon Jennings in 1983.

First Release: 'Keeps Rockin'' (1978) + Single A-side (1978)

I'll Find It Where I Can / Don't Let The Stars Get In Your Eyes
(No. 10 Country)

'Pop Goes The Country' (1978)

[256] I'LL FLY AWAY (1970)
(Albert E. Brumley)

Originally released by Rev. J.M. Gates in 1940, Jerry's studio version of 'I'll Fly Away' is one of his most rousing Gospel recordings, and really does sound like it was recorded at a Revival meeting. The song was performed numerous times over the years, often on special occasions. These include: The Memphis Church recording 1970; 'In Concert' taping, Los Angeles 1974 (song not broadcast); 'The Survivors' concert, Stuttgart 1981 (with Johnny Cash and Carl Perkins); '25 Years Of Jerry Lee Lewis' TV special 1982 (with Carl Perkins, Kris Kristofferson, Dottie West, Mickey Gilley, Charlie Rich and The Oak Ridge Boys); 'Salute To Jerry Lee Lewis' TV special 1983 (with Little Richard); and 'Live Man Standing Live' taping 2006 (with Willie Nelson, not broadcast). Perhaps its most unlikely outing though was in a sleazy Hamburg club in 1990, where Jerry responded to an audience request for the song.

First Release: 'In Loving Memories: The Jerry Lee Lewis Gospel Album' (1970)

[257] I'LL KEEP ON LOVING YOU (1957)
(Floyd Tillman)

First recorded by Cliff Bruner's Texas Wanderers in 1939, and initially wrongly titled 'If The World Keeps On Turning' when released by Jerry Lee Lewis in 1970, 'I'll Keep On Loving You' is a perfect example of just how much Jerry, Roland and Jimmy complimented each other when playing rocked-up oldies. The handful of live performances include Chatham 1972, Amsterdam 1978, Berlin 1983, Burlington 1986 and the 64th Birthday Show in Tunica 1999.

First Release: 'Ole Tyme Country Music' (1970)

[258a] I'LL MAKE IT ALL UP TO YOU (1958)
(Charlie Rich)

Initially recorded at an earlier session without a band, 'I'll Make It All Up To You' is a very slow Country-Pop ballad, enhanced by an overdubbed male vocal group. Released as the B-side of 'Break Up', it charted in its own right at No. 85 Pop and No. 19 Country. Later covers include Mickey Gilley (1967), Cliff Richard (1970) and Ivory Joe Hunter (1974).

First Release: Single B-side (1958)

[258b] I'LL MAKE IT ALL UP TO YOU (1963)

Played at a less funereal pace, in a higher key, and minus much of the over-production utilized on other songs from these sessions, The Smash 'Golden Hits' recording actually has the edge over the original. Later live performances include Nashville 1979, Bristol 1983, Las Vegas 1989, Memphis 1990 and New York 2008.

First Release: 'The Golden Hits of Jerry Lee Lewis' (1964)

[259] I'LL NEVER GET OUT OF THIS WORLD ALIVE (1994)
(Fred Rose / Hank Williams)

Originally recorded by Hank Williams in 1952, Jerry's fast version of 'I'll Never Get Out Of This World Alive' is wonderful, murky mix withstanding. Why he never played it live is a mystery.

First Release: 'Young Blood' (1995)

[260] I'LL SAIL MY SHIP ALONE (1958)
(Henry Glover / Lois Mann / Moon Mullican / Henry Thurston)

Aubrey Wilson 'Moon' Mullican was a Country music singer and pianist who occasionally rocked things up a little, and consequently, some people cite him as a major influence on Jerry Lee Lewis. The more likely truth though is that Moon was no more than an inspiration for him, signposting what was possible, before Jerry took things several stages further. One of his best-known recordings was 1949's 'I'll Sail My Ship Alone', a song Jerry cut 7 takes of a November 1958 session, and despite the somewhat incongruous saxophone, it is material that he was clearly familiar with and enjoying. Live performances over the years include Fort Worth 1966 (featured on the 'By Request' album, where Jerry mentions Moon Mullican by name), Toronto 1967, Stockholm 1977, San Francisco 1979, Deeside 1980, Gothenburg 1982, Nottingham 1983, Toronto 1987, Las Vegas 1989, Zurich 1990, Pwhelli 1994, the 66th Birthday Show in Memphis 2001 and Perth, Scotland 2004.

First Release: Single A-side (1958)

I'll Sail My Ship Alone / It Hurt Me So
(No. 93 Pop)

[261] I'LL SEE YOU IN MY DREAMS [INSTRUMENTAL] (1958)
(Isham Jones / Gus Kahn)

Originally released by Isham Jones with Ray Miller's Orchestra in 1925, later covers of 'I'll See You In My Dreams' include Ella Fitzgerald (1947), Bing Crosby (1949), Vic Damone (1950), Doris Day (1951), The Four Tunes (1951) and Anita O'Day (1956). Probably just a session warm-up number, 'I'll See You In My Dreams' is an enjoyable instrumental.

First Release: 'The Sun Years' (Box-Set, 1983)

[262] I'M A LONESOME FUGITIVE (1968)
(Casey Anderson / Liz Anderson)

A wonderful Merle Haggard, originally released as 'The Fugitive' in 1966, it is a real highlight of Jerry's 1968 so-called Country comeback album, 'Another Place, Another Time'. Gene Vincent covered the song the previous year, and it is open to debate whose version is the best.

First Release: 'Another Place, Another Time' (1968)

[263] I'M ALONE BECAUSE I LOVE YOU (1986)
(Ira Schuster / Joseph Young)

A ballad that was originally released by Joe Green and His Orchestra in 1930, Rock 'n' Roll fans will be more familiar with the song via Eddie Cochran's 1957 and Fats Domino's 1961 versions. Jerry's version from September 1986 is more than acceptable, and is available on the 'Rocket' album. He performed the song at a show in Reykjavik, Iceland, in November 1986.

First Release: 'Rocket' (1988)

[264] I'M FEELIN' SORRY (1957)
(Jack Clement)

A fast Country-Pop song penned by Sun staffer Jack Clement, Jerry recorded several takes over two sessions in July and September 1957, though curiously the released cut is from the earlier session. It was promoted on 'American Bandstand' in 1957, but is no record of other live performances. Both The Prowlers and Ricky Nelson covered it the following year.

First Release: 'The Great Ball of Fire' EP (1957)

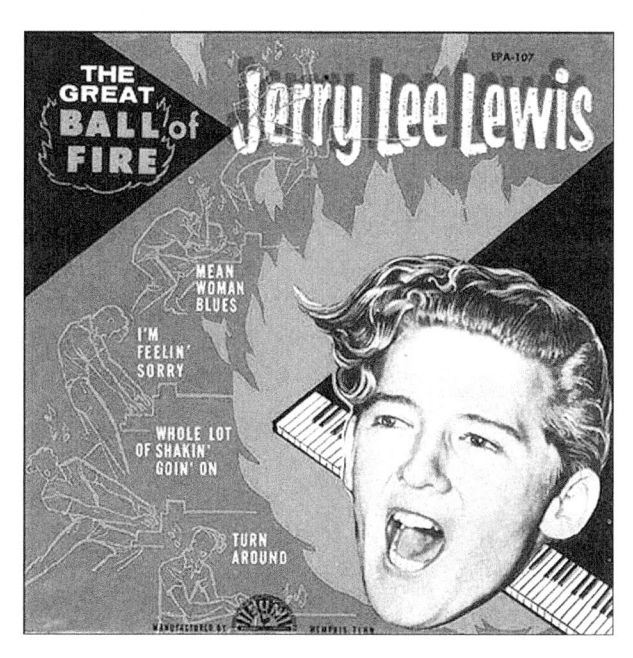

'The Ball Of Fire' (EP, 1957)

[265] I'M IN THE GLORYLAND WAY (1970) (L)
(James Samuel Torbett)

Originally released by The Jenkins' Sacred Singers in 1927, this is an up-tempo Gospel song very much in the 'I'll Fly Away' mode. The drummer on the live Memphis Church recording is Jerry's late son Jerry Lee Lewis Jr., who was taught how to play by Morris 'Tarp' Tarrant, coincidentally the same drummer who also taught Jerry's future wife Kerrie how to play the drums.

First Release: 'The Killer: 1969-1972' (box-set, 1986)

[266] I'M KNEE DEEP IN LOVING YOU (1975)
(Sonny Throckmorton)

Originally released by Roy Drusky in 1974, this modern mid-pace Pop-Rock song could've made a great single for Jerry, even if it did require some vocal overdubbing to give it a bit of polish. Instead, it remained locked firmly in the vaults for over a decade.

First Release: 'From The Vaults' (1986)

[267] I'M LEFT, YOU'RE RIGHT, SHE'S GONE (1973)
(Stan Kesler / Bill Taylor)

When Stan Kesler produced Jerry in 1973, they inevitably included the song he'd written 18 years earlier for Elvis Presley. For the first verse, it is easy to be fooled that The Killer's cut is the definitive one - until what sounds like the Royal Philharmonic Orchestra come in on strings. Jerry himself couldn't have thought much of it, as the only known live performance was as part of a medley in Birmingham, Alabama in 1974.

First Release: 'Sometimes A Memory Ain't Enough' (1973) + Single A-side (1973)

I'm Left, You're Right, She's Gone / I've Fallen To The Bottom
(No. 21 Country)

[268] I'M LONGING FOR HOME (1970)
(Rupert Cravens / O.S. Davis)

Originally released by Jerry's cousin David Beatty and The Oak Ridge Quartet in 1964, 'I'm Longing For Home' is passionately-sung Gospel ballad played in ¾ time. It was performed at the Memphis Church recording in 1970, as well as on the 40th Anniversary Show in Memphis in 1996.

First Release: 'In Loving Memories: The Jerry Lee Lewis Gospel Album' (1970)

[269] I'M LOOKING OVER A FOUR LEAF CLOVER (1983)
(Mort Dixon / Harry Woods)

Originally released by Sam Lanin's Dance Orchestra in 1927 and revived by Frankie Laine in 1948, Jerry's version kicks off with a 'Lucille' intro, and then proceeds along at a moderately-rocked-up pace. Not the greatest thing he did for MCA but certainly not the worst, live performances include Charlotte 1984, Toronto 1984, Pasadena 1984, Oslo 1985, Augusta 1985, Phoenix 1985, Montreal 1986, Memphis 1993, Dublin 1993 and Pwhelli 1994. On 1991's 'Honky Tonk Rock & Roll Piano Man' compilation, a remarkable alternate take re-titled 'I'm Looking Under A Skirt' came to light, with risqué but amusing lines like *"I'm looking under a skirt and I wonder, why I've never looked before!"*.

First Release: 'I Am What I Am' (1984)

[270a] I'M ON FIRE (1964)//(Bob Feldman / Jerry Goldstein / Richard Gottehrer)

Released as a single in 1964, 'I'm On Fire' was Jerry's best new Rock 'n' Roll song in years, summoning up the glory days of 'Great Balls Of Fire', 'Breathless' and 'Lovin' Up A Storm'. He gives it the treatment it deserves, and even the girly backing vocalists can't distract from its greatness. Stalling at No. 98 in the US Pop charts, Jerry did at least get to perform it on British TV's 'Whole Lotta Shakin' Goin' On' TV special, as well as on a couple of radio shows during the same tour. It was covered by The Strangeloves in 1964 and The Greenbeats in 1965, while an alternate take was issued on the 1969 European 'I'm On Fire' compilation.

First Release: Single A-side (1964)

I'm On Fire / Bread and Butter Man
(No. 98 Pop)

'Whole Lotta Shakin' Goin' On' (1964)

[270b] I'M ON FIRE (1988)

For just one day in early 1989, this author was an 'extra' in the 'Great Balls Of Fire' movie, and while it was very easy money getting paid to heckle Dennis Quaid, it was very obvious even then that a scene set in 1958 with a song not written until 1964 wasn't going to be the makings of a great movie! Still, 'I'm On Fire' is a nice re-cut, and if the vocal isn't quite as animated as it was in 1964, the more sympathetic backing more than makes up for it. Jerry even performed the song live again a couple of times, in Las Vegas in 1988 and Honefoss in 1989.

First Release: 'Great Balls Of Fire!' (1989)

[271] I'M SO LONESOME I COULD CRY (1969)
(Hank Williams)

Originally released by Hank Williams in 1949, later covers of Hank's most heart-breaking song include Marty Robbins (1957), Johnny Cash (1960), Ronnie Hawkins (1960), Johnny Tillotson (1962), The Everly Brothers (1963), Duane Eddy (1964), Hank Williams Jr. (1964), Del Shannon (1964), Wanda Jackson (1965) and Carla Thomas (1966). The most adventurously-arranged song on the 'Country Music Hall of Fame' albums, Jerry's beautiful version moderates over several keys. Although not released as a single at the time, in 1982 Mercury tastefully overdubbed it with subtle strings, and finally issued it on a 45, achieving a Top 50 Country hit in the process. Very occasional live performances include Stockholm 1972, Nashville 1973, Columbia (South Carolina) 1974, Pasadena 1981, London 1982, Bristol 1983 and Montreal 1986.

First Release: 'Sings The Country Music Hall of Fame Hits, Vol. One' (1969) + Single A-side (1982)

I'm So Lonesome I Could Cry / Pick Me Up On Your Way Down
(No. 43 Country)

[272] I'M SORRY, I'M NOT SORRY (1958)
(Wanda Ballman)

Originally released by Carl Perkins in 1956, Jerry's version is more than listenable. Most Sun fans though would prefer Carl's version.

First Release: 'The Sun Years' (Box-Set, 1983)

[273] I'M STILL JEALOUS OF YOU (1974)
(Jerry Foster / Bill Rice)

'I'm Still Jealous Of You' is one of the more memorable songs on 'Boogie Woogie Country Man', an album that in itself was a considerable improvement on the previous, 1974's 'I-40 Country'. For some reason, the song was performed several times in late 1978, including Owensboro, Margate, Bergen, Gothenburg, London and Birmingham, with Tulsa in 1980 was the only other known live performance. Perhaps the song resonated with whatever was going on in his private life at the time? Certainly late 1978 was when his growing alcoholism seemed to peak (he was often extremely drunk at the time), and by 1980 he'd straightened up considerably.

First Release: 'Boogie Woogie Country Man' (1975) + Single B-side (1975)

[274] I'M THE GUILTY ONE (1959)
(unknown, poss. Jerry Lee Lewis)

A wonderful Country song that Hank Williams would've been proud of, the composer credits are usually credited to Jerry Lee Lewis on releases, if only because no-one knows for sure who wrote it. If it really was The Killer, then this is his greatest song.

First Release: 'The Sun Years' (Box-Set, 1983)

[275a] I'M THROWING RICE (1958)
(Eddy Arnold / Ed Nelson, Jr. / Steve Nelson)

Originally released by Eddy Arnold in 1949, this sentimental ballad about lost love is amongst Jerry's finest early Country performances. The only known live performance was in Hollywood in 1979.

First Release: 'A Taste of Country' (1970)

[275b] I'M THROWING RICE (1980) *

Almost twice the length of the Sun cut and played in a lower key, for this 1980 re-cut Jerry opted for a fast Rock 'n' Roll arrangement, and whilst an interesting experiment, the song doesn't really lend itself to such a treatment.

First Release: 'The Caribou Ranch Sessions, 1980-1986' (2012) (bootleg)

[275c] **I'M THROWING RICE** (1988) *

In one scene of the 'Great Balls of Fire!' movie, a delightful mid-paced re-cut of 'I'm Throwing Rice' can be briefly heard. Surfacing on a bootleg a couple of years later, it is only slightly marred by the clumsy non-ending, which is probably why it wasn't included on the soundtrack album.

First Release: 'The Killer's Private Stash' (1991) (bootleg)

[276] **I'M USING MY BIBLE FOR A ROAD MAP - WAIT A LITTLE LONGER JESUS** (1987)
(Don Reno / Charles Schroder) + (Hazel Houser)

Originally released by Don Reno, Red Smiley and The Tennessee Cutups in 1952 and by Chester Smith in 1954, respectively, this Gospel medley would be very nice if it weren't for the horrible cheap keyboard and electronic drums. Surprisingly Jerry performed the same medley live at a 1988 show in Atlantic City.

First Release: 'At Hank Cochran's' (1995)

[276b] **I'M USING MY BIBLE FOR A ROAD MAP - I'M LONGING FOR HOME** (1988) *
(Don Reno / Charles Schroder) + (Rupert Cravens / O.S. Davis)

Released unofficially on the same 1991 bootleg as 'I'm Throwing Rice' from the same sessions, this impromptu Gospel medley is played solo without a band.

First Release: 'The Killer's Private Stash' (1991) (bootleg)

[277] **I'M WALKIN'** (1972)
(Dave Bartholomew / Fats Domino)

Originally released by Fats Domino in 1957 and covered by Ricky Nelson the same year, Jerry's version is played at an incredibly frantic pace, and would be very exciting indeed if it weren't for the diabolical strings. Instead, it sounds like two different records being played at once. The only known performance was live in Hamburg in 1972, a show that was released as one of the earliest Jerry Lee Lewis vinyl bootlegs.

First Release: 'The Killer Rocks On' (1972)

[278] **I'VE BEEN TWISTIN'** (1962)
(Herman Parker Jr.)

Based on Junior Parker's 'Feelin' Good' from 1953 (which in itself was based on a John Lee Hooker guitar riff), if it weren't for the dreaded "Twist" word, this would be regarded as one of Jerry's toughest later Sun recordings. Unfairly dismissed by many, for a long time there were thought to be at least 3 available versions, but instead there are just two takes, with the original single being an edit of the two.

First Release: Single A-side (1962)

I've Been Twistin' / Ramblin' Rose
(Not a hit)

[279] **I'VE FORGOT MORE ABOUT YOU (THAN HE'LL EVER KNOW)** (1974)
(Courtney Bentz / Jerry Grant)

Not to be confused with the vastly superior 'I Forgot More Than You'll Ever Know', 'I've Forgot More About You (Than He'll Ever Know)' is a forgettable song from Jerry's weakest album.

First Release: 'I-40 Country' (1974)

[280] **IF I EVER NEEDED YOU (I NEED YOU NOW)** (1954) *
(Al Jacobs / Jimmie Crane)

A predictable Pop ballad that was a 1954 hit for Eddie Fisher, Jerry's 1954 Demo is inevitably more impressive for his piano playing than it is vocally. As with the flipside, 'If I Ever Needed You (I Need You Now)', this surfaced on 1991's 'The Killer's Private Stash' bootleg.

First Release: 'The Killer's Private Stash' (1991) (bootleg)

[281] **IF I HAD IT ALL TO DO OVER** (1966)
(Paul Selph)

A very Soulfully-sung Pop ballad, when first issued as the B-side of 'Memphis Beat' it was overdubbed with sweeping but tasteful strings. Later issued in un-dubbed form, it somehow sounded a bit empty and far less enjoyable.

First Release: Single B-side (1958)

[282] **IF WE NEVER MEET AGAIN - I'LL MEET YOU IN THE MORNING** (1970)
(Albert E. Brumley)

Originally released by Brown's Ferry Four in 1946, and by the J. B. Whitmire Blue Sky Trio in 1937, respectively, this inspired Gospel medley played in ¾ 'waltz' time was actually recorded as two entirely separate pieces. The same medley was performed at the 1970 Memphis Church recording.

First Release: 'In Loving Memories: The Jerry Lee Lewis Gospel Album' (1970)

[283a] **IN LOVING MEMORIES** (1969)
(Cecil Harrelson / Linda Gail Lewis)

A song that is just as sad and downbeat as 'Gather 'Round Children', 'In Loving Memories' was first attempted in November 1969 at the same session where Jerry taped his rollicking version of 'Brown-Eyed Handsome Man'.

First Release: 'The Killer: 1969-1972' (box-set, 1986)

[283b] **IN LOVING MEMORIES** (1970)

Played in a higher key and at a suitably funereal tempo, this superior remake became the title track of Jerry's Gospel album of the same name. Also released as a single, it peaked at No. 48 in the Country charts. Conway Twitty covered the song in 1973.

First Release: 'In Loving Memories: The Jerry Lee Lewis Gospel Album' (1970) + Single A-side (1970)

In Loving Memories / I Can't Have A Merry Christmas, Mary (Without You)
(No. 48 Country)

[284a] IN THE GARDEN (1980) *
(Charles Austin Miles)

First recorded by Mrs. Wm. Asher and Homer Rodeheaver in 1916, 'In The Garden' was also covered by The Blackwood Brothers Quartet (1946), Gene Autry and Dinah Shore (1950), Roy Rogers and Dale Evans (1950), Tennessee Ernie Ford (1956), Jim Reeves (1959), Elvis Presley (1967), Willie Nelson (1976) and Mickey Gilley (1978). Played in ¾ time, Jerry's 1980 version would've made a nice inclusion on the proposed but cancelled Elektra Gospel album. He performed the song live on 'Austin City Limits' in 1983.

First Release: 'The Caribou Ranch Sessions, 1980-1986' (2012) (bootleg)

[284b] IN THE GARDEN (2022)

On the 16th of February 2019, Jerry Lee Lewis performed a concert at the Peace Center in Greenville, South Carolina, and though frail looking, he played some great piano and was in good spirits. It was his last show. Just days later, he suffered a debilitating stroke from which he never fully recovered, particularly affecting his walking and his right hand. On April 19th 2022, Jerry entered a recording studio in Baton Rouge, Louisiana, to record a long-promised Gospel album with his cousin Jimmy Swaggart, and although he was very weak, he managed to lay down vocal tracks for 5 songs that day, as well as contributing the occasional left-hand (only) piano work (Jerry reportedly also cut Gospel sessions in early 2020, but these remain unheard at time of writing). One of only two songs on the album sung without Jimmy, this sprightly version with slick but enjoyable production features Jerry sounding better than one might've thought, and he is clearly enjoying singing again.

First Release: 'The Boys From Ferriday' (2022)

[285] IN THE MOOD [INSTRUMENTAL] (1960)
(Joe Garland / Andy Razaf)

Originally released by Edgar Hayes and His Orchestra in 1938 and made famous by Glenn Miller and His Orchestra the following year, within the first few bars of this rocked-up version it is patently obvious who the pianist is, and any attempts to convince people otherwise under the name of 'The Hawk' clearly weren't going to work. Live performances include Toronto 1967, Amsterdam 1978, Madrid 1990, Memphis 1993, Dallas 1997, Perth (Scotland) 2004 and Farum 2006.

First Release: Single A-side (1960)

In The Mood / I Get The Blues When It Rains
(Not a hit)

[286] **INVITATION TO YOUR PARTY** (1963)
(Bill Taylor)

Taped at Jerry's final Sun session on 28th August 1963, this very contemporary-sounding Country song still sounded fresh when it was released 6 years later, getting to No. 6 in the Country charts. Live performances include Las Vegas 1970 and Birmingham, Alabama 1974.

First Release: 'The Golden Cream Of The Country' (1969) + Single A-side (1969)

Invitation To Your Party / I Could Never Be Ashamed Of You
(No. 6 Country)

[287a] IT ALL DEPENDS (WHO WILL BUY THE WINE) (1957)
(Billy Mize)

Originally released by Billy Mize in 1956 as 'Who Will Buy the Wine?', Jerry's excellent version from February 1957 made a very worthy album track, even if the overdubbed backing vocals weren't really needed. Six months later, he taped a less polished and inferior re-cut, and this was released on 2015's 'The Collected Works' box-set. Curiously, the Sun versions are generally entitled 'It All Depends'. It is only the later 1979 Elektra release which reverts to the original title.

First Release: 'Jerry Lee Lewis' (1958)

[287b] IT ALL DEPENDS (WHO WILL BUY THE WINE) (1979)

A bit faster, and with fiddle, steel guitar and strings, the 1979 cut is a perfectly fine modern-sounding Country recording, even if it could never replace the earlier Sun album track. A handful of live performances over the years include Chicago 1979, Tulsa 1980, Norrkoping 1985, Las Vegas 1989 and the 40th Anniversary Show in Memphis 1996.

First Release: 'When Two Worlds Collide' (1980) + Single B-side (1982)

[288] IT HURT ME SO (1958)
(Bill Justis / Charlie Rich)

A nice ballad that was issued as the flip side of 'I'll Sail My Ship Alone', an overdubbed vocal group, complete with a bass singer, make this the closest Jerry ever came to making a Doo Wop record. A total of 6 takes were recorded, of which the 1958 single was the last.

First Release: Single B-side (1958)

[289] IT IS NO SECRET [with Jimmy Swaggart] (2022)
(Stuart Hamblen)

Originally released by Stuart Hamblen in 1950 and covered by Elvis Presley in 1957 and Little Richard in 1963, Jerry's tenor nicely compliments Jimmy's deeper voice. Sadly though, he struggles a bit on this one, far more so than on 'In The Garden' cut the same day.

First Release: 'The Boys From Ferriday' (2022)

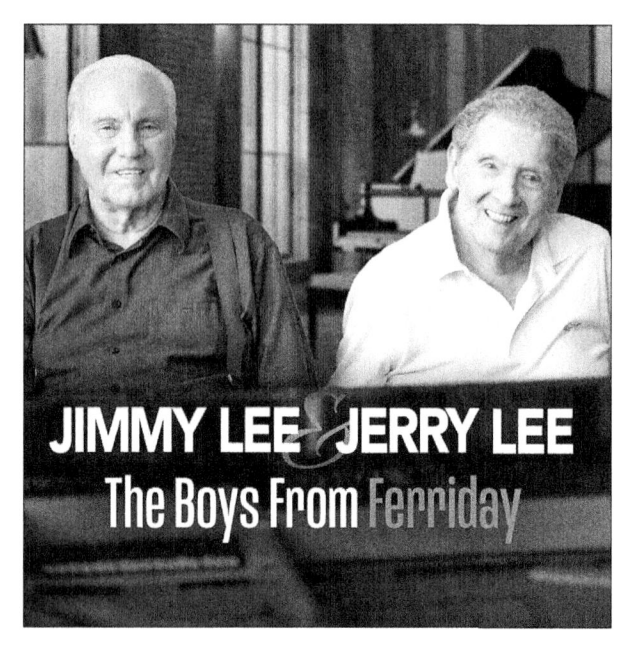

'The Boys from Ferriday' (2022)

[290] **IT MAKES NO DIFFERENCE NOW** (1969)

(Jimmie Davis / Floyd Tillman)

Originally released by Cliff Bruner's Texas Wanderers in 1938, others who covered 'It Makes No Difference Now' include Eddy Arnold (1947), Ernest Tubb (1959), Tommy Collins (1960), Ray Charles (1962), Don Gibson (1962), Carl Smith (1965) and Bill Monroe (1967). Jerry's version is like many of his Country recordings from around this time: clearly sung, nicely played, but just a little sterile and predictable.

First Release: 'Sings The Country Music Hall of Fame Hits, Vol. Two' (1969)

[291] **IT WAS THE WHISKEY TALKIN' (NOT ME)** (1990)

(Andy Paley / Jonathan Paley / Michael Kernan / Ned Claflin)

Following the relative success of the 1989 'Great Balls Of Fire' movie soundtrack, Jerry should've been swamped with offers of record contracts. That never quite happened, but it did lead to Sire wanting to include him on the soundtrack of 'Dick Tracy', the latest movie vehicle for the unfathomably popular Madonna. The song he was given, 'It Was The Whiskey Talkin' (Not Me),' is excellent, with a '30s 'Swing' feel and lyrics Jerry could've once identified with. It can be heard (briefly) in the movie, and appeared on both the 'Dick Tracy' soundtrack album and as a single. For the single's B-side, as well as also on the soundtrack album, Producer Andy Paley cut a '50s-styled Rock 'n' Roll version, complete with quasi-Sun echo. Jerry never performed the song live, but it was good enough to (eventually) persuade Andy Paley and Sire to record the 1995 'Young Blood' album, on which the Swing version also appeared.

First Release: Single (1990), also 'Young Blood' (1995)

It Was The Whiskey Talkin' (Not Me) / It Was The Whiskey Talkin' (Not Me)
(Not a hit)

[292] **IT WILL BE WORTH IT ALL WHEN WE SEE JESUS** (1970) (L)
(Bill Gaither)

Originally released by The Bill Gaither Trio in 1967, Jerry's performance from the 1970 Memphis Church recording is only about 50 seconds long, but it's nice while it lasts.

First Release: 'The Killer: 1969-1972' (box-set, 1986)

[293] **IT WON'T HAPPEN WITH ME** (1961)
(Ray Evans)

During the 1959-1967 era, there were many varied attempts to get Jerry back in the higher echelons of the charts, some of them inspired, and others bordering on desperation. The overtly teen-orientated 'It Won't Happen With Me', with lines like *"You say you can marry Fabian with help from the hands of fate!"* and *"The only thing that you may be for Ricky is just a fan!"* isn't suited to Jerry at all, though that said its nowhere near as awful as it looks on paper. Ironically, the few DJs who played the record preferred the hard-country 'Cold, Cold Heart' on the flip side, a moderate hit in its own right. There is no record of 'It Won't Happen With Me' ever being performed live.

First Release: Single B-side (1961)

[294] IT'LL BE ME (1957)
(Jack Clement)

Following the lack of real commercial success for Jerry's debut single 'Crazy Arms', Jack Clement thought he'd found the answer with 'It'll Be Me', but after stumbling upon 'Whole Lotta Shakin' Goin' On', it was relegated to the B-side. It is still a highly worthy Rock 'n' Roll song though, and the frantic-paced single version quickly became a fan favorite. When Sam Phillips compiled Jerry's debut album the following year, he selected a take from a slightly later session, which is slower, shorter, and features a drum intro. There are many outtakes from both sessions, some very different, but when 2015's 'The Collected Works' box-set was put together, compilers discovered a one-off take from a *third* session. Slow-ish and very playful, this alone is almost worth the price of the box-set! Amongst later cover versions were Johnny Cymbal (1960), Cliff Richard and The Shadows (1962), Gerry and The Pacemakers (1964), Bobby Vee (1965) and Tom Jones (1982), while infrequent live performances include Memphis 1961, Melbourne 1970, Belfast 1985 and Apeldoorn 1991.

First Release: Single B-side (1957) + 'Jerry Lee Lewis' (1958)

[295] IT'S A HANG UP BABY (1967)
(Eddie Reeves)

With funky bass guitar, a prominent electric piano motif, riffing horns, and lyrics like *"You do some mean-mean voodoo, you got a monkey's paw hangin' over you!"*, Sun traditionalists hated 'It's A Hang Up Baby'. But it is proof if needed that Jerry was an incredibly Soulful singer at his vocal peak, and didn't always *need* a piano. Remarkably, he opened several shows with the song during a series of concerts in Toronto in October 1967, but following his major success with Country music the following year, it was quickly forgotten. One person who did recognize the song's potential was Blues-Soul singer Z.Z. Hill, who cut an interesting cover in 1969.

First Release: Soul My Way (1967) + Single A-side (1967)

It's A Hang Up Baby / Holdin' On
(Not a hit)

[296] IT'S BEEN SO LONG [with Webb Pierce, Mel Tillis and Faron Young] (1984)
(Audrey Grisham)

Originally released by Webb Pierce in 1953, this is a traditional Country performance with the kind of backing and light production that sounds far more '50s than '80s. The highly enjoyable 'Four Legends' album contrasts greatly with the hugely disappointing 'Class of '55', recorded the following year.

First Release: 'Four Legends' (1985)

[297] IT'S THE REAL THING (1970) *
(Bill Backer)

During the March 1970 sessions for the 'There Must Be More To Love Than This' album, Jerry cut two short songs promoting Coca Cola, one of them Rock 'n' Roll the other Country, with 60 second and 30 second edits of each. The Rock 'n' Roll version appeared on a '70s bootleg, albeit wrongly listed as being from 1967; a big multi-national company like Coca Cola wouldn't have been interested in Jerry Lee Lewis during his wilderness years! Incidentally, Jerry also cut a radio advert for McDonalds in 1982, with the tag-line *"Goodness gracious, big mac 'n' fries!"*. Anyone got a recording of it?

First Release: 'Rockin' Jerry Lee Lewis' (1975) (bootleg)

[298] IVORY TEARS (1977)
(Mack Vickery)

In 1977, Jerry cut two versions of this excellent Mack Vickery-composed Country song, one in August and another one in December. With lines like *"I pour out my soul to my old piano, and I let those old ivories cry for me!"*, it was clearly tailor-made for him, but very strangely both takes stayed in the can for almost a decade. The August version, with a sparser arrangement, was released on 1986's '30th Anniversary Album', while the December take, a little slower and with a vocal group introduction, was issued on the following year's 'The Killer: 1973-1977' box-set.

First Release: '30th Anniversary Album' (1986)

[299] JACK DANIELS (OLD NUMBER SEVEN) (1973)
(Tony Colton / Chas Hodges / Albert Lee / Ray Smith)

Following the January 1973 London sessions, Heads, Hands and Feet band member Tony Colton arranged another session, this time in Memphis the following March. The main purpose of this was to record 'Jack Daniels (Old Number Seven)' a modern Country-Rock song that was first released by Heads, Hands and Feet in 1972. Jerry contributed one of his finest vocal performances on the song and it could've pushed him in a more contemporary 'Outlaw' direction, but unfortunately Mercury hid it on the B-side of 'No Headstone On My Grave', not even putting it on an album. Don Everly covered the song the following year.

First Release: Single B-side (1973)

[300] **JACKSON** [with Linda Gail Lewis] (1969)
(Gaby Rodgers / Billy Edd Wheeler)

First recorded by The Kingston Trio in 1963, and made famous by Johnny Cash and June Carter, and Nancy Sinatra and Lee Hazlewood, both in 1967, 'Jackson' is one of Jerry and Linda's most enduring duets. Live performances include Las Vegas 1970, 'The Midnight Special' 1973, New York 1986 (the show's opening number!), Cambridge 1987, Milan 1987 and Bridlington 1987.

First Release: 'Sings The Country Music Hall of Fame Hits, Vol. One' (1969) + 'Together' (1969)

[301a] **JAILHOUSE ROCK** (1958)
(Jerry Leiber / Mike Stoller)

The Elvis Presley classic from the previous year, 'Jailhouse Rock' was cut a 1958 session that also included 'Don't Be Cruel', 'Hound Dog' and 'Good Rockin' Tonight', and is just as thrilling as any of those other numbers. He was very like backed by his stage band, J.W. Brown on bass and Russell Smith on drums.

First Release: 'Monsters' (1971)

[301b] **JAILHOUSE ROCK** (1986)

Recorded in September 1986, this spirited performance is only slightly marred by the over-prominent Jordanaires.

First Release: 'Rocket' (1988)

'Rocket' (1988)

[302a] **JAMBALAYA (ON THE BAYOU)** (1958)
(Hank Williams)

Originally released by Hank Williams in 1952 with covers that include Moon Mullican (1952) and Brenda Lee (1956), Jerry's Sun version is given an exciting mid-tempo Rock 'n' Roll treatment with a prominent Roland Janes guitar riff, similar to 'Down The Line'. Sam Phillips was obviously impressed too, as he selected it for Jerry's debut album later that year.

First Release: 'Jerry Lee Lewis' (1958)

[302b] **JAMBALAYA (ON THE BAYOU)** (1969)

Very different from the Sun cut, Jerry's 1969 version of 'Jambalaya' is much faster yet more Country-fied, also having a few extra chords thrown in. For a couple of years at least, Jerry used this same arrangement for live performances, including on the 'Live at The International, Las Vegas' album. The song was still performed live very occasionally until well into the New Millennium.

First Release: 'Sings The Country Music Hall of Fame Hits, Vol. One' (1969)

[303a] **JEALOUS HEART** (1970)
(Jenny Carson)

Originally released by Tex Ritter in 1944, covers include Ivory Joe Hunter (1949), Bob Luman (1960), Connie Francis (1965), Loretta Lynn (1966), Wanda Jackson (1966) and Bonnie Owens (1969). Jerry's 1970 version oddly features an electric piano, and was not released at the time.

First Release: 'The Killer: 1969-1972' (box-set, 1986)

[303b] **JEALOUS HEART** (1977)

Thankfully with a real piano, as well as sympathetic backing that includes Kenny on fiddle, this is superior to the earlier cut in pretty much every way. Very occasional live performances include Wheeling 1977, Tulsa 1979, Atlantic City 1988 and Perth, Scotland 2004.

First Release: 'Country Memories' (1977)

[304] **JENNY, JENNY** (1964) (L)
(Enotris Johnson / Richard Penniman)

Originally released by Little Richard in 1957, this frantic live version makes a perfect opener to 'The Greatest Live Show on Earth' album, with Jerry and the band *really* cookin' throughout! Later live performances include 'Shindig!' 1964, Paris 1966, Lausanne 1966, Newcastle 1980 and London 1980, but more often it was only performed as part of Rock Medley.

First Release: 'The Greatest Live Show on Earth' (1964)

'The Greatest Live Show on Earth' (1964)

[305] JERRY LEE'S ROCK 'N' ROLL REVIVAL SHOW (1976)
(Jerry Foster / Bill Rice)

One of those contrived Rock 'n' Roll songs from writers who don't understand the genre but compensate by cramming in as many classic song titles as possible, it is noticeable that the only nod to Rock 'n' Roll on 'Country Class' is the weakest track on the album. Jerry performed the song in Rome in 1987 (and released it on the poorly-mixed 'Live in Italy' album), and with John Williams for the 40th Anniversary Show in Memphis in 1996. Freddie 'Fingers' Lee covered it as 'Freddie Lee's Rock and Roll Revival Show' in 1979.

First Release: 'Country Class' (1976) + Single B-side (1976)

[306] JERRY LEE'S BOOGIE (NEW ORLEANS BOOGIE) (1952)
(Jerry Lee Lewis)

The B-side of Jerry's very first Demo, 'Jerry Lee's Boogie' (aka 'New Orleans Boogie') is proof that Jerry Lee Lewis could play Rock 'n' Roll piano long before the term had even been invented! *See 'Don't Stay Away (Till Love Grows Cold)' for more background on this Demo!*

First Release: 'A Half Century Of Hits' (2006)

[307] JERRY'S GOT THE BLUES (1980) *
(Jerry Lee Lewis)

Little more than a mid-tempo Blues jam, this is worth hearing for some fine piano playing and guitar.

First Release: 'The Caribou Ranch Sessions, 1980-1986' (2012) (bootleg)

[308] JERRY'S PLACE (1975)
(Ray Griff)

'Jerry's Place' was the name of one of many short-lived night-clubs that Jerry invested in over the years, and the best thing about this mediocre song is the up-front boogie woogie piano playing. Writer Ray Griff recorded it as 'Raymond's Place' in 1977.

First Release: 'Odd Man In' (1975)

[309a] JESUS HOLD MY HAND (1980) *
(Albert E. Brumley)

Originally released by the Prairie Ramblers in 1936, this storming performance lasts over 5 minutes, with around 2 minutes devoted to an instrumental jam! One of several great Gospel performances cut for Elektra but kept in the can.

First Release: 'The Caribou Ranch Sessions, 1980-1986' (2012) (bootleg)

[309b] JESUS HOLD MY HAND [with Jimmy Swaggart] (2022)

Of the songs on 'The Boys from Ferriday', this fast number is the closest things came to Rock 'n' Roll, though of course with wholly spiritual lyrics. He and Jimmy are in quite good voice, with Jerry even playing some left-hand piano, alongside some excellent guitar and saxophone solos.

First Release: 'The Boys From Ferriday' (2022)

[310] JESUS IS ON THE MAINLINE (CALL HIM SOMETIME) (1974)
(Marijohn Wilkin)

Originally released by The Hopson Family in 1972 though based on an older song, 'Jesus Is On The Mainline' is one of Jerry's most exciting Gospel numbers, and is a highlight of the almost return to form 'Boogie Woogie Country Man' album. The song was performed live very occasionally as part of a longer Gospel medley during the mid '70s.

First Release: 'Boogie Woogie Country Man' (1975)

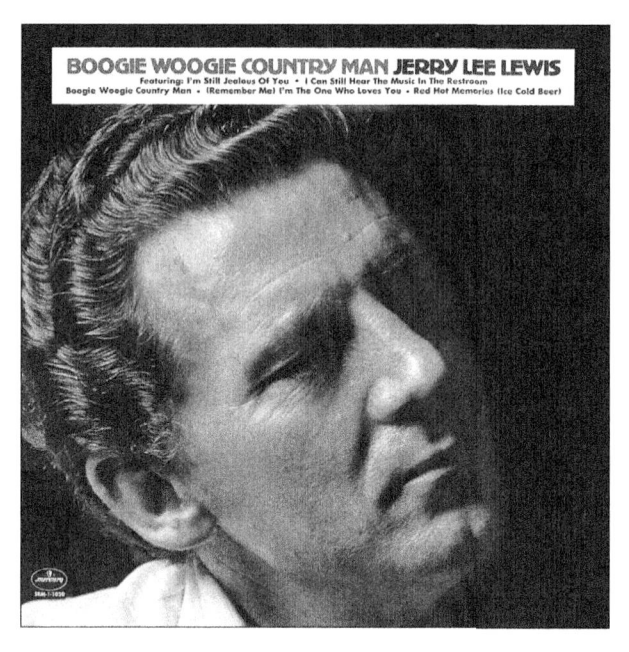

'Boogie Woogie Country Man' (1975)

[311] JOHN HENRY (1960)
(Traditional)

A very old song whose true origins are long lost, the earliest known recording is by Fiddlin' John Carson (as 'John Henry Blues') in 1924, and has been covered by Lead Belly (1943), Paul Robeson (1943), Josh White (1944), Merle Travis (1947), Burl Ives (1950), Woody Guthrie (1952), Lonnie Donegan (1954), Big Bill Broonzy (1954), Pete Seeger (1957) and Brownie McGhee and Sonny Terry (1958). Forgetting most of the lyrics, Jerry's loose but fun jam features a nice honking sax, and the worst thing about it is the track's short running time. *"It's too good to stop now!"* he says, just before the fade-out. He was right!

First Release: Single B-side (1960)

[312a] JOHNNY B. GOODE (1958)
(Chuck Berry)

The Chuck Berry Rock 'n' Roll standard from 1958, Jerry cut two very different versions at Sun that same year. The 2nd version, though the first to be released, features full guitar, bass and drums backing, and while good, there are some uncharacteristically sloppy stops and starts from Jimmy Van Eaton. When the 1983 'The Sun Years' box-set was released, it included an earlier version, taken from a solo session without a band, and it is *incredible*! As Jerry once said, when asked about other musicians on sessions *"I played on them, what the hell else do you need to know?!"*. Well this time, he didn't even *need* other musicians.

First Release: 'Rockin' Rhythm & Blues' (1969)

[312b] **JOHNNY B. GOODE** (1963)

Although the guitar's a bit tinny and the backing vocalists are annoying, this is a more than adequate version with a pounding piano solo. Taped at the September 1963 'Golden Hits' sessions, it didn't sound out of place when released on 1965's 'The Return Of Rock' two years later.

First Release: 'The Return of Rock' (1965)

[312c] **JOHNNY B. GOODE** (1973)

Kicking off with a piano intro, the lengthy and powerful version of 'Johnny B. Goode' recorded in January 1973 for 'The Session' is a real treat, and heavy-handed guitars aside, surpasses pretty much all earlier attempts. A rehearsal take circulates unofficially.

First Release: 'The Session' (1973)

'The Session' (1973)

[312d] **JOHNNY B. GOODE / CAROL** (1973/1974)

This lengthy, inspired but messy work-out, with prominent piano, steel guitar and harmonica, features a few snatches of Chuck's 'Carol' thrown in for good measure. As with Chuck's 'Roll Over Beethoven', 'Johnny B. Goode' remained a frequent crowd-pleaser at concerts well into the New Millennium.

First Release: 'The Knox Phillips Sessions: The Unreleased Recordings' (2014)

[313] **JUKEBOX** (1973)
(Tony Colton / Chas Hodges / Albert Lee / Ray Smith)

Of all the songs that ended up on 1973's 'The Session' double album, only two were completely new to Jerry (that is assuming that he was at least *vaguely* familiar with 'Early Morning Rain'!). Both were written by members of Heads, Hands and Feet, talented UK Country-Rockers that included Chas Hodges amongst their ranks. While perhaps not as strong a song as 'Music To The Man', Jerry sounds genuinely engaged. A lengthy rehearsal take, with largely improvised lyrics, circulates unofficially.

First Release: 'The Session' (1973)

[314] **JUKEBOX JUNKY** (1980)
(Danny Morrison / David Kirby)

There isn't too much filler on the three 1979-1980 albums Jerry cut for Elektra, but 'Jukebox Junky' is one of them. Annoyingly catchy and with awful lyrics like *"Jukebox Junky, play me something funky that really rocks!"*, its one redeeming point is a great piano solo.

First Release: 'Killer Country' (1980)

[315] **JUST A BUMMIN' AROUND** [with Merle Haggard] (2003-2006)
(Pete Graves)

Originally released by Jimmy Dean as 'Bumming Around' in 1952 and covered by T. Texas Tyler (1953), Hank Thompson (1959), Hank Snow (1965), Tex Ritter (1965), Dean Martin (1965) and Boxcar Willie (1982), Jerry and Merle's gloriously ragged revival is one of the absolute highlights of 'Last Man Standing'. The great thing about that album is that it finally got him together with a few like-minded individuals - people such as Merle, George Jones and Willie Nelson. Sadly, Waylon Jennings died in 2002, and Buck Owens had been in poor health for years before passing away in March 2006, otherwise they'd have probably been there too. Jerry and Merle performed the song together for 'Last Man Standing Live' in 2006.

First Release: 'Last Man Standing' (2006)

'Last Man Standing Live' (2006)

[316] **JUST A CLOSER WALK WITH THEE** (1980) *
(Traditional)

A song whose origins are lost, the earliest known recording was by The Selah Jubilee Singers in 1941, with later covers by Sister Rosetta Tharpe (1942), The Blackwood Brothers Quartet (1948), Little Richard (1960), Ruth Brown (1962), Patsy Cline (1963), The Seekers (1965), Ella Fitzgerald (1967), Cliff Richard (1967), Tammy Wynette (1968) and Charlie Rich (1976). Jerry's excellent interpretation could've been a highlight of the Gospel album he cut for Elektra, but the record company wasn't interested. On the 66th birthday concert in Memphis in 2001, Stephen Ackles performed the song as Jerry was entering the stage, and was then accompanied by The Killer on piano.

First Release: 'The Caribou Ranch Sessions, 1980-1986' (2012) (bootleg)

Peter Checksfield with Stephen Ackles and Kerrie Lewis (1993)

[317] **JUST A LITTLE BIT** (1973)
(Rosco Gordon)

Originally released by Rosco Gordon in 1959, 'Just A Little Bit' was also covered by Jerry Butler (1963), Gene Simmons (1964), Them (1965), Roy Head (1965), Mitch Ryder and The Detroit Wheels (1966), Etta James (1968), Freddie King (1973) and Elvis Presley (1973). Unlike some of 'Southern Roots', Jerry is clearly comfortable with this song, ad-libbing lines like *"There's a Whole Lotta Shakin' Goin' On baby, when you deliver to me, whoo! Great Balls Of Fire, mama!"*, and it's a very powerful version. It was performed occasionally as part of a closing medley up until around 2003.

First Release: 'Southern Roots' (1973) + Single B-side (1973)

[318] JUST BECAUSE (1963)
(Sydney Robin / Bob Shelton / Joe Shelton)

Originally released by Nelstone's Hawaiians in 1930 and covered by The Shelton Brothers (1935), Elvis Presley (recorded 1954, released 1956), Brenda Lee (1959), Conway Twitty (1960), Danny and The Juniors (1961) and Billy Fury with The Tornados (1963), Jerry's storming revival of 'Just Because' was one of the best things to come out of the September 1963 'Golden Hits' sessions, even if it did take three years to release it. The song was performed very occasionally until around 2000, but perhaps the most noteworthy is the version from Paris in 1966. Backed by Jerry's usual mid-'60s rhythm section of Herman 'Hawk' Hawkins on bass and Morris 'Tarp' Tarrant on drums, plus British guitarist Mick Stewart from Johnny Kidd's New Pirates (Jerry's American guitarist Charlie Freeman couldn't get a Visa owing to a recent drugs bust), the whole show is as crazed and wild as the Star Club album, and is highly worthy of official release.

First Release: 'Memphis Beat' (1966)

[319] JUST DROPPED IN (1967)
(Mickey Newbury)

Psychedelia completely passed Jerry Lee Lewis by. Indeed, the last time he took even the vaguest notice of passing trends was when he cut a couple of songs with the word "Twist" in it back in 1962, and later admitted that he never liked The Beatles' music much. That said, 'Just Dropped In', with lines like *"I tripped on a cloud and fell eight miles high, I tore my mind on a jagged sky!"* is the closest Jerry ever came to the spirit of '67, even if he does sound a bit bemused, and there's even a nice minor-key piano solo, albeit mixed too low and almost drowned out by horns. Needless to say, 'Just Dropped In' is not a song he ever attempted live. The following year, Kenny Rogers and The First Edition had a big hit with it, the same year Mickey Newbury released his own version, and later covers include Willie Nelson (2001) and Tom Jones (2012).

First Release: Soul My Way (1967)

[320] JUST IN TIME (1965)
(Leon Ashley / Margie Singleton)

A very good Country song with some nice acoustic guitar pickin', this was recorded at the January 1965 'The Return of Rock' sessions. Surprisingly not released on 'Country Songs For City Folks' where it would've been ideal, it first surfaced on an early '80s bootleg EP, before finally gaining official release in 1986.

First Release: 'The Killer: 1963-1968' (box-set, 1986)

[321] **JUST WHO IS TO BLAME** (1963)
(Arr: Jerry Lee Lewis)

A superior up-tempo Pop-Rocker with crisp drumming and honking saxophone, 3 quite polished takes were cut in August 1963, with a version first surfacing on a Dutch compilation in 1974 (it is hard to imagine now just how difficult it was to collect *every* Sun track prior to 'The Sun Years' box-set in 1983!).

First Release: 'Collectors' Edition' (1974)

[322] **KEEP ME FROM BLOWING AWAY** (1973)
(Paul Craft)

Originally released by The Seldom Scene in 1973, this passionately-sung Country-Pop song is made almost unlistenable by the heavy strings *(please, can someone re-mix the July 1973 Stan Kesler sessions?!).* Linda Ronstadt covered it in 1974, and Willie Nelson revived it in 2008.

First Release: 'Sometimes A Memory Ain't Enough' (1973)

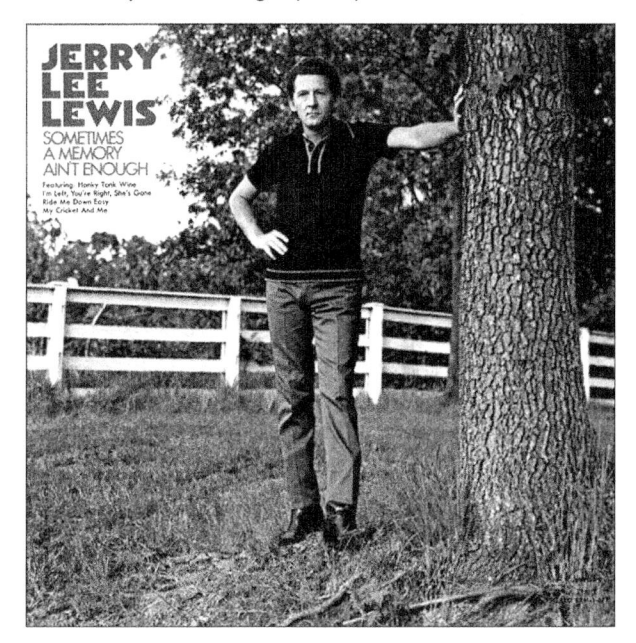

'Sometimes A Memory Ain't Enough' (1973)

[323] **KEEP ME IN MIND** (2008-2010)
(Mack Vickery)

A previously unrecorded Mack Vickery song (Mack died in 2004), this is a fine Country ballad that features largely unnecessary overdubs from vocalist and multi-instrumentalist Jon Brion (the un-dubbed version is available unofficially). Jerry performed the song live just once, at a 2014 show in New York.

First Release: 'Rock & Roll Time' (2014)

[324a] **KEEP MY MOTOR RUNNING** (1980) *
(Randy Bachman)

A Rock 'n' Roll song with slightly forced lyrics *("I got fuel injection, with chromed wheels!")*, the unreleased Elektra version is rushed, with an almost 'Heavy Metal' guitar solo plus a sloppy ending, though the potential was there. It was performed most nights on the April 1981 European Tour 5 months later, and more occasionally afterwards until around 1989.

First Release: 'The Caribou Ranch Sessions, 1980-1986' (2012) (bootleg)

[324b] **KEEP MY MOTOR RUNNING** (1985)

Re-recorded as one of two songs *without* Cash, Perkins and Orbison on 'Class of '55' (the other being 'Sixteen Candles'), it is largely an improvement, albeit with some annoying horns. Jerry can be seen recording an alternate version on a TV documentary filmed at the sessions.

First Release: 'Class of '55' (1986)

'Class of '55: A Rockin' Reunion' (1985)

[325] **KEEP ON THE FIRING LINE** (1970) (L)
(Bessie F. Hatcher)

Originally released by Howard Haney in 1928 and covered by The Carter Family in 1942, Jerry's live version of this Gospel song is very fast, and at around 80 seconds, very short.

First Release: 'The Killer: 1969-1972' (box-set, 1986)

[326] **KEEP YOUR HANDS OFF OF IT! (BIRTHDAY CAKE)** (1960)
(Priscilla Bowman / Jay McShann)

It is hard to pin-point the exact origins of 'Keep Your Hands Off Of It!', alternatively called 'Birthday Cake'. It shares at least some similarities with Jay McShann and Priscilla Bowman's 'Hands Off' from 1955, but also with Skeet's McDonald and Benny Walker's 1952 'Birthday Cake Boogie'. Maybe he combined the two, or perhaps he heard it somewhere else completely? Whatever, it's a rockin' Rhythm 'n' Blues tune with highly suggestive lyrics, and stood about as much chance of a '50s release as 'Big Legged Woman' and 'Sixty Minute Man'. As always, we should be forever thankful to Sam Phillips for keeping the tapes rollin'! The song was performed live in San Francisco in 1979 and in Berlin in 1991.

First Release: 'Keep Your Hands Off Of It!' (1987)

[327] **KING OF THE ROAD** (1965)
(Roger Miller)

Originally a hit for composer Roger Miller earlier the same year, Jerry's version is fine, though without adding much to the original.

First Release: 'Country Songs For City Folks' (1965)

[328] **LADY OF SPAIN** (1980) *
(Robert Hargreaves / Tolchard Evans / Stanley Damerell / Henry Tilsley)

Originally released by The New Mayfair Dance Orchestra in 1931, 'Lady Of Spain' was covered by Eddie Fisher (1952), Teddy Randazzo (1961), Paul Anka (1963) and Ray Stevens (1975). Complete with a Bossa Nova beat, Jerry's lengthy version is largely an instrumental (he doesn't start singing until almost 2 minutes in), and is more of a fun jam than a serious attempt at recording the song. It was performed live at a show in Goldston, North Carolina in 1996.

First Release: 'The Caribou Ranch Sessions, 1980-1986' (2012) (bootleg)

[329] **LATE NIGHT LOVIN' MAN** (1980)
(Rick Klang)

A good solid Rock 'n' Roll song with solid pumpin' piano throughout, which Jerry is clearly into *("I ain't into watchin' no TV baby, Jerry Lee's got his eye on you!")*, it's a little surprising that this isn't more well-known. He performed a wild version of the song at a show in Providence, Rhode Island in 1981, but sadly it never became a concert regular.

First Release: 'Killer Country' (1980)

[330] **LAWDY MISS CLAWDY - C.C. RIDER** (1981) (L) *
(Lloyd Price) + (Chuck Willis / Ma Rainey / Lena Arent)

Originally released by Lloyd Price in 1952 and covered by Elvis Presley in 1956, Jerry performed a medley of the song together with an up-tempo 'C.C. Rider' at 'The Survivors' taping in Stuttgart in 1981, though unfortunately it wasn't included on the album. Live performances have been rare, but they date back as far as Jerry's 1958 UK concerts, and as recently as the early '90s. In 1992, this author was very fortunate to witness Jerry perform a few songs at a Private Party in a London night club, where he was backed by Little Richard's musicians (Richard himself wasn't there). After Jerry had finished his set, he sat down to watch the legendary Lloyd Price take the stage, and when Lloyd performed 'Lawdy Miss Clawdy', the overweight 58-year-old Jerry Lee Lewis in a track-suit somehow became that teenage Rhythm 'n' Blues fan again, and clearly loved every second of it.

First Release: 'The Real Thing: Rare and Unreleased' (2008) (bootleg)

Peter Checksfield with Jerry Lee Lewis and (behind him) Lloyd Price (1992)

[331] **LET A SOLDIER DRINK** (1967)
(Charles Fonteyn Manney)

In 1991, a couple of great quality studio run-throughs of songs from 'Catch My Soul' surfaced via a bootleg, both with Shakespeare-influenced lyrics! The less interesting of these is 'Let A Soldier Drink', which unlike the newer 'Lust Of The Blood', was first published back in 1907. The correct title is probably 'Let Me The Cannikin Clink'. <u>See 'Give Me Some Action' for more on 'Catch My Soul'!</u>

First Release: 'The Killer's Private Stash' (1991) (bootleg)

[332] **LET ME ON** (1980)
(Layng Martine Jr.)

Whereas in 'Keep My Motor Running' a man is compared to a car, in 'Let Me On' the woman is compared to a train! Despite the contrived lyrics (and the annoying *"Choo choo"* backing singers) Jerry gives the song his best, with some strong piano.

First Release: 'Killer Country' (1980)

[333] **LET THE GOOD TIMES ROLL** (1958)
(Fleecie Jordan / Sam Theard)

Originally released by Louis Jordan and His Tympany Five in 1946, 'Let The Good Times Roll' is a storming Rock 'n' Roll performance that incredibly stayed in the can for 17 years before popping up on a 1975 compilation. Maybe the reason Sam overlooked it is because Jerry throws in a verse from 'Mean Woman Blues'? The song was performed live in Keanesburg in 1962.

First Release: '16 Songs Never Issued Before 1' (1975)

[334] **LET'S HAVE A PARTY** (1981) (L) *
(Jessie Mae Robinson)

Originally released by Elvis Presley as 'Party' in 1957 and covered by The Collins Kids (1957) and Wanda Jackson (1958), Jerry performed an impromptu but good version at a 1981 Nashville concert. Broadcast on radio, it became a popular bootleg. Despite the mixed messages The Killer gave over the years, Jerry clearly *loved* Elvis, and loved his early music.

First Release: 'Live At The Grand Ole Opry' (1982) (bootleg)

[335] LET'S LIVE A LITTLE (1977)
(Ruth E. Coletharp)

Originally released by Carl Smith in 1951, this is one of around a dozen excellent recordings that Jerry recorded during his final few Mercury sessions, which stayed unreleased for several years. A shame, as they would've made a great final album for the company. Perhaps they just didn't want to compete with his Elektra releases? The song was performed live in Oslo in 1985, and became the title track of a popular vinyl bootleg of the show.

First Release: 'The Mercury Sessions' (1985)

[336] LET'S PUT IT BACK TOGETHER AGAIN (1976)
(Jerry Foster / Bill Rice)

A modern, excellent Country-Pop song, 'Let's Put It Back Together Again' clearly clicked with the public, becoming his biggest Country hit in several years. Not a song that was performed much live, it did make an appearance at a show in Sacramento in 1976.

First Release: 'Country Class' (1976) + Single A-side (1976)

Let's Put It Back Together Again / Jerry Lee's Rock and Roll Revival Show
(No. 6 Country)

[337] LET'S SAY GOODBYE LIKE WE SAID HELLO (1977)
(Jimmie Skinner / Ernest Tubb)

Originally released by Ernest Tubb in 1947 and covered by Wanda Jackson in 1966, Jerry's relaxed version is a highlight of the rather good 'Country Memories' album. The song was performed in Plymouth in 1983 and Las Vegas in 1989.

First Release: 'Country Memories' (1977)

[338a] LET'S TALK ABOUT US (1959)
(Otis Blackwell)

'Let's Talk About Us' is a song that was worked on diligently over two separate sessions in March and June 1959 before being considered worthwhile for release. Many of the early versions have an exciting drum intro, but that's about as good as it gets, as Jerry's delivery is often monotone and very bored-sounding. The final single take has a distinctive boogie woogie introduction and a much better lead vocal, only for it to be all but ruined by some particularly irritating girl vocals. The un-dubbed master, first released on a limited edition fan club EP in 1985, is well worth checking out instead. The song was promoted on the TV shows 'Richard Haye's Big Beat Show' and 'Alan Freed's Big Beat Party' in 1959, quite a big deal as these were Jerry's *only* major TV appearances during the 1959-1961 era, while later live performances include Memphis 1961, Hull 1972, Birmingham (Alabama) 1974, Worcester (Massachusetts) 1984 and Las Vegas 1989. Cover versions include Billy Lee Riley (recorded 1959, not released until 1977), Grady Chapman (1959), Johnny Kidd and The Pirates (1961), Dave Edmunds (1977) and Van Morrison and Linda Gail Lewis (2000).

First Release: Single A-side (1959) + 'Jerry Lee's Greatest!' (1961)

Let's Talk About Us / The Ballad Of Billy Joe
(Not a hit)

[338b] LET'S TALK ABOUT US (1968)

The most distinctive thing about 'Let's Talk About Us' has always been the piano intro, so it's a disappointment to find that missing on the Mercury re-cut. Did a musician or engineer make a mistake? Otherwise, this is largely superior to the Sun cut.

First Release: 'She Still Comes Around' (1969) + Single B-side (1968)

[339a] **LEWIS BOOGIE** (1957)
(Jerry Lee Lewis)

A much loved Jerry Lee Lewis original, in the USA 'Lewis Boogie' was thrown away as the B-side to the ludicrous 'The Return of Jerry Lee', but in the UK it was belatedly issued in 1964 as an A-side, and was eagerly promoted alongside Jerry's latest Smash single 'I'm On Fire'. Although never a concert regular, he'd perform 'Lewis Boogie' very occasionally throughout his career, including his very last concert in 2019, though to hear it at its best check out the 1964 Star Club version. Incidentally, in 1983, an earlier take was issued on 'The Sun Years' box-set, and is distinguished by the substitution of the words *"Natchez town"* instead of *"Memphis town"*; a few weeks later when Jerry performed it in Plymouth on his European Tour, he reprised the "Natchez" lyrics!

First Release: Single B-side (1958)

[339b] **LEWIS BOOGIE** (1988) *

After sitting through the 'Great Balls of Fire!' movie at cinemas, most Jerry Lee Lewis fans couldn't wait to get out, but those who hung around were in for a treat: at the very end of the closing credits, a unique version of 'Lewis Boogie' can be heard, featuring just Jerry alone at the piano.

First Release: bootleg only

[340] **LEWIS WORKOUT [INSTRUMENTAL]** (1961)
(Jerry Lee Lewis)

An instrumental jam with a 'What'd I Say' riff and distinctive Saxophone, the name 'Lewis Workout' was given by compilers of the mid '70s compilation where it first appeared (a good title though!). Long thought to be taped at the June 1960 session where Jerry also cut 'Hang Up My Rock 'n' Roll Shoes', 2015's 'The Collected Works' puts it a full year later at the June 1961 session where the best-known version of 'Hello Josephine' was recorded, and it does indeed sound less out of place there.

First Release: '16 Songs Never Issued Before 1' (1975)

[341] **LIFE'S LITTLE UPS AND DOWNS** (1970)
(Margaret Ann Rich)

A wonderful song first recorded by Charlie Rich in 1969 and composed by his wife Margaret, if anything Jerry's version is even better, and makes a great closing track to the 'There Must Be More To Love Than This' album.

First Release: 'There Must Be More To Love Than This' (1970)

[342a] LIFE'S RAILWAY TO HEAVEN (1977)
(M.E. Abbey / Charlie Tillman)

First recorded by Edward Allen and Charles Hart in 1918, 'Life's Railway To Heaven' is a popular Gospel song, and was covered by The Blackwood Brothers Quartet (1948), Burl Ives (1950), Bill Monroe (1958), Tennessee Ernie Ford (1959), Roy Acuff (1965), The Oak Ridge Boys (1965), Jimmie Davis (1966) and J.D. Sumner (1968), amongst many others. Jerry first attempted the song at the 1970 Memphis Church recording (where it was wrongly titled 'Blessed Saviour Thou Wilt Guide Us' on first release), and his 1977 studio recording is suitably accompanied by backing vocalists that sound like a church choir. The song was still performed live once in a while well into the 21st century.

First Release: 'From The Vaults' (1986)

[342b] LIFE'S RAILWAY TO HEAVEN [with Solomon Burke] (2008-2010)

Re-titled 'Railroad To Heaven', this is a fine re-make, even if Solomon Burke's very obviously overdubbed vocals don't really add much (the pair reached their true potential on 'Last Man Standing Live', where they performed inspired duets of 'Who Will The Next Fool Be' and 'Today I Started Loving You Again').

First Release: 'Mean Old Man' (2010)

'Mean Old Man' (2010)

[343] LINCOLN LIMOUSINE (1966)
(Jerry Lee Lewis)

Perhaps the strangest song Jerry ever recorded, and certainly the most unlikely ever to come from The Killer's pen, this Folk-Rock number was supposed to be a loving tribute to assassinated President John F. Kennedy. Trouble is, the song's main hook *"They shot him in the back seat of a Lincoln Limousine!"* makes it sound like a car commercial, and what *did* he mean by the ominous *"It would have been better if he had stayed at home!"*? Not long afterwards, Jerry and Linda were happily seen posing for photos with George Wallace, the controversial Governor of Alabama.

First Release: 'Memphis Beat' (1966)

[344] LISTEN, THEY'RE PLAYING MY SONG (1968)
(Glen Garrison / Charlie Williams)

Originally released by Waylon Jennings in 1967, 'Listen, They're Playing My Song' is a very slow Country ballad with a slight Bluesy touch. There is little doubt that Jerry really was at his vocal peak in 1968-1969, but it's just a pity that after hitting with 'Another Place, Another Time', he pretty much stuck to the same formula; fine on singles, but on album after album, things did start to all blend into one.

First Release: 'She Still Comes Around' (1969)

[345] LITTLE GREEN VALLEY (1957)
(Carson J. Robison)

Originally released by Vernon Dalhart and Carson Robison in 1928, 'Little Green Valley' is the kind of rocked-up oldie that Jerry excelled at during his early days at Sun. Incredibly, on 'The Collected Works' box-set, there are 9 largely very similar takes, and great though they are, this author must confess that he hasn't been able to get through them all without pressing the 'skip' button. The song was played at a hotel jam session in Stockholm in 1985.

First Release: 'Rockin' and Free' (1974)

[346a] LITTLE QUEENIE (1959)
(Chuck Berry)

We have Jerry's mother Mamie to thank for his version of 'Little Queenie'. A fan of Chuck Berry's original, she was constantly playing the record and raving about how great it is, until Jerry could take no more. So, determined to prove that he could do it better, he arranged a quick session at Sun on the 28th May. Was he right? Well, no disrespects to Chuck's great original, but Jerry's version may *just* have the edge, and Sam Phillips was impressed enough to release it as a single. Memorably performed as the opening number on 1966's 'By Request' album, 'Little Queenie' was played occasionally throughout his career.

First Release: Single A-side (1959)

Little Queenie / I Could Never Be Ashamed Of You
(Not a hit)

[346b] **LITTLE QUEENIE** (2008-2010)

Complete with a too-loud but otherwise great Keith Richards guitar overdub, Jerry's re-cut is fine - particularly when remembering the fact that it was recorded around *50 years* after the Sun version. The un-dubbed take is available unofficially, as is an alternate take.

First Release: 'Rock & Roll Time' (2014)

[347] **LIVE AND LET LIVE** (1958)
(Wiley Walker / Gene Sullivan)

Originally released by Wiley and Gene in 1941 and covered by Carl Smith in 1956, Jerry's version is just a brief snippet that was taped without a band. It had potential.

First Release: 'The Sun Years' (Box-Set, 1983)

[348] **LIVIN' LOVIN' WRECK** (1961)
(Otis Blackwell)

The B-side to the 'What'd I Say' single, 'Livin' Lovin' Wreck' is a good commercial up-tempo Pop song. It was covered by at least three different artists in 1964, namely The Searchers, Ian and The Zodiacs and Dig Richards, while the only known live performance was in Northampton in 1987 - by special request of this author!

First Release: Single B-side (1961)

[349] **LIVING ON THE HALLELUJAH SIDE** (1970)
(J. Howard Entwisle / Johnson Oatman Jr.)

First recorded by The C. and M. A. Gospel Quintette as 'The Hallelujah Side' in 1923, 'Living On The Hallelujah Side' is a fast Gospel number, complete with fiddle and vocal chorus. Jimmy Swaggart would record the song in 1977.

First Release: '30th Anniversary Album' (1986)

[350] **LONELY WEEKENDS** (1972)
(Charlie Rich)

Originally released by Charlie Rich in 1959, covers include Emile Ford and The Checkmates (1960), Wanda Jackson (1961), P.J. Proby (1965), Billy Lee Riley (1965), The Everly Brothers (1965), Trini Lopez (1968), Waylon Jennings (1969) and Ronnie Hawkins (1971). Jerry's version is a little too fast, but it's still one of the better tracks on 'The Killer Rocks On', and at least the string orchestra sat this one out. Jerry performed it live as early as a show in Lausanne, Switzerland in 1966, while other performances include Memphis 1972, 'The Midnight Special' 1973 and Sacramento 1976. *First Release: 'The Killer Rocks On' (1972) + Single A-side (1972)*

Lonely Weekends / Turn On Your Love Light
(No. 11 Country / No. 95 Pop)

[351] **LONESOME FIDDLE MAN** (1971)
(Dallas Frazier / Sanger D. Shafer)

Specially written with Kenny Lovelace in mind, he never sounded better than on this song about lost love. Only rarely played live, performances include Reno 1976, Dartford 1985 and Reykjavik 1986.

First Release: 'Would You Take Another Chance On Me' (1971)

[352] **LONG GONE LONESOME BLUES** (1957)
(Hank Williams)

Originally released by Hank Williams in 1950 and covered by Marty Robbins in 1956, Jerry's version is a little disappointing in comparison to his usual Hank Williams covers. It's not *bad* though, despite the loss of some of the lyrics, with a great piano solo and distinctive guitar from Roland Janes.

First Release: 'Rockin' and Free' (1974)

[353] **LONG TALL SALLY** (1964) (L)
(Enotris Johnson / Richard Penniman)

Originally released by Little Richard in 1956, covers include Pat Boone (1956), Marty Robbins (1956), Elvis Presley (1956), Eddie Cochran (recorded 1956, released 1962), The Johnny Otis Show (1957), Wanda Jackson (1958), Carl Perkins (1958), Vince Taylor and The Play-Boys (1961), The Isley Brothers (1963), The Beatles (1964) and The Kinks (1964). Jerry featured the song on his two 1964 live albums, and it's hard to choose between them; both are frantic and wild, but the Star Club version probably wins for being better recorded. He recorded a studio version for BBC radio in 1964, and the song was regularly performed as parts of longer medleys well into the '90s.

First Release: 'Live at The Star Club, Hamburg' (1964) / 'The Greatest Live Show on Earth' (1964)

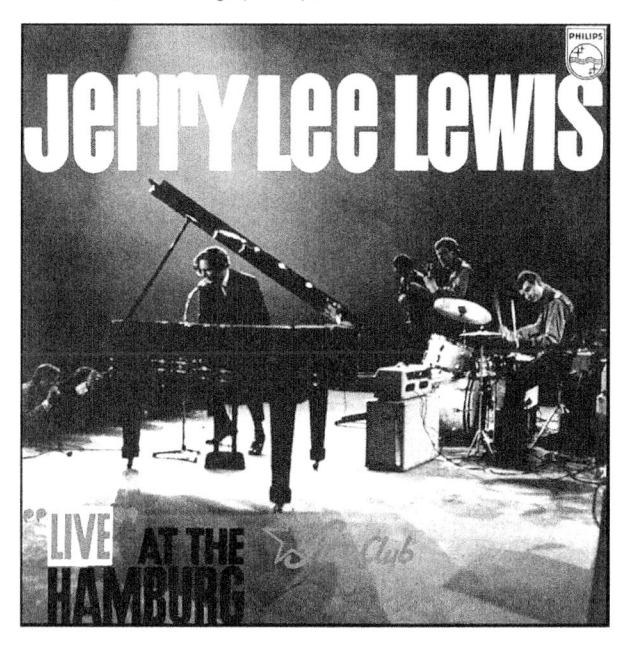

'Live at The Star Club, Hamburg' (1964)

[354] **LOOKING FOR A CITY** (1970) (L)
(Marvin P Dalton / W. Oliver Cooper)

Originally released by The Chuck Wagon Gang in 1949, this up-tempo number kicked off proceedings for his 1970 Memphis Church recording. Jimmy Swaggart recorded the song in 1979.

First Release: 'The Killer: 1969-1972' (box-set, 1986)

[355] **LORD, I'VE TRIED EVERYTHING BUT YOU** (1977)
(Carl Knight)

A great old-time Country song with Gospel-tinged lyrics, Jerry is in particularly good form vocally, and it would've been more than worthy of release at the time. Instead, it stayed in the can for 9 years. The only known live performance of the song was at a show in Long Beach in 1978.

First Release: 'From The Vaults' (1986)

[356] **LORD, WHAT'S LEFT FOR ME TO DO** (1975)
(Cecil Harrelson)

Not really a Gospel song despite the title, 'Lord, What's Left For Me To Do' is a mid-tempo Country song with great lyrics like *"How many roads are there left to travel, or am I just living in my last and final hour?"* from Cecil Harrelson. Jerry first recorded it at the 'Jack Daniels Old No. 7' session in March 1973, but it remains unreleased and is unfortunately lost. The issued cut is instead from the June 1975 session that produced 'A Damn Good Country Song'. Vernon Oxford covered the song in 1981.

First Release: 'From The Vaults' (1986)

[357] **LOST HIGHWAY** [with Delaney Bramlett] (2003-2006)
(Leon Payne)

Originally released by Leon Payne in 1948 and made famous by Hank Williams the following year, covers include Skeets McDonald (1958), Johnny Horton (1959), Hank Thompson (1961), Leon Russell (1973), Ray Campi and His Rockabilly Rebels (1977), Sleepy LaBeef (1981) and David Allan Coe (1997). A great song of course, Jerry is on fine form both vocally and on piano, and Delaney Bramlett contributes some superb electric slide guitar. Where it goes downhill slightly is when Delaney joins in *vocally*, with his Dylan-esque voice being a very acquired taste. There is no record of Jerry playing the song live, though no-one would've been too surprised if he'd dug it out once in a while during the '70s or '80s.

First Release: 'Last Man Standing' (2006)

[358] **LOUISIANA MAN** (1968)
(Doug Kershaw)

Originally released by Rusty and Doug Kershaw in 1960, cover versions include Bob Luman (1962), Buck Owens and His Buckaroos (1964), P.J. Proby (1964), George Jones and Gene Pitney (1965), Rick Nelson (1966), The Seekers (1966) and Bobbie Gentry (1968). Jerry's version is one of the more exciting tracks he recorded in the late '60s, with a Rock 'n' Roll piano solo and predictably superb fiddle from Kenny Lovelace. He performed the song live in Mannheim, Germany in 1991.

First Release: 'She Still Comes Around' (1969)

[359] **LOVE GAME** (1979)
(Hugh Moffatt)

A ballad that is far more Pop than Country, 'Love Game' is one of the weaker moments on 'When Two Worlds Collide', and is notable for being the *only* song on the album never to have been played live.

First Release: 'When Two Worlds Collide' (1980)

[360] **LOVE INFLATION** (1974)
(Sanger D. Shafer)

Although Jerry does quite a good job with it, 'Love Inflation' is a Country song with some rather dodgy lyrics *("Love inflation, Lord the price is high!")*. Jerry did play it once though, at a hotel jam session in London in 1982. Composer Whitey Shafer recorded his own version in 1976.

First Release: 'Boogie Woogie Country Man' (1975)

[361] **LOVE LETTERS IN THE SAND** (1957)
(J. Fred Coots / Chas Kenny / Nick Kenny)

Originally released by The Majestic Dance Orchestra in 1931 and covered by Pat Boone in 1957, Jerry's mid-paced version features some nice pumpin' piano and a *"Roland Boy!"* guitar solo. Although not his finest moment at Sun, 'Love Letters In The Sand' deserved to be issued far earlier than 1983.

First Release: 'The Sun Years' (Box-Set, 1983)

[362] **LOVE MADE A FOOL OF ME** (1960)
(Henry Sledd / York Wilburn)

If you ask Jerry Lee Lewis fans to name their least favorite Sun recording, chances are they'll say 'Love Made A Fool Of Me'. Recorded in October 1960 alongside 'When I Get Paid' and 'No More Than I Get', it doesn't even feature Jerry on piano - that honor went to Larry Muhoberac. The Killer gives it his best shot, but you can't polish a turd! For those who want to suffer even further, an extended uncut version is also available.

First Release: Single B-side (1960)

[363] **LOVE FOR ALL SEASONS** (1969)
(Linda Gail Lewis)

Linda Gail Lewis has said that 'Love For All Seasons' is the first song she ever wrote, and if true, she became a very accomplished songwriter very quickly. A mid-paced pure Pop ballad that one could imagine Andy Williams singing, Jerry does a fantastic job on it despite this, and the reason it wasn't released probably had more to do with how very different it is rather than any quality issues. Incidentally, there is some confusion over what the correct title is: Some releases call it 'Love *Of* All Seasons', but when Linda Gail Lewis cut her own version for an aborted Mercury single in 1974, it was listed as 'Joy & Love You Bring'.

First Release: 'The Killer: 1969-1972' (box-set, 1986)

[364] **LOVE ON BROADWAY** (1963)
(Dub Allbritten / Ronnie Self)

Written by Rockabilly artist Ronnie Self, the modern Country-Pop of 'Love On Broadway' couldn't be further from that genre. It sounded contemporary enough to scrape to No. 31 in the Country charts when finally issued 8 years later.

First Release: 'Original Golden Hits Volume III' (1971) + Single A-side (1971)

Love On Broadway / Matchbox
(No. 31 Country)

[365] **LOVERS HONEYMOON** (1979) *
(unknown)

A slow waltz, Jerry seems to struggle vocally on this one as the key is a bit too low for him, and the song isn't that great either. 'Lovers Honeymoon' deserved to remain in the can.

First Release: 'Honky Tonk Stuff - A Collection Of Rare and Unreleased Recordings' (2007) (bootleg)

[366] LOVESICK BLUES (1958)
(Cliff Friend / Irving Mills)

Originally released by Elsie Clark in 1922 and more famously covered by Hank Williams in 1949, 'Lovesick Blues' is a song that Jerry would've known for years. Moderately Rocked-up, it could've made a perfect album track. The song was performed in Atlantic City in 1988 and Oslo in 1989.

First Release: 'Johnny Cash & Jerry Lee Lewis Sing Hank Williams' (1971)

[367] LOVIN' CAJUN STYLE (1973/1974)
(James Kenneth Donley)

Originally released by Jimmy Donley in 1963 and long rumored to have been recorded by Jerry at some point in his career, a version of 'Lovin' Cajun Style' from the '70s finally surfaced in 2014. Unfortunately, although it starts off fine, the song very quickly breaks down into a stop-start rehearsal. In 1987, this writer was fortunate enough to witness an after-show 'hotel session' in Cambridge, where Jerry played to a handful of fans whilst accompanied by Kenny Lovelace on fiddle. One of the songs he did was a word-perfect version of 'Lovin' Cajun Style', something he repeated on stage in Northampton the very next night.

First Release: 'The Knox Phillips Sessions: The Unreleased Recordings' (2014)

Peter Checksfield with Johannes 'Tex' Sipkema, Jonny Williams and Jerry Lee Lewis (1987)

[368] **LOVIN' UP A STORM** (1959)
(Luther Dixon / Allyson R. Khent)

A song that is amongst Jerry's very greatest recordings (this author would put it above *any* of his biggies), several takes of 'Lovin' Up A Storm' were taped at a session around December 1958/January 1959, of which the final one was issued as a single. A complete flop in the USA, at least some people in the UK recognized its greatness, as it got to No. 28 in the charts. Jerry performed a fantastic version at the 'By Request' taping in Fort Worth in 1966 (a track that was not included on the original album but was thankfully issued on 1994's 'The Locust Years... And The Return To The Promised Land' box-set), while other performances include Toronto in 1967 and the 66th birthday show in Memphis in 2001. 'Lovin' Up A Storm' was covered by Colin Hicks and His Cabin Boys (1960), Vince Taylor and The Play-Boys (1961) and Jerry Williams (1964).

First Release: Single A-side (1959)

Lovin' Up A Storm / Big Blon' Baby
(Not a hit)

[369a] **LUCILLE** (1977)
(Al Collins / Little Richard)

Originally released by Little Richard in 1957 and covered by The Everly Brothers (1960), Bobby Vee and The Crickets (1962), The Hollies (1964), Otis Redding (1964), Peter and Gordon (1964), Tom Jones (1965), The Animals (1966) and Bill Haley and The Comets (1968), whereas Little Richard's original is uninhibited and wild, Jerry's is cool and controlled. 'Lucille' was occasionally performed live until well into the New Millennium.

First Release: 'Keeps Rockin'' (1978)

[369b] **LUCILLE** (1986)

Sounding a bit more animated than on the 1977 version, this version of 'Lucille' from September 1986 was released 2 years later.

First Release: 'Rocket' (1988)

[369c] **LUCILLE** (1990) *

During a warm-up for a 1990 'It Was The Whiskey Talkin' (Not Me)' vocal overdub session, Jerry jammed on numerous songs. These were largely just short snippets and playful jams, but one song worthy of release is 'Lucille'. Backed only by bass and drums, it is tight, concise and inspired.

First Release: 'Ivory Tears' (1994) (bootleg)

[369d] **LUCILLE - ALL SHOOK UP** (1990) (L) *
(Al Collins / Little Richard) + (Otis Blackwell)

At a concert in Athens, Greece in December 1990, Jerry combined 'Lucille' with Elvis Presley's 'All Shook Up', and this medley turned up on a bootleg a few years. 'All Shook Up' was performed several times around this period (sometimes as a stand-alone song and other times as a medley), though it is debatable how well his slower arrangement worked.

First Release: 'On Fire Live!' (2018) (bootleg)

[370] **LUST OF THE BLOOD** (1967)
(Ray Pohlman / Emil Dean Zoghby)

One of two intriguing 'Catch My Soul' rehearsals that surfaced on a 1991 bootleg, 'Lust Of The Blood' is basically a Blues (the melody and riff are very similar to Elvis Presley's 'Trouble'), but with quasi-Shakespeare lyrics like *"I'll plague him with flies, Poison with lies. And everywhere he goes, I'll lead him gently by the nose!"*. The combination of the two sounds a little odd, but it must've *really* been something seeing Jerry perform these songs on a theatre stage! The correct title is probably 'That's What You Call Love', but the bootlegger's title is far more fitting. See 'Give Me Some Action' for more on 'Catch My Soul'!

First Release: 'The Killer's Private Stash' (1991) (bootleg)

[371] **MAMA, THIS ONE'S FOR YOU** (1980)
(Ray Griff)

Although a modern song, 'Mama, This One's For You' sounds like the kind of thing Al Jolson would've sung, and is enhanced even further by some Dixieland backing. Jerry performed it live very occasionally up until around 1996.

First Release: 'Killer Country' (1980)

[372] MAMA'S HANDS (1973)
(Frank Dycus / Larry Kingston)

Originally released by Johnny Bush in 1971, 'Mama's Hands' with lyrics like *"Now mama's hands are cold with age, they tremble when she prays!"* is an almost unbearably sad song, and Jerry half-speaks and half-sings the song with real feeling. George Jones recorded it in 1974.

First Release: 'Sometimes A Memory Ain't Enough' (1973)

[373] MARGIE (1973)
(Con Conrad / Benny Davis / J. Russel Robinson)

Originally released by The Rega Dance Orchestra in 1920, 'Margie' was covered by Al Jolson (1946), Jim Reeves (1958), Fats Domino (1959), Louis Prima (1960) and Ray Charles (1961). Jerry's superb version is one of the best songs from the 1973 'Southern Roots' sessions, but sadly remained unreleased for 14 years.

First Release: 'The Killer: 1973-1977' (box-set, 1987)

[374] MATCHBOX (1958)
(Carl Perkins)

Originally released by Carl Perkins in 1957 (though loosely based on an older song), Jerry taped two Bluesy takes of 'Matchbox' in early 1958. The best version with alternative lyrics remained in the can until 1983, but the other version, rather heavy-handedly overdubbed with a male vocal group, was issued on Jerry's debut album. It was performed very occasionally into the New Millennium, most notably in Hamburg in 1964.

First Release: 'Jerry Lee Lewis' (1958)

[375a] MATHILDA (1965)
(George Khoury / Huey Thierry)

Originally released by Cookie and His Cupcakes in 1958, in Jerry's hands 'Mathilda' is a powerful Rhythm 'n' Blues number, with soulful singing and pounding piano. Never a song that was played much live, he did perform it in Frankfurt in 1982.

First Release: 'Memphis Beat' (1966)

[375b] MATHILDA (1986)

Far less intense than the version from 21 years earlier, this relaxed but good performance from September 1986 was issued on 'Rocket'.

First Release: 'Rocket' (1988)

[376] MAYBELLENE (1965)
(Chuck Berry)

Jerry rarely disappointed when covering Chuck Berry, and such was the case with his inspired version of ol' Chuckles' 1955 debut single. Released on the consistently brilliant 'The Return Of Rock' in 1965, occasional live performances include Wheeling 1975, Reno 1976, Sacramento 1976, Las Vegas 1985, Oslo 1989 and Las Vegas 1989.

First Release: 'The Return of Rock' (1965)

[377] ME AND BOBBY MCGEE (1971)
(Fred Foster / Kris Kristofferson)

Originally released by Roger Miller in 1969, 'Me and Bobby McGee' was also recorded by Kenny Rogers and The First Edition (1969), Gordon Lightfoot (1970), Kris Kristofferson (the song's writer, 1970) and Janis Joplin (1971). Jerry's up-tempo version is a near-perfect combination of Rock 'n' Roll, Country and mainstream Pop-Rock, and after years of mostly concentrating on Country ballads and Gospel, it was a real breath of fresh air. Reaching the Pop Top 40, it was still performed live very occasionally well into the 21st Century.

First Release: 'Would You Take Another Chance On Me' (1971) + Single Double-A-side (1971) + 'The Killer Rocks On' (1972)

Me and Bobby McGee / Would You Take Another Chance On Me
(No. 40 Pop, No. 1 Country / No. 1 Country)

'The Glen Campbell Show' (1971)

[378] **ME AND JESUS** [with Linda Gail Lewis] (1972)
(Tom T. Hall)

Originally released by Tom T. Hall earlier the same year, 'Me and Jesus' was specially recorded at a stand-alone session on 31st May 1972. A rousing Gospel number that is one of Jerry and Linda's best duets, it flopped disastrously when issued as a single. Jerry would never again record another studio duet with Linda Gail Lewis. The song was performed as part of a Gospel medley in Cincinnati in 1975.

First Release: Single A-side (1972)

Me and Jesus / Handwriting On The Wall
(Not a hit)

[379] **MEAN OLD MAN** [with Ronnie Wood] (2008-2010)
(Kris Kristofferson)

Originally released by Kris Kristofferson in 1986 (though performed by him live at least as early as 1982), 'Mean Old Man' is a great piece of 'Outlaw' Country music, with simplified lyrics that somehow suit the song perfectly. The title track of his 2010 album, the song was performed live a handful of times, including in Belo Horizonte (Brazil) 2009, Paris 2009 (the closing number!) and Linz 2009.

First Release: 'Mean Old Man' (2010)

[380] **MEAN WOMAN BLUES** (1957)
(Claude DeMetrius)

In the USA, the 'Great Balls Of Fire' B-side was 'You Win Again', but in the UK, fans had something *far* more exciting - the legendary 'Mean Woman Blues'! Originally recorded and released by Elvis Presley earlier the same year, Jerry only utilized the chorus from the song, and instead re-wrote (or improvised) completely different verses. It is the piano playing which *really* thrilled though: the late great Chas Hodges was no slouch on the ol' Joanna (piano), but even he would tell friends that there was one bit that he could never *quite* work out. And Jerry was just *22 years old* when he recorded it! There are no alternate takes, and the only other studio version was recorded for BBC radio's 'Saturday Club' in 1964, but notable early live versions include 'American Bandstand' 1957, Hamburg 1964, Birmingham, Alabama 1964, 'Shindig!' 1964, Fort Worth 1966, Toronto 1969 and Las Vegas 1970. 'Mean Woman Blues' was very occasionally performed live well into the New Millennium.

First Release: 'The Great Ball of Fire' EP (1957)

'Shindig!' (1964)

[381a] **MEAT MAN** (1973)
(Mack Vickery)

Basically a song about cunnilingus, something which the lyrics only thinly disguise *("I've been down to Macon, Georgia, ate the fuzz off a Georgia peach!")*, 'Meat Man' rivals 'Big Legged Woman' for explicitness, and makes 'The Urge' and 'Sixty Minute Man' sound like innocent nursery rhymes! Originally released by the song's writer under the name Atlanta James in 1970, the September 1973 'Southern Roots' version is only slightly diminished by the over-busy production. Released as a single, even in 1973, it was a bit too much for most DJs, and the record didn't chart. The song was performed live very occasionally up until around 2004.

First Release: 'Southern Roots' (1973) + Single A-side (1973)

Meat Man / Just A Little Bit
(Not a hit)

[381b] **MEAT MAN** (1973/1974) *

On an undated studio session with Knox Phillips, Jerry attempted a much slower arrangement of 'Meat Man'. It circulates unofficially in poor quality.

First Release: bootleg only

[381c] **MEAT MAN** (1979) *

In direct contrast to the Knox Phillips re-cut, in 1979 Jerry cut a *very* wild version, which sounds just like a concert finale! It is more than deserving of official release, but currently only circulates unofficially.

First Release: bootleg only

[381d] **MEAT MAN** (1986)

Following an unusual drum and bass intro with double tracked vocals, for the 'Rocket' album Jerry performed a straight-ahead Rock 'n' Roll version of the song, and it is *almost* as rockin' as the Elektra cut.

First Release: 'Rocket' (1988)

[382] **MEETING IN THE AIR** (1970)
(A.P. Carter)

Originally released by The Carter Family in 1940, Jerry's version of 'Meeting In The Air' is played *very* fast, but like all six songs from the 15th December 1970 studio session in Memphis, it wasn't released until the mid-'80s.

First Release: '30th Anniversary Album' (1986)

[383] **MELANCHOLY BABY** (1987)
(Ernie Burnett / George A. Norton)

Originally released by Walter Scanlan in 1915, with later revivals including Connie Francis (1958), The Crew Cuts (1959), The Marcels (1962) and Chas 'n' Dave (1983), unfortunately Jerry's version from the 1987 Hank Cochran session is played on a truly horrible Casio keyboard.

First Release: 'At Hank Cochran's' (1995)

[384] **MEMORIES** (1987)
(Egbert Van Alstyne / Gustave Kahn)

Originally released by Harry McClaskey in 1916, and later revived by Gene Austin (1930), Bing Crosby (1949), The Platters (1962) and Mike Berry (1981), 'Memories' is a Pop ballad with old-time chord changes. Jerry's version from the December 1987 Hank Cochran session is pleasant enough.

First Release: 'At Hank Cochran's' (1995)

[385] **MEMORY NUMBER ONE** (1984)
(Max Powell / Wayne Walker)

Originally released by Webb Pierce in 1964, the nicely old-fashioned and unobtrusive backing make this one of Jerry's best Country recordings of the '80s. He had previously performed the song at a show in Nashville in 1981.

First Release: 'Four Legends' (1985)

'Four Legends' (1985)

[386] **MEMORY OF YOU** (1958)
(Jimmy Swan)

When first released on 1983's 'The Sun Years' box-set, compilers assumed that this solo (without a band) performance was of a self-composed Country number. However, it later emerged that the song is actually Jimmy Swan's 1952 hit 'I Love You Too Much'.

First Release: 'The Sun Years' (Box-Set, 1983)

[387] **MEMPHIS BEAT** (1966)
(Milton Addington / Dickey Lee Lipscomb / Allen Reynolds)

Original released by Sam The Sham and The Pharaohs in 1965 and covered by The RPM's the same year, in Jerry's hands 'Memphis Beat' sounds like a hybrid of 'Memphis, Tennessee' and 'Breathless'. A little too contrived to be an out-and-out classic, it still made a great title track for his 1966 album release, and also a great name for his road band, who were called The Memphis Beats from herewith! Not entirely satisfied with the January 1966 album cut, in July Jerry attempted it again, cutting two similar takes. With a distinctive guitar/bass riff, whereas Jerry sounds cheerful and upbeat on the album cut, this time he comes across as frustrated and grumpy. One of the takes was released as a single, but with minimal promotion, failed to chart.

First Release: 'Memphis Beat' (1966) + Single A-side (1966)

Memphis Beat / If I Had It All To Do Over
(Not a hit)

[388a] **MEMPHIS, TENNESSEE** (1964) (L)
(Chuck Berry)

One of several new (to Jerry) songs on 'The Greatest Live Show on Earth', this loose and inspired version of Chuck's classic hit features pounding piano, a solo that elicits crowd cheers - and mixed up lyrics! Somehow it doesn't matter, and Tom Jones loved the arrangement so much, a couple of years later he cut a carbon copy in the studio.

First Release: 'The Greatest Live Show on Earth' (1964)

[388b] **MEMPHIS, TENNESSEE** (1973)

A tight-but-loose version from January 1973, this time with the verses in the right order, is one of the better remakes on 'The Session', despite the slightly messy false ending (a rare Japanese Quadrophonic release called 'Rock 'n' Roll Supersession' includes a slightly longer edit). Though not a song that was played live with any frequency, Jerry very occasionally dug it out well into the 21st Century.

First Release: 'The Session' (1973)

[388c] **MEMPHIS, TENNESSEE** (1980) *

A slightly ragged but fun run-through, this sounds more like a warm-up than a serious attempt at re-recording the song.

First Release: 'The Caribou Ranch Sessions, 1980-1986' (2012) (bootleg)

[389a] **MEXICALI ROSE** (1960) *(parts 1 & 2)*
(Helen Stone / Jack Tenney)

Originally released by Lewis James in 1923 and covered by Gene Autry in 1936, it was via the latter that Jerry learnt the song. He plays the song both slow and fast, trying (and failing!) to convince Sam Phillips that this would make a hit record. The fast section *only* was released in 1974, with the full slow-fast take only surfacing 13 years later, while it was performed live occasionally for the rest of his career, albeit usually fast only.

First Release: 'Rockin' and Free' (part 2 only - 1974) + 'Keep Your Hands Off Of It!' (1987)

[389b] **MEXICALI ROSE** (1980) *

A marginally more polished version complete with steel guitar and backing vocalists, and again played both slow and fast, Jerry is clearly having fun here. It *still* doesn't sound like a hit though!

First Release: 'The Caribou Ranch Sessions, 1980-1986' (2012) (bootleg)

[389c] **MEXICALI ROSE** (1987)

Played on a cheap Casio keyboard and accompanied by Bossa Nova drums, this mid-tempo version of the song from the 1987 Hank Cochran sessions is best avoided.

First Release: 'At Hank Cochran's' (1995)

[389d] **MEXICALI ROSE** (2006)

Taped live in the studio, Jerry's voice sounds a little worn out but otherwise this is just fine.

First Release: CMT.com (exclusive download) + 'Rock 'n' Roll Resurrection' (2007) (bootleg)

[390a] **MIDDLE AGE CRAZY** (1977)
(Sonny Throckmorton)

A ballad that is a lot more Pop than Country with lyrics about ageing that Jerry could clear identify with *("Today he's forty years old going on twenty!")*, 'Middle Age Crazy' was a major success, becoming his biggest hit in 5 years. Also recorded by songwriter Sonny Throckmorton in 1978 and Billy Joe Royal in 1982, the song even inspired a 1980 movie of the same name starring Bruce Dern and Ann-Margret. 'Middle Age Crazy' was performed live with increasingly less frequency into the New Millennium, but it is a song that always worked far better on record than it did in concert.

First Release: 'Country Memories' (1977) + Single A-side (1977)

Middle Age Crazy / Georgia On My Mind
(No. 4 Country)

'Pop Goes The Country' (1977)

[390b] **MIDDLE AGE CRAZY** [with Tim McGraw and Jon Brion] (2008-2010)

Featuring a more modern 'Americana' Country-Rock backing, this is a nice enough re-make, even if it can no way match up to the Mercury original.

First Release: 'Mean Old Man' (2010)

[391] **MILK COW BLUES** (1979) *
(Kokomo Arnold)

Originally released by Kokomo Arnold in 1934, covers of 'Milk Cow Blues include Joe Williams' Washboard Blues Singers (1935), Moon Mullican and The Showboys (1947), Elvis Presley (as 'Milkcow Blues Boogie' 1955), Ricky Nelson (1960), Eddie Cochran (recorded 1960, released 1962) and The Kinks (1965). From the opening intro and the *"You know down in ol' Louisiana, we call this gut bucket Blues!"* ad-lib onwards, and with able support from James Burton, this is one of the greatest Blues performances Jerry ever put on record. It was played live in Las Vegas in 1977, and again at the 66th Birthday concert in Memphis in 2001.

First Release: 'Alive and Rockin'' (1986) (bootleg)

[392] **MILKSHAKE MADEMOISELLE** (1958)
(Jack Hammer)

What song made the perfect follow-up to 'Great Balls Of Fire'? The answer is 'Milkshake Mademoiselle' of course! At least, that was seriously considered at one point. Problem was, it turned out a little *too* uninhibited and wild, with Jerry giving the rather trite lyrics a treatment they didn't quite deserve. Of the 5 full surviving takes, the version first issued in 1974 is one of the more subdued, but far better takes surfaced on later releases.

First Release: 'Rockin' and Free' (1974)

[393] **MILWAUKEE HERE I COME** [with Linda Gail Lewis] (1969)
(Lee Fikes)

Originally released by George Jones and Brenda Carter in 1968, 'Milwaukee Here I Come' is a jovial and up-tempo Country song. Surprisingly, Jerry Lee Lewis is mentioned in the original, but whereas George Jones sings *"Which one you love the best, me or Jerry Lee?"*, Jerry changes it to *"Which one you want the most, George Jones or Jerry Lee?!"*.

First Release: 'Together' (1969)

[394a] **MISS THE MISSISSIPPI AND YOU** (1994)
(William Halley / Eric Schoenberg)

Originally released by his early idol Jimmie Rodgers in 1932, the 1994 version of 'Miss The Mississippi and You' is amongst Jerry's very best old time Country revivals. It even received a one-off live outing, in Danville, West Virginia in 1995.

First Release: 'Young Blood' (1995)

[394b] **MISS THE MISSISSIPPI AND YOU** (2003-2006)

Recorded some time during the 'Last Man Standing' sessions, the remake of 'Miss The Mississippi and You' was instead held over for 2010's 'Mean Old Man'. Played alone at the piano, his inevitably older and more fragile voice just adds to the poignancy of the performance.

First Release: 'Mean Old Man' (2010)

[395] **MISSISSIPPI KID** (2008-2010)
(Al Kooper / Bob Burns / Ronnie Van Zant)

Originally released by Lynyrd Skynyrd in 1973, 'Mississippi Kid' is an OK mid-tempo Rocker with hot but over-loud overdubs by Derek Trucks and Doyle Bramhall II. Released on 'Rock & Roll Time', the un-dubbed version can be found on the 'Come Sundown' bootleg.

First Release: 'Rock & Roll Time' (2014)

[396] MOM AND DAD'S WALTZ (1969)
(Lefty Frizzell)

Originally released by Lefty Frizzell in 1951 and covered by Faron Young (1959), Patti Page (1961), Ernest Tubb (1966) and Merle Haggard (1968), 'Mom and Dad's Waltz' is a beautiful but over-sentimental ballad. With lighter production (no backing singers!), it is a highlight of the 'Country Music Hall of Fame' sessions. Live performances include Ipswich in 1972 and Atlantic City in 1988.

First Release: 'Sings The Country Music Hall of Fame Hits, Vol. One' (1969)

[397] MONA LISA (1987) (L)
(Ray Evans / Jay Livingston)

Originally released by Charlie Spivak and His Orchestra in 1950 and made famous by Nat 'King' Cole the same year, cover versions include Moon Mullican (1950), Carl Mann (1959), Conway Twitty (1959), Sam Cooke (1960), Johnny Burnette (1961), James Brown (1964), Orion (1979), Willie Nelson (1981) and Shakin' Stevens (1981). It is rumored to have been recorded in the studio for Elektra around 1980, but if so it hasn't surfaced yet, and the only 'official' version is on the poorly-mixed 'Live in Italy' album. 'Mona Lisa' was performed live very occasionally from 1980 to around 2004.

First Release: 'Live in Italy' (1987)

[398a] MONEY (THAT'S WHAT I WANT) (1961)
(Janie Bradford / Berry Gordy, Jr.)

Originally released by Barrett Strong in 1959, Jerry's original studio recording of 'Money (That's What I Want)' is a strange affair, with pounding drums, and shrill horns with backing vocals that are sometimes hard to tell apart. It did make an interesting single though, and full kudos to Jerry for recording the song long before The Beatles and The Rolling Stones made it a much-covered standard. Where it *really* came alive was on stage though, and never more so than on the 'Live at The Star Club, Hamburg' album *("Why don't you break down honey and give me just a little bit of that money?!")*. It was still performed once in a while up until around 2005, though perhaps the most unusual version was for 1997's 'Monday Night Concert' TV show, where his daughter Phoebe sung it while Jerry backed her.

First Release: Single A-side (1961) + 'Jerry Lee's Greatest!' (1961)

Money / Bonnie B.
(Not a hit)

[398b] **MONEY (THAT'S WHAT I WANT)** [with Levi Kreis] (2010)

Ragged but enjoyable, Jerry's re-cut of 'Money (That's What I Want)' would be OK if it weren't for the horrible overdubbed duet vocals by Levi Kreis, the actor who played him in the 'Million Dollar Quartet' stage show. Initially available exclusively to those who saw the show, it received wider exposure via a bootleg single, while the un-dubbed version circulates among collectors.

First Release: Single A-side (2012) (bootleg)

Peter Checksfield with Phoebe Lewis (2006)

[399] **MORE AND MORE** (1969)
(Merle Kilgore / Webb Pierce)

Originally released by Merle Kilgore in 1954 and by Webb Pierce later the same year, this is a typically good track from the 'Country Music Hall of Fame' sessions.

First Release: 'Sings The Country Music Hall of Fame Hits, Vol. Two' (1969)

[400a] **MOTHER, THE QUEEN OF MY HEART** (1971)
(Slim Bryant / Jimmie Rodgers)

Originally recorded by Jimmie Rodgers in 1932, 'Mother, The Queen Of My Heart' was covered by Ernest Tubb (1951), Ramblin' Jack Elliott (1960), Stonewall Jackson (1968), Merle Haggard (1969) and Hank Snow (1970). Jerry's heart-felt version was recorded while his beloved mother Mamie was dying of cancer, and you can really hear the emotion in his voice. The song itself is beautifully arranged, and is a highlight of the 'Touching Home' album.

First Release: 'Touching Home' (1971)

[400b] **MOTHER, THE QUEEN OF MY HEART** (1987)

Played on a real piano and backed by unobtrusive acoustic guitar, bass and drums, this unrehearsed but very good performance is one of the better tracks from the December 1987 Hank Cochran session.

First Release: 'At Hank Cochran's' (1995)

[401] **MUSIC! MUSIC! MUSIC! - CANADIAN SUNSET** (1973/1974)
(Bernie Baum / Stephan Weiss) + (Eddie Heywood / Norman Gimbel)

Performed alone at the piano without a band, an entertaining performance of Teresa Brewer's 'Music! Music! Music' is abandoned half-way through in favor of an instrumental version of Andy Williams' 'Canadian Sunset'.

First Release: 'The Knox Phillips Sessions: The Unreleased Recordings' (2014)

[402] **MUSIC TO THE MAN** (1973)
(Tony Colton)

Written by a member of Heads, Hands and Feet, 'Music To The Man' is perhaps the kind of material he should've recorded more often, as he does a more than credible job. A rehearsal take circulates unofficially, while Heads, Hands and Feet released their own version (as 'Taking My Music To The Man') later the same year.

First Release: 'The Session' (1973)

[403] **MY BABE** (1962) (L) *
(Willie Dixon)

A Rhythm 'n' Blues standard, 'My Babe' was first recorded by Little Walter in 1955, and later covered by Ricky Nelson (1958), Dale Hawkins (1958), Cliff Richard and The Drifters (1959) and even Mickey Gilley (1961). A very poor quality live recording - later revealed to be from Keanesburg, New Jersey, in July 1962 - appeared on a bootleg in 1972. Incidentally, though almost unlistenable, the half-dozen or so shows circulating on tape from Keanesburg in 1962 reveal some real eye-popping, mouth-watering, song titles: 'Tennessee Waltz', 'Set My Mind At Ease', 'Georgia On My Mind', 'My Blue Heaven', 'The Twist', 'Beautiful Dreamer' (instrumental), 'There Stands The Glass', 'San Antonio Rose' (instrumental), 'Hello Hello Baby', 'Bill Bailey Won't You Please Come Home', 'Shake Rattle and Roll', 'Let The Good Times Roll'... why oh *why* didn't Sam Phillips ever tape Jerry properly at a series of club dates?! 'My Babe' was later performed in Hamburg in 1980.

First Release: 'With Jerry Lee Rock and Roll' (1972) (bootleg)

[404a] **MY BLUE HEAVEN** (1959)
(Walter Donaldson / George A. Whiting)

Originally released by Paul Whiteman and His Orchestra in 1927 and covered by Glenn Miller and His Orchestra (1941), Frank Sinatra (1950) and Fats Domino (1956), it was probably the latter version that inspired Jerry to record the song. 4 takes were recorded at a March 1959 session, though one sounds hesitant and the other three are a little rushed. The song was performed in Keanesburg in 1962 and Copenhagen in 1977.

First Release: 'Ole Tyme Country Music' (1970)

[404b] **MY BLUE HEAVEN** (1961)

Slower than most of the 1959 versions, Jerry's 2 takes from June 1961 are notable for some excellent saxophone courtesy of Ace Cannon of 'Yakety Sax' fame.

First Release: 'Sun: Into The Sixties' (various artists box-set, 1989)

[404c] **MY BLUE HEAVEN** (1969)

A really lovely version, this is noticeable for including an opening verse *("Day is ending, birds are wending...")* that is missing from Jerry's earlier versions. From the 'Country Music Hall of Fame' sessions but not released until much later, when Jerry heard it again in 1987, he complained that there's a mistake in the solo. If true, only *he* could hear it, as to mere mortals like everyone else, it sounds like the work of genius.

First Release: 'The Killer: 1969-1972' (box-set, 1986)

[405] MY BONNIE (1960)
(Charles E. Pratt)

An ancient song that was first recorded by The Haydn Quartet in 1901, it is probable that Jerry was inspired to record a Rock 'n' Roll version via Ray Charles' 1958 cover. Recorded with backing that includes saxophone, it's a great version, even if there are a little too many 'stops' in it. Later performances include Wheeling 1975, Bremen 1977 and (appropriately) Perth, Scotland 2004.

First Release: 'Collectors' Edition' (1974)

[406] MY CAROLINA SUNSHINE GIRL (1957)
(Jimmie Rodgers)

Originally released by Jimmie Rodgers in 1929, probably the best thing about 'Carolina Sunshine Girl' is the Bluesy piano intro. Otherwise, the fast 'pumpin' piano' treatment just doesn't suit the material, and Roland Janes' little guitar run at the end indicates that this wasn't a serious attempt at making a good record.

First Release: 'Rockin' and Free' (1974)

[407] MY CRICKET AND ME (1973)
(Leon Russell)

Originally released by Leon Russell as 'My Cricket' in 1972, Jerry gives a far better vocal performance than this string-laden waltz is worth.

First Release: 'Sometimes A Memory Ain't Enough' (1973)

[408] MY FINGERS DO THE TALKIN' (1982)
(Billy Taylor / Buck Moore)

The A-side of his first single on MCA and the title track of his first album for the label, after the 1979-1980 Elektra era it came as a bit of a disappointment. Yes, Jerry's voice is good, and the song is OK, but it is obvious that it's not Jerry playing piano, and is swamped with horns and some truly horrendous backing vocals. It did scrape to No. 44 in the Country charts though, surprising for a song that mentions erogenous zones. The handful of live performances include Pasadena 1982, Chase City 1982, 'Johnny Carson's Tonight Show' 1982, 'Wogan' 1983 and New York 1983. An alternate take was issued on 1992's 'Pretty Much Country' compilation.

First Release: 'My Fingers Do The Talkin'' (1982) + Single A-side (1982)

My Fingers Do The Talkin' / Forever Forgiving
(No. 44 Country)

'Wogan' (1983)

[409a] **MY GOD IS REAL** (1980) *
(Kenneth Morris)

An ancient hymn that was later covered by Red Foley (1952), The Prisonaires (1953), Pat Boone (1957), Jimmie Davis (1959), Johnny Cash (1962) and Mahalia Jackson (1963), legend has it that Jerry was thrown out of the Southwestern Bible Institute in Waxahachie, Texas for playing a boogie-woogie version of 'My God Is Real'. His 1980 recording though, can best be described as a little sprightly rather than Rockin'. Occasional live performances of the song (apart from in Waxahachie) include the Memphis Church recording 1970, 'Nashville Now' 1982 and 'Music City Tonight' 1995.

First Release: 'The Caribou Ranch Sessions, 1980-1986' (2012) (bootleg)

[409b] **MY GOD IS REAL** (1988) *

Recorded solo without a band, this brief version from the 1988 'Great Balls of Fire!' movie soundtrack sessions is played both slow and fast.

First Release: 'The Killer's Private Stash' (1991) (bootleg)

[410] MY GOD'S NOT DEAD (1970)
(Thomas LaVerne / Don Pittman / Bill Taylor)

From the 'In Loving Memories' Gospel album, 'My God's Not Dead' is an enjoyably fast number about religious devotion *("My God, my God, my God's not dead, sorry 'bout yours my friend!")*.

First Release: 'In Loving Memories: The Jerry Lee Lewis Gospel Album' (1970)

[411] MY MAMMY (1987)
(Walter Donaldson / Joe Young / Sam M. Lewis)

Along with Country music pioneers Jimmie Rodgers and Hank Williams, one of Jerry's biggest early heroes was Al Jolson. So it's a real shame that Jerry's only known studio recording of the song is played on a cheap Casio keyboard. From the largely unlistenable December 1987 Hank Cochran session, it was released on CD in 1995. Performed just a handful of times over the years, this writer witnessed a large group of Teds (Teddy Boys) walk out of a show in Northampton in 1987 when Jerry played it, despite the fact that he'd also performed gems like 'Ubangi Stomp' and 'Money' earlier in the show! Other performances include Sacramento 1976, Oslo 1985 and Goldston 1996.

First Release: 'At Hank Cochran's' (1995)

[412] MY ONLY CLAIM TO FAME (1969)
(Glenn Sutton)

Even on album as good as 'She Even Woke Me Up To Say Goodbye' (arguably the very pinnacle of Jerry's 'Country Comeback') the odd turkey gets through, and although 'My Only Claim To Fame' is very nicely sung and played, one can't help but cringe with lyrics like *"Each time we kiss I make a small deposit, in an endless bank of happy memories"*!

First Release: 'She Even Woke Me Up To Say Goodbye' (1970)

[413] MY PRETTY QUADROON (1962)
(Traditional)

An ancient song that was first released on record by Bud Billings and Carson Robison in 1930, 'My Pretty Quadroon' is a song which would've been considered racially-insensitive even in the early '60s (a 'quadroon' is a person of one-quarter black descent). So, it's surprising that it got as far as a well-polished and all-round excellent take - and it was even more of a surprise when Jerry performed the song on stage in Nottingham in 1983!

First Release: 'Collectors' Edition' (1974)

[414] **MYSTERY TRAIN** (1969) (L)
(Junior Parker / Sam Phillips)

Originally released by Little Junior Parker in 1953 and made famous by Elvis Presley in 1955, for Jerry's appearance at the Toronto Peace Festival in 1969, he performed a fabulous live version of the song while playing guitar with Kenny Lovelace on fiddle. His whole set was comprised largely of Elvis songs: one reason is because he didn't want to upset bill-sharers Little Richard and Chuck Berry by performing their songs (though that didn't stop him from doing that at the London Rock 'n' Roll Show 3 years later), and another reason is because he'd seen Elvis play in Las Vegas recently, so he probably felt the need to prove that he could do the songs better! Other live performances of 'Mystery Train' include Chatham 1972 and Bremen 1977.

First Release: 'The Killer: 1969-1972' (box-set, 1986)

[415] **NEAR YOU [INSTRUMENTAL]** (1959)
(Francis Craig / Kermit Goell)

Originally released by Francis Craig and His Orchestra in 1947, Jerry's version is a nice mid-paced boogie woogie instrumental.

First Release: 'Jerry Lee Lewis and His Pumping Piano' (1974)

[416] **NEVER TOO OLD TO ROCK 'N' ROLL** [with Ronnie McDowell] (1988)
(Ronnie McDowell / Joe Meador / Richard O. Young)

Recorded in a Memphis studio in January 1988, Jerry taped two quite different versions of 'Never Too Old To Rock 'n' Roll' with Ronnie McDowell, the superior single take and a longer but slower version that appeared on Ronnie's 'I'm Still Missing You' album. A Pop-Rock Elvis-lite pastiche, the song is nothing special, though it's well-intentioned. An unexceptional Promo Video was made, but more exciting was a one-off live performance of the song on the 'Nashville Now' TV show.

Never Too Old To Rock and Roll / Rock and Roll Kiss
(No. 50 Country)

'Nashville Now' (1989)

[417] **NIGHT TRAIN TO MEMPHIS** (1959)
(Owen Bradley / Marvin Hughes / Beasley Smith)

A Roy Acuff song from 1942, Jerry forgets most the lyrics but still manages to come up with an exciting record. *"We'll have a Jubilee, down in Memphis, Tennessee!"*, indeed!

First Release: 'A Taste of Country' (1970)

[418a] **NO HEADSTONE ON MY GRAVE** (1973)
(Charlie Rich)

First released by Little Esther Phillips in 1962, 'No Headstone On My Grave' is a great bluesy Charlie Rich song that could've been written for Jerry. Part-slow Blues and part-fast Rock 'n' Roll, The Killer is clearly having a ball, as are all the 'Rock' musicians with him, and the song remained a concert favorite for the rest of Jerry's career. Charlie Rich's own previously unreleased recording from 1962 was finally issued in 1981.

First Release: 'The Session' (1973) + Single A-side (1973)

No Headstone On My Grave / Jack Daniels (Old Number Seven)
(No. 60 Country)

[418b] **NO HEADSTONE ON MY GRAVE** (2006)

A no-nonsense live-in-the-studio performance, this was one of the better 'Last Man Standing' exclusive bonus tracks.

First Release: iTunes (exclusive download) + 'Rock 'n' Roll Resurrection' (2007) (bootleg)

[419] **NO HONKY TONKS IN HEAVEN** (1971)
(Thomas LaVerne / Bill Taylor)

A Country weeper with lyrics like *"Daddy there ain't no honky tonks in heaven, I know because that's where my mama's gone!"*, the song probably meant a lot to Jerry at the time of recording. Despite this, it was kept in the can for a full 15 months, finally appearing as the B-side to 'Who's Gonna Play This Old Piano' in September 1972 (it wasn't issued on an album until 1974's UK-only 'Fan Club Choice' LP). The song was performed in Attica, Indiana in July 1971.

First Release: Single B-side (1972)

[420] **NO LOVE HAVE I** [with Webb Pierce, Mel Tillis and Faron Young] (1984)
(Mel Tillis)

Originally released by Webb Pierce in 1959, this mid-paced honky tonk song is another highly enjoyable track from the over-looked 'Four Legends'.

First Release: 'Four Legends' (1985)

[421] **NO MORE HANGING ON** (1972)
(Jerry Chesnut)

By 1972, the hard Country of Jerry's 1968-1970 comeback was gradually being superseded by more Pop-orientated material, and while there's no criticizing his vocal delivery on 'No More Hanging On', the piano playing by Hargus 'Pig' Robbins is far closer to Elton John than it is to Jerry Lee Lewis. The biggest problem with this is that he was starting to have big Country hits that never become part of his live repertoire, almost as if the two were becoming separate entities.

First Release: 'Who's Gonna Play This Old Piano' (1972) + Single A-side (1972)

No More Hanging On / The Mercy Of A Letter
(No. 19 Country)

[422] **NO MORE THAN I GET** (1960)
(Stan Kesler)

A catchy Pop-Rocker from the same October 1960 session that produced 'When I Get Paid' and 'Love Made A Fool Of Me', this is at least far preferable to the latter!

First Release: '16 Songs Never Issued Before 2' (1975)

[423] **NO ONE BUT ME** (1964) *
(Peter Gage / Geoff Pullum)

During a UK tour in November 1964, Jerry took time out to record a song in a London studio, and then film a cameo for a forthcoming low-budget movie called 'Be My Guest'. Backed by British pick-up band The Plebs, 'No One But Me' is similar to Charlie Rich's 'Rebound', and whilst not the greatest song ever written it's certainly not the worst either. Never released on record at the time, it turned up on a '70s bootleg, though these days the movie itself is easily available thanks to an official DVD release.

First Release: 'With Jerry Lee Rock and Roll' (1972) (bootleg)

'Be My Guest' (1965)

[424] **NO ONE KNOWS ME** (1974)
(Charlie Owens)

Written by the steel guitar player in Jerry's early '70s road band, the song was taped at an October 1974 session but remained unreleased for years, probably due to The Killer's rather hoarse vocals. On some releases it is titled 'Nobody Knows Me'.

First Release: 'From The Vaults' (1986)

[425] **NO ONE WILL EVER KNOW** (1976)
(Mel Foree / Fred Rose)

A Roy Acuff from 1945, Jerry's beautifully played version is a highlight of the aptly-titled 'Country Class', arguably Jerry's finest post-1970 Country album. It's not a song that was performed very often, but he still dug it out very occasionally until as recently as 2006.

First Release: 'Country Class' (1976)

[426] **NO PARTICULAR PLACE TO GO** (1964) (L)
(Chuck Berry)

A Chuck Berry song from the same year (which was basically a rewrite of his earlier 'School Days'), Jerry's live cover is even more thrilling than the original. Surprisingly, there is no record of other live performances, though he did play a live-in-the-studio version for BBC radio's 'Top Gear' show later that year.

First Release: 'The Greatest Live Show on Earth' (1964)

[427] **NO TRAFFIC OUT OF ABILENE** (1972)
(Woodrow Webb)

Originally released by We Too in 1971, Jerry's wonderful cover of this fast Folky number was cut at the same January 1972 session as 'Chantilly Lace' and 'Think About It Darlin'', and would've made a great single. Instead, it is a highlight of the 'Who's Gonna Play This Old Piano' album.

First Release: 'Who's Gonna Play This Old Piano' (1972)

[428] **NORTH TO ALASKA** [with Linda Gail Lewis] (1965)
(Tillman Franks)

Originally released by Johnny Horton in 1960, Jerry and Linda's duet was only the 2nd time they ever sang together in the studio, yet it is infinitively better than 'Seasons Of My Heart' 2 years earlier, fitting perfectly onto Jerry's first Country album.

First Release: 'Country Songs For City Folks' (1965)

[429] **NUMBER ONE LOVIN' MAN** (1979)
(Jim Cottengim)

The most musically-thrilling track on Jerry's debut Elektra album, 'Number On Lovin' Man' is played with a drive and power that no-one could've expected in the late '70s, and the backing of musicians like James Burton and Hal Blaine is just sublime. The song was played in Hamburg 1980, Amsterdam 1980, Lyon 1980, Stockholm 1980, Rotterdam 1981 and Paris 1981, and was a concert highlight every time.

First Release: 'Jerry Lee Lewis' (1979)

[430] **OH LONESOME ME** (1969)
(Don Gibson)

Originally released by Don Gibson in 1957, covers of 'Oh Lonesome Me' include Bob Luman (1960), Johnny Burnette (1960), George Jones (1961), Clyde McPhatter (1962), Ray Charles (1962), Ann-Margret (1962), The Everly Brothers (1963), Wanda Jackson (1965), Nancy Sinatra with Lee Hazlewood (1967) and Roy Acuff (1967). Jerry's version rocks along nicely, even if the backing singers water things down a bit. Live performances were infrequent, but he performed it as recently as a New Year's Eve concert in Memphis in 2017, while other memorable live outings include a duet with wife Kerrie in Orange, France in 1995, and a duet with daughter phoebe at the 40th Anniversary Show in Memphis in 1996.

First Release: 'Sings The Country Music Hall of Fame Hits, Vol. One' (1969)

[431] **OKLAHOMA HILLS** (1990) (L) *
(Jack Guthrie / Woody Guthrie)

In 2006 a bootleg CD appeared featuring mixing desk recordings of two previously-uncirculated shows from Knott's Berry Farm, Los Angeles in 1990. Included is a full-length version of 'Oklahoma Hills', a song that dates back to Jack Guthrie and His Oklahomans in 1945, and although the tape is running a little fast, with some pitch adjustment it is well worth a listen.

First Release: 'Knott's Berry Farm' (2006) (bootleg)

[432] **OLD BLACK JOE** (1960)
(Stephen Foster)

A very old song, 'Old Black Joe' is a Stephen Foster composition that was published in 1853, though the likeliest version to influence Jerry was Al Jolson's 1951 recording. At least 4 full takes were cut at a January 1960 session, and although he forgets most of the original lyrics and it is overdubbed with a vocal chorus, the song gained almost mythical status amongst British fans when it was reissued on a '70s single. 'Old Black Joe' was performed live very occasionally from the late '70s until around 2001.

First Release: Single B-side (1960)

Peter Checksfield at Sun studios, Memphis (2005)

[433] **OLD GLORY** [with Toby Keith] (2003-2006)
(Paul Roberts / Shelby Darnell / Jerry Lee Lewis)

An 'original' song that is strongly based on Elton Britt's 1942 'There's A Star Spangled Banner Waving Somewhere', Jerry had performed the song live as far back as a 1995 show in Myrtle Beach, South Carolina. An album highlight, for a while it was considered as the title track, until someone came up with 'Last Man Standing' instead.

First Release: 'Last Man Standing' (2006)

[434] **OLD SWEET MUSIC (SWEET JESUS)** (1979) *
(unknown)

The problem with illicit bootleg recordings is that sometimes it is difficult to know the correct title of a song, and such is the case with 'Old Sweet Music' or 'Sweet Jesus'. Whatever it's called, it's a Gospel song played with a Rock 'n' Roll fervor, accompanied by prominent horns and backing vocalists.

First Release: 'Honky Tonk Stuff - A Collection Of Rare and Unreleased Recordings' (2007) (bootleg)

[435] **OLD TIME CHRISTIAN** (1987)
(Hal Reeves)

Played on a proper piano and with excellent backing that includes a vocal chorus, the partly rocked-up 'Old Time Christian' is arguably the highlight of the December 1987 Hank Cochran session.

First Release: 'At Hank Cochran's' (1995)

[436a] OLD TIME RELIGION (1957)
(Traditional)

First recorded by the Haydn Quartet with Orchestra in 1906, two fast but short takes of this old Gospel number were taped at Sun around February 1957. Unlike 'When The Saints Go Marching In' from the same session, 'Old Time Religion' was kept in the vaults until the '70s.

First Release: 'Sunday Down South' (1970)

[436b] OLD TIME RELIGION (1980) *

Far slower and longer, the 1980 re-cut of 'Old Time Religion' is one of several songs that would've helped make an interesting Elektra-era Gospel album.

First Release: 'The Caribou Ranch Sessions, 1980-1986' (2012) (bootleg)

[437] OLD TIME ROCK AND ROLL (1979) *
(George Jackson / Thomas E. Jones)

A strangely popular modern commercial Rock song originally released by Bob Seger and The Silver Bullet Band in 1978, Jerry's version has no piano but it does have some good James Burton guitar and prominent male backing vocals. Although there is no record of any live concert performances, in Manchester in 1980 Jerry did a lengthy rehearsal (something that is almost unheard of!), and included this song.

First Release: 'Alive and Rockin'' (1986) (bootleg)

[438] OLE PAL OF YESTERDAY (1957)
(Gene Autry / Jimmy Long)

Recorded by Gene Autry and Jimmy Long in 1932, Jerry cut 4 similar takes of the song in February 1957, complete with a 'Crazy Arms'-like intro and superb pumpin' piano.

First Release: 'Rockin' and Free' (1974)

[439] ON THE BACK ROW (1968)
(Jerry Chesnut / Norris 'Norro' Wilson)

Although otherwise a pretty average Country song, Jerry's vocal delivery at times is extremely soulful, hitting notes that he could only dream of just a few years later. The song was covered by Del Reeves in 1969 and George Jones in 1972.

First Release: 'Another Place, Another Time' (1968)

[440] ON THE JERICHO ROAD (1980) *
(Don McCrossan)

Originally released by The Propes Quartet in 1934, 'On The Jericho Road' is a song Jerry would've been very familiar with, jamming on it at the 1956 'Million Dollar Quartet' session and performing it live at the Memphis Church recording in 1970, on 'Kerrie Live!' (a TV show hosted by Jerry's wife Kerrie) in 2000, and on both his 66th and 67th Birthday concerts in Memphis. This version is as good as any of those, and is a highlight of the unreleased 1980 Gospel sessions that he cut for Elektra.

First Release: 'The Caribou Ranch Sessions, 1980-1986' (2012) (bootleg)

[441] ONCE MORE WITH FEELING (1969)
(Kris Kristofferson / Shel Silverstein)

One of Jerry's greatest Country hits, 'Once More With Feeling' was recorded twice in the studio, first of all on 15th October 1969 (a version that wasn't released until the '80s) and a far superior re-make on 18th November 1969. He promoted the song on 'The Johnny Cash Show' in 1970, and it was played live very occasionally until well into the '90s. Unlikely cover versions include Sheb Wooley (under the name Big Ben Colder) in 1970 and UK Pop singer Susan Maughan in 1974, while Kris Kristofferson recorded his own version in 1979.

First Release: 'She Even Woke Me Up To Say Goodbye' (1970) + Single A-side (1970)

Once More With Feeling / You Went Out Of Your Way (To Walk On Me)
(No. 2 Country)

'The Johnny Cash Show' (1970)

[442] ONE HAS MY NAME (THE OTHER HAS MY HEART) (1969)
(Hal Blair / Dearest Dean / Eddie Dean)

A song that was first recorded by The Frontiersmen with Eddie Dean in 1948, Jerry's stand-out version from the 'Country Music Hall of Fame' sessions made an ideal single. Promoted on 'Hee Haw' and 'The Mike Douglas Show', 'One Has My Name' was a concert regular up until 1981, and performed far less frequently up to around 1993.

First Release: 'Sings The Country Music Hall of Fame Hits, Vol. Two' (1969) + Single A-side (1969)

One Has My Name (The Other Has My Heart) / I Can't Stop Lovin' You
(No. 3 Country)

[443] ONE MINUTE PAST ETERNITY (1963)
(Stan Kesler / Bill Taylor)

A memorable mid-tempo Country song from Jerry's final Sun session in August 1963, 'One Minute Past Eternity' almost topped the Country charts when released 6 years later. It was covered by such Country giants as Hank Locklin (1970), Ernest Tubb (1970), Kitty Wells (1970), Wanda Jackson (1970) and Hank Snow (1974), while very occasional live performances include Las Vegas 1970, Raleigh 1981, Las Vegas 1989 and Memphis 1993. Incidentally, when interviewed by this author, guitarist Buck Hutcheson swore that he played on this session, despite never being credited. Jerry's other road musicians at the time Herman 'Hawk' Hawkins and Morris 'Tarp' Tarrant are also on the session, so it certainly makes perfect sense that he would've been there.

First Release: 'The Golden Cream Of The Country' (1969) + Single A-side (1969)

One Minute Past Eternity / Frankie and Johnny
(No. 2 Country)

[444] ONE MORE TIME (1970)
(Larry Butler / Jan Crutchfield / Buddy Killen)

A predictable but well played Country song, 'One More Time' was later covered by Ferlin Husky (1971), Connie Smith (1971) and Conway Twitty (1971).

First Release: 'There Must Be More To Love Than This' (1970)

[445a] ONE OF THEM OLD THINGS (WE ALL GO THROUGH) (1987) *
(Hoy Lindsey / Joel Sonnier)

An above average Country ballad, Jerry cut a great version of the song for Producer Eddie Kilroy in 1987.

First Release: 'The Caribou Ranch Sessions, 1980-1986' (2012) (bootleg)

[445b] ONE OF THEM OLD THINGS (WE ALL GO THROUGH) (1994)

With the earlier cut still unreleased, Jerry liked the song enough to re-cut it at a slightly slower tempo for 1995's 'Young Blood'. It was performed several times on the 1987 European Tour (including on the 'Live in Italy' album), again for a show in London in 1995, and at the 40th Anniversary show in Memphis in 1996, where he was joined by composer Joel Sonnier.

First Release: 'Young Blood' (1995)

Jonny Williams and John Pearce with Jerry Lee Lewis (1995)

[446] ONLY LOVE CAN GET YOU IN MY DOOR (1976)
(Ric Marlow / Michel Rubini)

Originally released by Ric Marlow in 1975, 'Only Love Can Get You In My Door' starts as a pretty ballad with old-fashioned chord changes; then halfway through, it changes gear and turns into an up-tempo Country-Rock song. Very occasional live versions include St. Louis 1980, Wheeling 1982, Toronto 1987, Skien 1989 and Oslo 1989.

First Release: 'Country Class' (1976)

[447] ONLY YOU (AND YOU ALONE) (1983)
(Buck Ram)

Originally released by The Platters in 1954, cover versions include Carl Perkins (1958), Brenda Lee (1962), Little Richard (1964), James Brown (1964), Roy Orbison (1969), The Shirelles (1972), P.J. Proby (1973) and Ringo Starr (1974). Jerry's nice Country-fied version appeared on his 2nd MCA album, while an alternate take was released in 1991. Jerry performed the song live as early as Birmingham, Alabama in 1974, while very occasional later performances include Toronto 1984, Norrkoping 1985, Atlantic City 1988, Memphis 1988 and Dublin 1993. Most significant of all though was a performance in Oslo in 1985 where he was joined by wife Kerrie, who surprised the audience with her beautiful and powerful voice.

First Release: 'I Am What I Am' (1984)

Peter Checksfield with Kerrie Lewis (1993)

[448] **OOBY DOOBY** (1957)
(Wayde Lee Moore / Dick Penner)

Originally released by Roy Orbison with his group The Teen Kings in 1956 and covered by both Sid King and The Five Strings and Janis Martin the same year, Jerry cut two inspired takes of this Rockabilly song around August 1957. Not released until the '70s, it might've been a candidate for his debut album if the piano intro wasn't so similar to 'Ubangi Stomp'.

First Release: 'Rockin' and Free' (1974)

[449] **OUT OF MY MIND** (1968)
(Kenneth Lovelace)

First employed by Jerry in early 1967, Kenny Lovelace quickly proved himself a fine guitarist and fiddle player, an excellent band leader, and a very loyal friend. He also quickly became a useful songwriter, and 'Out Of My Mind' is as strong as anything else on the 'She Still Comes Around' album.

First Release: 'She Still Comes Around' (1969)

[450] **OVER THE RAINBOW** (1980)
(E.Y. Harburg / Harold Arlen)

The Judy Garland classic from 1939, cover versions from the Rock 'n' Roll era include The Del Vikings (1957), Gene Vincent and His Blue Caps (1959), Little Anthony and The Imperials (1959), The Marcels (1961), Connie Francis (1963), Ray Charles (1963) and Jackie Wilson (1965). Jerry's version is notable for its superb piano and fiddle, and when issued as a single became a Top 10 Country hit. Promoted on 'The Tomorrow Show', it remained a concert regular for the rest of Jerry's career.

First Release: 'Killer Country' (1980) + Single A-side (1980)

Over The Rainbow / Folsom Prison Blues
(No. 10 Country)

'The Tomorrow Show' (1980)

[451] **PARTING IS SUCH SWEET SORROW** (1972)
(Cecil Harrelson / Linda Gail Lewis)

On the 'Who's Gonna Play This Old Piano' album there's an interesting and melodic Country instrumental called 'Parting Is Such Sweet Sorrow'. It later emerged that he'd *also* cut a vocal track for the song, but this had been kept in the can, finally surfacing on the 'From The Vaults' compilation in 1986.

First Release: 'Who's Gonna Play This Old Piano' (1972)

[452] **PASS ME NOT, O GENTLE SAVIOR** (1973/1974)
(William H. Doane / Fanny J. Crosby)

An old Gospel song that was published in 1870, this heartfelt performance with prominent piano and steel guitar is one of the highlights of his sessions with Knox Phillips.

First Release: 'The Knox Phillips Sessions: The Unreleased Recordings' (2014)

[453] **PEACE IN THE VALLEY** (2008-2010) *
(Thomas A. Dorsey)

Original released by The Flying Clouds Of Detroit in 1947 and later covered by Elvis Presley (1957), Johnny Cash and The Carter Family (1962), Ruth Brown (1962) and Duane Eddy (1963), the only studio recording by Jerry comes from the 'Mean Old Man' sessions. He was highly familiar with it of course, singing it as part of the 'Million Dollar Quartet' sessions in 1956, at the Memphis Church recording in 1970, in Dalton in 1979, and in Stuttgart with Johnny Cash and Carl Perkins for 'The Survivors' album. The 21st century version is played alone at the piano, where he is accompanied by a female singer who may or may not be Mavis Staples.

First Release: 'Come Sundown' (2014) (bootleg)

[454] **PEACH PICKING TIME DOWN IN GEORGIA** (1985) (L) *
(Clayton McMichen / Jimmie Rodgers)

A Jimmie Rodgers song from 1933, Jerry performed a great version of 'Peach Picking Time In Georgia' at an Oslo concert in 1985, a show that was released as a popular bootleg. It wasn't the first time he'd performed it, as one fan recalled him playing the song in Birmingham (UK) in 1972.

First Release: 'Let's Live A Little' (1985) (bootleg)

[455] **PEE WEE'S PLACE** (1977)
(Harvey Faglier)

Written by Jerry's guitarist (later bassist) Harvey 'Duke' Faglier, 'Pee Wee's Place' has the distinction of being the last song The Killer cut for Mercury. He does a good job on it with some pretty nifty piano work, even if the mix could be better.

First Release: 'Keeps Rockin'' (1978)

[456] **PEN AND PAPER** (1963)
(Dianne Kilroy / Eddie Kilroy)

Released as one side of his debut Smash single in 1963, there is some debate over whether this or 'Hit The Road, Jack' was meant to be the A-side. As it turned out, it was 'Pen and Paper', a nicely-sung Country song with prominent strings and backing vocals that got the most attention. Faron Young covered the song in 1965, and Mickey Gilley did the same in 1975.

First Release: Single A-side (1963)

Pen and Paper / Hit The Road Jack
(No. 36 Country)

[457] **PERSONALITY** (1979)
(Harold Logan / Lloyd Price)

Originally released by Lloyd Price in 1959 and covered by Anthony Newley (1959), Pat Boone (1961), Bill Haley and The Comets (1973) and The Platters (1974), Jerry's version is one of the weaker moments on his mostly brilliant first Elektra album.

First Release: 'Jerry Lee Lewis' (1979)

[458] **PICK ME UP ON YOUR WAY DOWN** (1969)
(Harlan Howard)

Originally released by Charlie Walker (1958) and covered by Webb Pierce (1959), Ernest Tubb (1960), Warren Smith (1961), Buck Owens (1961), Porter Wagoner (1963), Hank Thompson (1964) and Harlan Howard (1965), 'Pick Me Up On Your Way Down' is one of those great honky tonk Country songs that one could easily imagine being played at Sun, albeit not with the fiddle and steel guitar backing featured here. A song Jerry clearly liked, it was performed live occasionally up until around 1996.

First Release: 'Sings The Country Music Hall of Fame Hits, Vol. Two' (1969) + Single B-side (1982)

[459] **PINK CADILLAC** [with Bruce Springsteen] (2003-2006)
(Bruce Springsteen)

Originally released by Bruce Springsteen in 1984 and covered by Natalie Cole in 1987 and Carl Perkins in 1992, Jerry's duet with JLL fan Bruce is one of the more successful duets on 'Last Man Standing'. Promoted by an interesting animated Promo Video, sadly there were no live performances of the song.

First Release: 'Last Man Standing' (2006)

'Pink Cadillac' Promo Video (2006)

[460] **PINK PEDAL PUSHERS** (1958)
(Carl Perkins)

A great Carl Perkins song that the composer recorded both at Sun and Columbia, Jerry's version of 'Pink Pedal Pushers' was cut at the February 1958 session when he mostly recorded songs associated with Elvis. It is just as inspired.

First Release: 'Monsters' (1971)

[461] **PLAY ME A SONG I CAN CRY TO** (1968)
(Jerry Chesnut)

A real tear-jerker, 'Play Me A Song I Can Cry To' is basically about an old man in a club requesting a song, and then dying while listening to it. Not the jolliest of ditties then, but perfectly in keeping with Jerry's initial 'Country Comeback' period.

First Release: 'Another Place, Another Time' (1968)

[462] PLEASE DON'T TALK ABOUT ME WHEN I'M GONE (1971)
(Sidney Clare / Sam H. Stept)

Originally released by Ernie Golden and His Orchestra in 1931, notable covers of 'Please Don't Talk About Me When I'm Gone' include Johnnie Ray (1953), Bill Haley and His Comets (1957), Ann-Margret (1962) and Connie Francis (1968). On Jerry's previous album 'There Must Be More To Love Than This', he included an incredibly fast version of 'Sweet Georgia Brown'; this time he Rocks-up another oldie, if anything even harder than before, giving name-checks to musicians Kenny Lovelace on fiddle and Pete Drake on steel guitar along the way. Not a song that was generally played live, a rare exception was at a 1979 New Year's Eve show in St. Louis.

First Release: 'Touching Home' (1971)

[463] PLEDGING MY LOVE (1973)
(Don Robey / Ferdinand Robinson)

A Johnny Ace song from 1954, as with 'No Headstone On My Grave', it's a number that was performed several times during the Spring 1972 tour, prior to being recorded for 'The Session' in January 1973. It works well too, despite being the only ballad on the original double album. Subsequently performed very occasionally live, it largely disappeared after the late '80s, though as late as 2006 it was a surprise inclusion at a show in Istanbul, Turkey. Incidentally, on an old and long-deleted Linda Gail Lewis website, there was a detailed Discography. Listed in the 'Unreleased' section was this intriguing entry: *acetate - Forever My Darling (Duet with Jerry Lee) - 1960's*. This author once asked Linda Gail about this, and she confirmed that the song is actually 'Pledging My Love', but had no further details.

First Release: 'The Session' (1973)

[464] POISON LOVE (1994)
(Elmer Laird)

Original recorded by Johnnie and Jack in 1950 and covered by Bill Monroe (1951), Hank Snow (1957) and Webb Pierce (1960), it is the kind of rocked up Country song that Jerry excels at, and a more than worthy inclusion of the underrated 'Young Blood'.

First Release: 'Young Blood' (1995)

[465] PRECIOUS MEMORIES (1980) *
(J.B.F. Wright)

First released by the Simmons Sacred Singers in 1929, this Gospel song was also recorded by Roy Rogers (1952), Bill Monroe (1958), Jim Reeves (1959), Tennessee Ernie Ford (1959), LaVern Baker (1959), Duane Eddy (1963) and J.D. Sumner and The Stamps Quartet (1968). Jerry's otherwise fine version is a little too slow, not helped by the rather heavy-handed drumming. A faster and more natural-sounding version was performed at the 1970 Memphis Church recording.

First Release: 'The Caribou Ranch Sessions, 1980-1986' (2012) (bootleg)

[466a] **PRIDE DON'T MEAN A THING** (1980) *
(unknown)

A good Country song whose writer is unknown, with a bit more work it could've been hit material.

First Release: 'The Caribou Ranch Sessions, 1980-1986' (2012) (bootleg)

[466b] **PRIDE DON'T MEAN A THING** (1987) *

Jerry liked the song enough to give it a 2nd try a seven years later, and, although it's fairly similar in arrangement, his 1987 voice sounds in better shape.

First Release: 'The Caribou Ranch Sessions, 1980-1986' (2012) (bootleg)

[467] **PROMISED LAND** (2008-2010)
(Chuck Berry)

Originally released by Chuck Berry in 1964, covers of 'Promised Land' include Johnny Rivers (1965), Johnnie Allan (1971), Dave Edmunds (1972), Elvis Presley (1974) and Dale Hawkins (1999). Jerry rarely disappointed with Chuck Berry numbers, and this is largely the case here, with some pretty good piano played at a brisk tempo. Shame about the faded ending though!

First Release: 'Rock & Roll Time' (2014)

'Rock & Roll Time' (2014)

[468] **PUMPING PIANO ROCK** (1957)
(Jerry Lee Lewis)

A song that is often strangely dismissed, 'Pumpin' Piano Rock' actually lives up to its title. With a little more work and a longer running time, it could've been another 'Lewis Boogie'.

First Release: 'Rockin' and Free' (1974)

[469] **PUT ME DOWN** (1958)
(Roland Janes)

Written by guitarist Roland Janes, at least 7 takes of 'Put Me Down' were cut at a March 1957 session, some of them very different from each other. Ironically for a song written by a guitarist, it is drummer Jimmy Van Eaton who *really* shines on the originally released cut. Cover versions include Marty Wilde (1959), Colin Hicks and His Cabin Boys (1960) and Matt Lucas (1963).

First Release: 'Jerry Lee Lewis' (1958)

[470] **RAGGED BUT RIGHT** (1973/1974)
(Traditional)

First recorded by the Blue Harmony Boys in 1930, Jerry probably learnt the song via George Jones' 1956 or Moon Mullican's 1961 recording. Performed with only piano plus a little harmonica and steel guitar (presumably the other musicians had passed out in a corner somewhere), the song could've been tailor-made for Jerry, and with a little more polish and fuller backing it is easy to imagine this on 'Boogie Woogie Country Man' or 'Odd Man In'. Circulating unofficially in poor quality for years, it was finally issued with pristine sound in 2014.

First Release: 'The Knox Phillips Sessions: The Unreleased Recordings' (2014)

[471] **RAINING IN MY HEART** (1973)
(Jerry Moore / James West)

Originally released by Slim Harpo in 1961 and covered Dorsey Burnette (1961), Clyde McPhatter (1962), The Pretty Things (1965) and Hank Williams Jr. (1970), 'Raining In My Heart' can best be described as a Blues ballad. Jerry clearly feels at home with the material *("Baby, try Jerry Lee's love just one more time!")*, and it would've made a far more commercial single than 'Meat Man', as well as a great inclusion on 'Southern Roots'. Instead, it was kept in the can until the '80s.

First Release: 'The Killer: 1973-1977' (box-set, 1987)

[472] **RAMBLIN' ROSE** (1961)
(Fred Burch / Marijohn Wilkin)

Not to be confused with Nat 'King' Cole's ballad of the same name, Jerry's 'Ramblin' Rose' is a soulful mid-tempo song with driving saxophones, and something it is easy to imagine Ray Charles singing. As it was, any '60s covers were left to Ted Taylor (1965), The Motions (1967) and MC5 (1969). An alternate take slipped out on 1969's 'Golden Cream Of The Country' compilation.

First Release: Single B-side (1962)

[473] **RED HOT MEMORIES (ICE COLD BEER)** (1975)
(Tom T. Hall)

Jerry recorded several Tom T. Hall numbers during the '70s, sometimes because they were great songs, and sometimes because Tom was a Mercury label-mate. 'Red Hot Memories (Ice Cold Beer)' falls firmly into the latter category. The composer released his own version in 1983.

First Release: 'Boogie Woogie Country Man' (1975)

[474a] **RELEASE ME** (1959)
(Eddie Miller / Dub Williams / Robert Young)

Originally released by Eddie Miller and His Oklahomans in 1950 and covered by Ray Price (1954) and Kitty Wells (1954), 'Release Me' became forever associated with Engelbert Humperdinck after his giant 1967 hit with the song. Jerry's mid-tempo Sun cut is just a rough run-through, with the heavy-handed drummer who is definitely *not* Jimmy Van Eaton audibly dragging at times. Some have speculated that it is actually Jerry Lee Lewis playing drums and someone else playing piano, but this is unlikely.

First Release: 'Rockin' and Free' (1974)

[474b] **RELEASE ME** (1968)

Beautifully sung and played, slower and more majestic, the 1968 cut is the definitive version of the song. It was performed live occasionally up until the late '90s.

First Release: 'She Still Comes Around' (1969)

[474c] **RELEASE ME** [with Gillian Welch] (2008-2010)

A little faster than the Mercury cut, this lengthy version is enhanced by Gillian Welch's lovely harmony vocal, which contrasts nicely with Jerry's rather ragged delivery.

First Release: 'Mean Old Man' (2010)

[475] (REMEMBER ME) I'M THE ONE WHO LOVES YOU (1974)
(Stuart Hamblen)

Originally released by Stuart Hamblen in 1950 and covered by Ray Price (1957), Johnny Cash (1957), Pat Boone (1960) and Johnny Burnette (1962), Jerry's great version features a particularly good vocal for the time. Live performances of the song include Augusta, Maine in 1985 and Las Vegas in 2001.

First Release: 'Boogie Woogie Country Man' (1975) + Single B-side (1975)

[476] RESTLESS HEART (1994)
(Andy Paley / James Burton / Julie Richmond / Kenny Lovelace)

A nice Country song that could've easily fit onto any late '70s Mercury album, it can be found on 1995's 'Young Blood'. Co-writer Julie Richmond was a regular songwriting partner of Kenny Lovelace, so it is probable that Andy Paley and James Burton just added ideas later.

First Release: 'Young Blood' (1995)

[477] REUBEN JAMES (1970)
(Barry Etris / Alex Harvey)

Originally released by Kenny Rogers and The First Edition in 1969, 'Reuben James' is a mid-paced Country-Rock song about a poor but kind 'colored' man who was misunderstood by the white folks, and is something refreshingly different for Jerry at a time when his albums were becoming increasingly formulaic. It is highly unlikely that it was ever performed live.

First Release: 'There Must Be More To Love Than This' (1970)

[478] RIDE ME DOWN EASY (1973)
(Billy Joe Shaver)

Originally released by Bobby Bare in 1973 and covered by Waylon Jennings the same year, 'Ride Me Down Easy' is a modern 'Outlaw' Country song, and the best thing to come out of the July 1973 Stan Kesler sessions. Jerry performed the song at shows in Halden, Norway 1989 and in Las Vegas 1989, while Billy Joe Shaver released his own version in 1976.

First Release: 'Sometimes A Memory Ain't Enough' (1973)

[479] RING OF FIRE (1965)
(June Carter Cash / Merle Kilgore)

First recorded by Anita Carter as 'Love's Ring Of Fire' in 1962 and made famous by Johnny Cash in 1963, Jerry's version is excellent, even if he largely imitates Cash's version, right down to the Mariachi trumpets.

First Release: 'Country Songs For City Folks' (1965)

[480] RITA MAY (1979)
(Bob Dylan / Jacques Levy)

Originally released by Bob Dylan in 1976, 'Rita May' is an excellent mid-paced Rock 'n' Roll song that ideally suits Jerry. Apparently when he expressed his admiration for the song and asked who'd wrote it, he showed no recognition when told it was Bob Dylan, something he may or may not have been serious about! Live performances include Rotterdam 1981, Frankfurt 1981, Berlin 1985, Las Vegas 1989 and Reno 1990.

First Release: 'Jerry Lee Lewis' (1979) + Single B-side (1979)

[481] ROCK 'N' ROLL FUNERAL (1986)
(Blackie Ferrell)

First recorded by Commander Cody the same year, this amusing modern Rock 'n' Roll song features Jerry accompanied just by Bob Moore's bass and Buddy Harman's drums, with no guitars or backing vocals.

First Release: 'Rocket' (1988)

[482] ROCK 'N' ROLL IS SOMETHING SPECIAL (1987) *
(Jerry Lee Lewis)

Kicking off with a 'Lucille' intro, 'Rock 'n' Roll Is Something Special' is a song full of self-mythologizing lyrics, and could've been another 'Lewis Boogie' or 'Rockin' Jerry Lee' if it had been released. Despite this, he performed it live very occasionally, including Cambridge 1987, Rome 1987, Newport 1987, Southport 1987, Atlantic City 1988, Nice 1990, Hamburg 1991 and Sarpsborg 1993.

First Release: 'The Caribou Ranch Sessions, 1980-1986' (2012) (bootleg)

[483] ROCK 'N' ROLL MEDLEY: GOOD GOLLY, MISS MOLLY - LONG TALL SALLY - JENNY, JENNY - TUTTI FRUTTI - WHOLE LOTTA SHAKIN' GOIN'ON (1973)
(Robert 'Bumps' Blackwell / John Marascalco) + (Enotris Johnson / Richard Penniman) + (Dorothy LaBostrie / Joe Lubin / Richard Penniman) + (Sunny David / David Williams)

Apart from the Chuck Berry-styled guitar intro, this Medley from January 1973 sounds almost like a concert finale, and was therefore the perfect way to close side four of the double album from his London sessions.

First Release: 'The Session' (1973) + Single B-side (1973)

[484] ROCK 'N' ROLL MONEY (1982)
(Hellard / Garvin / Jones)

When the 'Get Out Your Big Roll Daddy' compilation LP of MCA material was released in 1986, it included one completely new track, namely a Rock 'n' Roll song called 'Rock 'n' Roll Money'. Collectors of live tapes however would've heard it before, as he'd previously performed the song in Charlotte 1984, Toronto 1984, Pasadena 1984 and New Jersey 1985, amongst others. It would later be played in Houston and Zwolle, both in 1987, but by the end of the '80s it had been forgotten.

First Release: 'Get Out Your Big Roll Daddy' (1986)

[485] ROCK AND ROLL [with Jimmy Page] (2003-2006)
(Robert Plant / John Bonham / Jimmy Page / John Paul Jones)

Originally released by Led Zeppelin in 1971, 'Rock & Roll' is an interesting experiment that is only partially successful. Jerry puts in an exciting Rock 'n' Roll performance and Jimmy Page adds some great guitar, but without the distinctive drum intro and guitar riff of the original (both absent here) the actual *song* isn't up to much. Jerry performed it live on 'The Today Show' in 2006.

First Release: 'Last Man Standing' (2006)

Peter Checksfield with Jimmy Page (1992)

[486] ROCK AND ROLL (FAIS-DO-DO) [with Johnny Cash, Carl Perkins and Roy Orbison] (1985)
(Michael Smotherman)

Although a great idea on paper, the problem with the 'Class of '55' album is that much of the material is so damn weak. Add the horrible horn-driven '80s production, and the results are barely listenable. 'Rock and Roll (Fais-Do-Do)' is the perfect example of this (for those wondering, a 'Fais Do-Do' is a Cajun dance party).

First Release: 'Class of '55' (1986) + Single B-side (1986)

[487] ROCK AND ROLL RUBY (1957)
(Johnny Cash)

Originally released by Warren Smith, and taped at the same early 1958 session as Warren Smith's 'Ubangi Stomp' and 'So Long I'm Gone', this is a fine Rock 'n' Roll performance. Some might even call it Rockabilly, but Jerry Lee Lewis *hated* being called that *("I'm Rock 'n' Roll, boy!")*. It was performed live in Las Vegas in both 1985 and 1998, and at the 66th Birthday Show in Memphis in 2001.

First Release: 'Collector's Edition' (1974)

[488] ROCK AND ROLL TIME (2008-2010)
(Kris Kristofferson / Roger McGuinn / Bob Neuwirth)

Originally released by Kris Kristofferson in 1974, Bob Neuwirth the same year, and Roger McGuinn in 1976, 'Rock and Roll Time' is a slow-ish Country-Rock song with lyrics like *"If sometimes it seems I'm falling behind, remember I'm running on rock and roll time!"* that Jerry could clearly identify with. The title track of his final non-Gospel album, the only live performance was on 'The Late Show with David Letterman', though rather rudely it was cut short by resident band leader Paul Shaffer, a person who clearly does *NOT* run on Rock and Roll Time!

First Release: 'Rock & Roll Time' (2014)

'The Late Show with David Letterman' (2014)

[489a] ROCKIN' JERRY LEE (1966)
(Jerry Lee Lewis)

An excellent self-composed Rock 'n' Roll song with a stop-start rhythm, 'Rockin' Jerry Lee' is the story of his rise to fame condensed into 2 minutes and 40 seconds: *"I worked at a night spot they called 'The Wagon Wheel', in Natchez Mississippi set up back upon a hill!"*. Recorded during the 'Memphis Beat' album sessions, it first surfaced on a bootleg in 1975, finally getting an official release in 1986.

First Release: 'The Killer: 1963-1968' (box-set, 1986)

[489b] ROCKIN' JERRY LEE (1979)

Faster and wilder but missing the stops and starts of the earlier version, this would be a more than worthwhile remake... except that it features the most irritating, puke-inducing female backing vocals ever put on tape! An un-dubbed version surfaced recently, and it is a thousand times better.

First Release: 'When Two Worlds Collide' (1980) + Single B-side (1980)

[490a] ROCKIN' MY LIFE AWAY (1979)
(Mack Vickery)

Despite or because of some of the most obscure and bizarre lyrics Jerry Lee Lewis ever uttered (*"A streamline feline a military brat, she knows she's the general's daughter but The Killer's top brass!"*), 'Rockin' My Life Away' is the most enduring new-written Rock 'n' Roll song Jerry recorded after leaving Sun, with some of his most inspired piano playing. Initially promoted on 'The CMA Awards', the song became a live regular for the rest of Jerry's career, long after he'd stopped playing big hits like 'Breathless', 'High School Confidential' and 'What'd I Say'. Mickey Gilley covered it in 1980, the same year Mack Vickery released his own version.

First Release: 'Jerry Lee Lewis' (1979) + Single A-side (1979)

Rockin' My Life Away / I Wish I Was Eighteen Again
(No. 18 Country)

'The CMA Awards' (1979)

[490b] **ROCKIN' MY LIFE AWAY** [with Kid Rock & Slash] (2008-2010)

A faster but shorter version than the 1979 cut, Jerry sounds fine, and Slash proves himself a very good Rock 'n' Roll guitarist even if he ain't no James Burton. The less said about Kid Rock's shouty non-singing though, the better.

First Release: 'Mean Old Man' (2010)

[491] **ROCKIN' THE BOAT OF LOVE** (1961)
(Carl Mann)

Written by the late Carl Mann, 'Rockin' The Boat Of Love' is a saxophone-accompanied Pop-Rock song with a Mexican feel and a vocal that hits some almost falsetto high notes. It was taped at the same September 1961 session as 'Money (That's What I Want)' and 'Ramblin' Rose', but unlike those songs, it stayed in the can until the '70s.

First Release: 'Collectors' Edition' (1974)

[492] **ROCKIN' WITH RED (SHE KNOWS HOW TO ROCK ME)** (1958)
(Willie Perryman)

Originally released by Piano Red (Willie Perryman) in 1950 and covered by 'Little' Jimmy Dickens in 1954, this impromptu but highly enjoyable run-through clearly needed a bit more polish to make it a candidate for '50s release. As it was, it stayed in the can until 1983.

First Release: 'The Sun Years' (Box-Set, 1983)

[493] **ROCKING LITTLE ANGEL** (1979)
(Jimmie Rogers)

Originally released by Ray Smith in 1959, 'Rocking Little Angel' is basically a Rocked-up nursery rhyme, which would've been more suited to Bill Haley than Jerry Lee Lewis. Despite this, he gives it a harder Rock 'n' Roll treatment than it probably deserves.

First Release: 'Jerry Lee Lewis' (1979)

[494] **ROCKING PNEUMONIA AND BOOGIE WOOGIE FLU** (1965)
(Huey 'Piano' Smith / John Vincent)

Originally released by Huey 'Piano' Smith and The Clowns in 1957, Jerry's fine revival is only slightly marred by him playing a harpsichord rather than a piano. Released as an A-side, it failed to chart, despite a performance on the 'Shindig!' TV show.

First Release: Single A-side (1965)

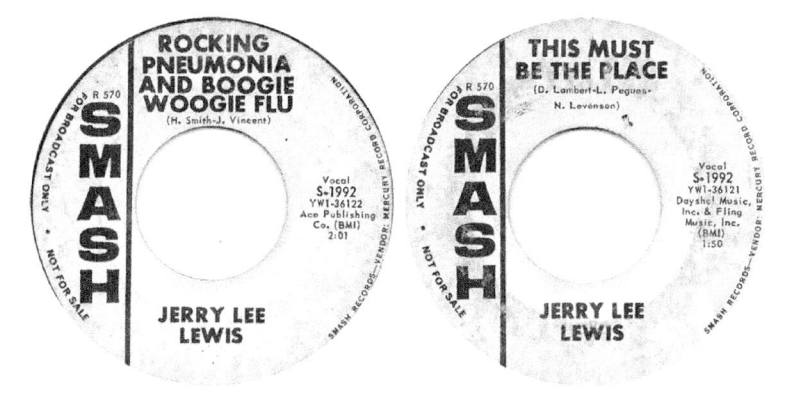

Rocking Pneumonia and Boogie Woogie Flu / This Must Be The Place
(Not a hit)

'Shindig!' (1965)

[495] ROLL ON (2008-2010) *
(J.J. Cale)

First released by Jessi Colter in 1978, with composer J.J. Cale recording it with Eric Clapton in 2009, 'Roll On' is a mid-paced but laid-back Country-Rock song. Clearly just a run through, without piano but with a full band, Jerry's version needed more polish to make it releasable.

First Release: 'Come Sundown' (2014) (bootleg)

[496a] ROLL OVER BEETHOVEN (1965)
(Chuck Berry)

Originally released by Chuck Berry in 1956 and revived by The Beatles in 1963, 'Roll Over Beethoven' has been performed by Jerry Lee Lewis many, many times, in the studio and on stage, but *none* are quite as powerful as his 1965 recording on 'The Return Of Rock'. The only surprising thing is that he didn't tackle the song years earlier! 'Roll Over Beethoven' became a live regular for the rest of his career.

First Release: 'The Return of Rock' (1965)

[496b] ROLL OVER BEETHOVEN [with Linda Gail Lewis] (1969)

Jerry and Linda had been performing 'Roll Over Beethoven' as a duet on stage for quite some time - indeed, footage surfaced a few years back of them playing it on 'Cowtown Jamboree' in 1967 (also notable as the earliest footage to feature Kenny Lovelace as a band member). So it made perfect sense to record it as the one token Rock 'n' Roll song on 'Together', despite it being a little on the short side. It was even a minor Country hit, though the single's B-side would've been far more suitable for the Country market.

First Release: 'Together' (1969) + Single B-side (1969)

Roll Over Beethoven / Secret Places
(No. 71 Country)

'Cowtown Jamboree' (1967)

[496c] **ROLL OVER BEETHOVEN** [with Ringo Starr and Jon Brion] (2004-2006)

A song that Jerry could've played in his sleep by the New Millennium, this lively version featuring Ringo Starr on drums (but *not* vocals) made a welcome addition to the 'Mean Old Man' album when finally issued some years later.

First Release: 'Mean Old Man' (2010)

[497a] **ROOM FULL OF ROSES** (1973)
(Tim Spencer)

A song originally released by Dick Haymes in 1949 that Jerry would've known for years, unfortunately Jerry's 1st recorded version is less than satisfactory. Recorded in July 1973 at the mammoth sessions produced by Stan Kesler that resulted in the bulk of the 'Sometimes A Memory Ain't Enough' and 'I-40 Country' albums, the extremely over-powering strings, and an overdubbed vocal where the original can still be faintly heard underneath, render it a disappointment. By the time it was in the shops, his cousin Mickey Gilley had a major hit with it, his big breakthrough after years of struggling beneath Jerry's mighty shadow.

First Release: 'I-40 Country' (1974)

[497b] **ROOM FULL OF ROSES** (1973/1974)

Although a little ragged at times, this far sparser and longer version with lots of improvisation is infinitively more listenable than the more widely heard version released by Mercury. Jerry performed the song live very occasionally during the '70s and '80s, including a partly up-tempo version in Long Beach in '78, and he revived it in 1995 for a 'Music City Tonight' TV tribute to Mickey Gilley.

'The Knox Phillips Sessions: The Unreleased Recordings' (2014)

[498] SAIL AWAY [with Charlie Rich] (1959)
(Charlie Rich)

A slightly ragged duet with Charlie Rich that isn't without its charms, their version wasn't released for 15 years. Instead it served as a demo for Ray Smith's recording and release of the song later in the year.

First Release: 'Jerry Lee Lewis and His Pumping Piano' (1974)

[499a] SAN ANTONIO ROSE (1970) (L)
(Bob Wills)

Originally released by Bob Wills and His Texas Playboys as 'New San Antonio Rose' in 1940 (the first 'San Antonio Rose' was an instrumental from the previous year), covers include Moon Mullican (1955), Patsy Cline (1961), Ray Price (1962), Gene Autry (1962), George Jones (1962), Faron Young (1964), Willie Nelson (1966) and Webb Pierce (1966). The live version from the 'Live at The International, Las Vegas' is the wildest thing on the album, with drummer Morris 'Tarp' Tarrant *almost* upstaging Jerry and Kenny! Other live vocal versions have been infrequent, but include Wheeling in 1975 and the 66th Birthday Show in Memphis in 2001.

First Release: 'Live at The International, Las Vegas' (1970)

[499b] SAN ANTONIO ROSE [INSTRUMENTAL] (1980) *

Jerry had very occasionally performed an instrumental version of 'San Antonio Rose' at concerts for decades (including in Keansburg in 1962), so this storming version with fabulous piano and fiddle wasn't too much of a surprise. Maybe someday, some enterprising record company like Bear Family will finally put together a box-set covering Jerry's post-Mercury era, as there are *lots* of great outtakes out there!

First Release: 'The Caribou Ranch Sessions, 1980-1986' (2012) (bootleg)

[500] SAVE THE LAST DANCE FOR ME (1961)
(Doc Pomus / Mort Shuman)

Originally released by The Drifters in 1960, 'Save The Last Dance For Me' isn't an obvious choice of song for Jerry Lee Lewis. Nevertheless, he does a surprisingly good job on it, enough for Sam Phillips to put it out as a single, after which it was largely forgotten. Then, in 1978, Shelby Singleton overdubbed Elvis 'sound-alike' Jimmy Ellis' vocal onto it (under the mysterious name of 'Orion'), releasing this obviously faked duet as a single. Many people were actually convinced that it was Elvis, so much so, it got to No. 26 in the Country charts! What Jerry thought about this deception at the time is unknown, but he couldn't have held too much of a grudge, as he invited Orion/Ellis on stage to perform the song live at a 1983 show in Orrville, Alabama.

First Release: Single B-side (1961)

Save The Last Dance For Me / As Long As I Live
(Not a hit)

[501] **SEA CRUISE** (1973)
(Huey 'Piano' Smith / John Vincent)

The Frankie Ford classic from 1958, after a brief acoustic guitar intro, Jerry and the band cook up a version that manages to straddle that fine line between rehearsal and spontaneity without things getting *too* messy. 'Sea Cruise' was performed live in Geneva in 1991, the only known performance.

First Release: 'The Session' (1973)

[502a] **SEASONS OF MY HEART** [with Linda Gail Lewis] (1963)
(Darrell Evans / George Jones)

A George Jones song from 1955, 'Seasons Of My Heart' is rumored to have been played at Jerry's initial Sun audition, but if so there is no evidence to support it. Instead, he cut it at a March 1963 session, as an ill-advised duet with his 15-year-old sister Linda Gail Lewis. Jerry sounds fine, playing the song in a far more Bluesy style than the original, but Linda's harmony vocal doesn't work *at all*. She would improve enormously by the time she joined Jerry in the studio again two years later.

First Release: Single B-side (1963)

[502b] **SEASONS OF MY HEART** (1965)

Without Linda Gail, the 1965 cut is a major improvement, apart from the strange choice of a harpsichord instead of a proper piano. Live performances include Memphis 1972, Owensboro 1978, Oslo 1985 and Goldston 1996.

First Release: 'Country Songs For City Folks' (1965)

[503] **SECRET PLACES** [with Linda Gail Lewis] (1969)
(Cecil Harrelson / Linda Gail Lewis / Kenneth Lovelace)

A song written about a secret love affair by Linda Gail Lewis together with her ex-and-future-husband Cecil Harrelson and current husband Kenny Lovelace (and you thought *Jerry's* life was complicated?!), 'Secret Places' is the best song any of them ever wrote. A highlight of the 'Together' album, it would've made a great single A-side, but was instead wasted on the back of 'Roll Over Beethoven'.

First Release: 'Together' (1969) + Single B-side (1969)

[504a] **SEND ME THE PILLOW YOU DREAM ON** (1980) *
(Hank Locklin)

Original released by Hank Locklin in 1949, cover versions include The Browns (1960), Johnny Tillotson (1962), The Everly Brothers (1963), Anita Bryant (1963), Connie Francis and Hank Williams Jr. (1964), Dean Martin (1965), Webb Pierce (1966), Linda Gail Lewis (on her 'Two Sides of Linda Gail Lewis' album, 1969) and Charlie Feathers (1976). Jerry cut two takes at the 'Caribou' sessions, one slow and one in a mid-paced honky tonk style, and both are excellent. The song was performed live in Amsterdam 1978, Stockholm 1978 and Merrillville 1980.

First Release: 'The Caribou Ranch Sessions, 1980-1986' (2012) (bootleg)

'The Two Sides of Linda Gail Lewis' (1969)

[504b] **SEND ME THE PILLOW YOU DREAM ON** (1983)

Although in good voice and with a nice piano intro, very disappointedly, the MCA version features no piano or fiddle solos, unlike the largely superior Elektra takes.

First Release: 'I Am What I Am' (1984)

[505] **SET MY MIND AT EASE** (1962)
(Red West)

Written by Elvis Presley associate Red West, 'Set My Mind At Ease' is an excellent mid-tempo Pop-Rocker which was highly worthy of release. It instead stayed in the vaults, but this didn't prevent Jerry from including it in his set when performing in Keanesburg the following month.

First Release: 'Collectors' Edition' (1974)

[506] **SETTIN' THE WOODS ON FIRE** (1958)
(Ken Nelson / Fred Rose)

A Hank Williams song from 1952, Jerry's slightly hesitant recording was taped at a solo session without a band, with other instrumentation overdubbed onto it shortly afterwards. The dubbed version was first released in 1971, and fans got so used to hearing bass and drums, it sounded a little strange when the un-dubbed version finally surfaced 12 years later.

First Release: 'Johnny Cash & Jerry Lee Lewis Sing Hank Williams' (1971)

[507] **SEVENTEEN** (1986)
(Boyd Bennett)

Originally released by Boyd Bennett and His Rockets in 1955, Jerry's sprightly version from September 1986 features prominent backing vocals by the Jordanaires, and was released on 'Rocket'. It was performed in Oslo in 1989.

First Release: 'Rocket' (1988)

[508a] **SEXY WAYS (COOL, COOL WAYS)** (1958)
(Hank Ballard)

Originally released by Hank Ballard and The Midnighters in 1954, Jerry was keen to record the song at the peak of his early success in January-March 1958. Trouble is, even *he* knew that it would be commercial suicide to release such a title, so tried two alternatives in sessions a couple of months apart. 'Cool Cool Ways' might've had a watered-down title, but with Jerry growling and drooling like a dog on heat, everyone knew *exactly* what he was on about!

First Release: 'Jerry Lee Lewis and His Pumping Piano' (1974)

[508b] **SEXY WAYS (CARRYIN' ON)** (1958)

With a 'Whole Lotta Shakin'' Going On' intro and a frantic tempo, 'Carrin' On' is the wildest of the 'Sexy Ways' attempts, even if it's also the least sleazy.

First Release: 'Rockin' and Free' (1974)

[508c] **SEXY WAYS** (1965)

By 1965 the word "Sexy" wasn't *quite* so controversial, even if it was unlikely to be played on mainstream Pop radio. Kicking off with a drum intro, Jerry's vocal is more soulful and 'black' sounding than on the '50s versions, and it is by far the most lascivious *("I want you to get down on your knees one time, and shake for Jerry Lee Lewis honey!")*.

First Release: 'The Return of Rock' (1965)

[509] **SHAKE, RATTLE AND ROLL** (1974)

(Charles E. Calhoun)

Originally released by Big Joe Turner in 1954 and covered by Bill Haley and His Comets (1954), Elvis Presley (1956), Carl Perkins (1958), Chubby Checker (1961), Conway Twitty (1961) and Sam Cooke (1963), Jerry's energetic but slightly hoarse version would be even better without the too-loud backing vocals and prominent harmonica. Although never a concert regular, the song was performed very occasionally well into the New Millennium.

First Release: 'Odd Man In' (1975)

[510] **SHAME ON YOU** (1957)

(Spade Cooley)

Originally released by Spade Cooley in 1945, this is a typically good run-through from Jerry's early days at Sun. Sam Phillips was clearly perfectly happy to let the musicians play whatever they wanted until something caught his ear.

First Release: 'Rockin' and Free' (1974)

[511] **SHANTY TOWN** (1959)

(Jack Little / John Siras / Joe Young)

Originally released by Ted Lewis and His Band in 1932, unfortunately Jerry's 1959 recording features the same heavy-handed and slightly amateurish drumming as 'Release Me' from the same session, and eventually the take breaks down completely. He performed the song with Mickey Gilley on 'Pop Goes The Country' in 1978, as well as at concerts in Goldston in 1996 and Las Vegas in 2001.

First Release: 'Jerry Lee Lewis and His Pumping Piano' (1974)

[512] SHE EVEN WOKE ME UP TO SAY GOODBYE (1969)
(Doug Gilmore / Mickey Newbury)

The very pinnacle of the late '60s 'Country Comeback', Mickey Newbury's composition with poetic lines like *"Just like the dawn my heart is silently breaking, with my tears it goes tumbling to the floor!"* was clearly a song that meant a lot to Jerry. Promoted on both 'Music Scene' and 'The Ed Sullivan Show' in late 1969, of all Jerry's late '60s/early '70s Country hits, 'She Even Woke Me Up To Say Goodbye' is the *only* one that remained a concert regular right until the very end. Mickey Newbury released his own version that year, while later covers include Lynn Anderson (1970), Kenny Rogers and The First Edition (1970), Del Shannon (recorded 1970, released 2004), Johnny Tillotson (1972), Brook Benton (1972), Hank Snow (1975), Ronnie Milsap (1975) and Tony Sheridan (1978).

First Release: Single A-side (1969) + 'She Even Woke Me Up To Say Goodbye' (1970)

She Even Woke Me Up To Say Goodbye / Echoes
(No. 2 Country)

'The Ed Sullivan Show' (1969)

[513] SHE NEVER SAID GOODBYE (1983)
(unknown)

A good Country song with unknown authorship from the 'I Am What I Am' sessions, featuring Hargus 'Pig' Robbins on piano, 'She Never Said Goodbye' didn't surface until an early '90s compilation.

First Release: 'Pretty Much Country' (1992)

[514] SHE SINGS AMAZING GRACE (1982)
(Jerry Foster / Bill Rice)

Originally released by Stan Hitchcock in 1981 and covered by Gary Stewart the following year, 'She Sings Amazing Grace' (with its *"While I played those old honky tonk songs, she sang amazing grace!"* tag-line) is a well recorded Country song, albeit with the backing vocalists a little too loud in the mix. Jerry performed the song at a show in Wheeling in 1982, complaining afterwards *"I can't identify with that song!"*.

First Release: 'My Fingers Do The Talkin'' (1982) + Single B-side (1983)

[515] SHE STILL COMES AROUND (TO LOVE WHAT'S LEFT OF ME) (1968)
(Glenn Sutton)

Although not quite up there with 'She Even Woke Me Up To Say Goodbye', 'She Still Comes Around' is another top-notch hard Country song, with a wonderful vocal from Jerry. A concert regular throughout the '70s, the song largely disappeared after 1983. Johnny Bush covered 'She Still Comes Around' in 1969.

First Release: 'She Still Comes Around' (1969) + Single A-side (1968)

She Still Comes Around (To Love What's Left Of Me) / Slipping Around
(No. 2 Country)

[516] SHE SURE MAKES LEAVING LOOK EASY (1982)
(Sonny Thockmorton)

Original released by Sonny Throckmorton in 1978, 'She Sure Makes Leaving Look Easy' is a lushly-stringed ballad with a crooning Jerry Lee Lewis vocal. He promoted the song on 'Johnny Carson's Tonight Show' (an absolutely terrible version, with Jerry and the studio band just grinding to a halt), as well as in Rotterdam 1982, Wheeling 1982, Nashville 1982 and New York 1983. Incidentally, a version was recorded in 1980 with Kenny Lovelace on guide lead vocals, so the song was obviously considered a couple of years earlier.

First Release: 'My Fingers Do The Talkin'' (1982)

'Johnny Carson's Tonight Show' (1982)

[517] SHE THINKS I STILL CARE (1966)
(Dickey Lee Lipscomb)

Original released by George Jones in 1962 and covered by Little Willie John (1962), Connie Francis (1962), Eddy Arnold (1963), Cher (1965) and The Carter Family (1965), 'She Thinks I Still Care' is of the very few true Country songs cut in the studio during the 1966-1967 era (the only other one was 'Swinging Doors', and that was kept in the can for 5 years). Jerry sings it wonderfully of course, even if it did sound a bit incongruous when released on the 'Memphis Beat' album.

First Release: 'Memphis Beat' (1966)

[518] SHE WAS MY BABY (HE WAS MY FRIEND) (1964)
(Joy Byers)

A robust mid-tempo rocker that one could easily imagine The Coasters doing around this time, 'She Was My Baby (He Was My Friend)' was released as a single A-side. UK group The Shouts covered the song in 1964, a band who had backed Gene Vincent both on record and on tour. Could they have heard Jerry play the song live?

First Release: Single A-side (1964)

She Was My Baby (He Was My Friend) / The Hole He Said He'd Dig For Me
(Not a hit)

[519] SHE'S REACHIN' FOR MY MIND (1972)
(Dallas Frazier / A.L. Owens)

A lushly-stringed middle-of-the-road Pop song with Jerry doing his best middle of the road crooner impersonation, the best thing about it is the closing ad-lib *"She's reachin' for something, God, I hope she finds it!"*.

First Release: 'Who's Gonna Play This Old Piano' (1972)

[520] SHOESHINE MAN (1970) (L)
(Tom T. Hall)

Originally released by Tom T. Hall in 1969, in Jerry's hands 'Shoeshine Man' is a tough up-tempo Rhythm 'n' Blues song. If the 'Live at The International, Las Vegas' LP had been a double (if only!), then this would've been a good candidate for inclusion. Instead, it is one of many previously unreleased live goodies that first surfaced in 1986.

First Release: 'The Killer: 1969-1972' (box-set, 1986)

[521] SHOTGUN MAN (1967)
(Cecil Harrelson)

Jerry's friend, manager and on-and-off brother-in-law Cecil Harrelson wrote some wonderful Country and Gospel songs, but funky Soul? Featuring a riff straight out of a James Brown song, one almost expects Jerry to come out dancing on one foot, but it actually works much better than expected, and at least lyrics like *"Well I ain't no 007, I ain't no 00-Soul!"* show that this was written in the '60s rather than the 19th Century. Released as a single along with 'Turn On Your Lovelight', it is fun to speculate what might've happened to Jerry's career if this had been a hit instead of the follow-up 'Another Place, Another Time'.

First Release: Soul My Way (1967) + Single B-side (1967) + 'The Killer Rocks On' (1972)

[522] SHOULDER TO LEAN ON - MAKE THE WORLD GO AWAY (1987)
(Anna Lee Murrell) + (Hank Cochran)

Originally released by The Anna Murrell Singers in 1964, and Timi Yuro in 1963, respectively, this Casio keyboard-accompanied medley from the December 1987 Hank Cochran session goes on for over 8 minutes. For those who really must hear everything, it was released on 'At Hank Cochran's' in 1995. In 2001, an edit with real piano of 'Shoulder To Lean On' *only* was released an obscure German CD entitled 'Rock Right Now With The Piano Man'. However, on close examination, the piano had been overdubbed by a so-so impersonator rather than by the real thing.

First Release: 'At Hank Cochran's' (1995)

[523] SHOUT [with Linda Gail Lewis and Greg Todd] (1969) (L)
(O'Kelly Isley / Rudolph Isley / Ronald Isley)

Originally released by The Isley Brothers in 1959 and covered by Joey Dee and The Starliters (1961), Dion (1962), Lulu and The Luvvers (1964), The Shangri-Las (1964), The Kingsmen (1965), Tommy James and The Shondells (1967) and Cliff Richard (1967), Jerry and guests opened an episode of 'The Many Sounds of Jerry Lee' with a wild but short version of the song.

First Release: 'The Many Sounds of Jerry Lee' (DVD, 2010)

[524a] SICK AND TIRED (1959)
(Dave Bartholomew / Chris Kenner)

Original released by Chris Kenner in 1957 and covered by Fats Domino in 1958, Jerry's Sun cut features some very iffy drumming (*not* Jimmy Van Eaton!), and piano that may or may not be Jerry. The song was performed a few times, including Zurich 1985, Phoenix 1985, Montreal 1986 and Lake Charles 2006.

First Release: 'Rockin' and Free' (1974)

[524b] SICK AND TIRED (2008-2010)

Although a little monotone vocally, this Rocks along quite nicely, and it was nice to get a more polished version at last! It circulates unofficially without Jon Brion's overdubs.

First Release: 'Rock & Roll Time' (2014)

[525] SILENT NIGHT [with Johnny Cash, Carl Perkins and Roy Orbison] (1977) (L)
(John Freeman Young / Franz Gruber / Joseph Mohr)

Published in 1859, the first recording was in German by Hans Hofmann as 'Stille Nacht, Heilige Nacht' in 1902, with The Haydn Quartet being the first to record an English language version in 1909. Performed with Johnny Cash, Carl Perkins and Roy Orbison for 1977's 'The Johnny Cash Christmas Show', even a hackneyed old song like 'Silent Night' is preferable to at least 75% of 'Class of '55'.

First Release: 'Johnny Cash - Christmas Special 1977' (DVD, 2008)

[526a] **SILVER THREADS AMONG THE GOLD** (1956)
(Hart Pease Danks / Eben Eugene Rexford)

Published in 1873 and first released on record by Henry Burr in 1904, 'Silver Threads Among The Gold' is just one of many very old songs that Jerry recorded at Sun. It was first issued on 1970's 'Sunday Down South', an album he shared with Johnny Cash.

First Release: 'Sunday Down South' (1970)

[526b] **SILVER THREADS AMONG THE GOLD** (1973)

A mid-tempo bluesy performance from the September 1973 'Southern Roots' sessions, this is perhaps marred by the dominant steel guitar and organ. He performed the song in a very similar style for 'The Midnight Special' TV show in 1973, while later performances include Oslo in 1989 and Hamburg in 1990.

First Release: 'The Killer: 1973-1977' (box-set, 1987)

[527a] **SINCE I MET YOU BABY** (1969)
(Ivory Joe Hunter)

Originally released by Ivory Joe Hunter in 1956 and covered by Freddy Fender (1959), Sam Cooke (1961), Bruce Channel (1962), Wanda Jackson (1963), Brook Benton (1964), The Spencer Davis Group (1966) and Solomon Burke (1968), the Blues ballad 'Since I Met You Baby' is amongst Jerry's very finest recordings, with Kenny Lovelace on particularly great form *("Ahhh, play your fiddle Mr. Kenneth Lovelace, I wanna hear those blues son!")*. If *only* he'd recorded more Blues-orientated songs in this era instead of so much often mediocre Country.

First Release: 'She Even Woke Me Up To Say Goodbye' (1970)

[527b] **SINCE I MET YOU BABY** (1980) *

A little faster and with a nice piano solo, this would be just fine if it weren't compared to the 1969 cut, even if the backing singers here are a little too prominent.

First Release: 'The Caribou Ranch Sessions, 1980-1986' (2012) (bootleg)

[528a] **SINGING THE BLUES** (1956)
(Melvin Endsley)

First released by Marty Robbins in 1956 and covered by both Guy Mitchell and Tommy Steele the same year, Jerry's Sun cut features a nice shuffle drum beat and prominent guitar. Perhaps surprisingly for such a well known song, there is no record of any live performances.

First Release: 'Monsters' (1971)

'She Even Woke Me Up To Say Goodbye' (1970)

[528b] **SINGING THE BLUES** (1973)

Slower, more bluesy, and with a slide guitar solo, this was cut during the January 1973 London sessions for 'The Session'. Rejected at the time, it surfaced 13 years later.

First Release: 'The Complete Session Volume Two' (1986)

[529] **SITTIN' AND THINKIN'** (1977)

(Charlie Rich)

Originally released by Charlie Rich in 1962 and covered by Ray Price (1963), Bobby Bare (1964), Johnnie Allan (1974) and Lefty Frizzell (1975), Jerry's outtake from the 'Keeps Rockin'' sessions is as good as anything on the released album. This isn't the first time he had played the song in the studio, as at Sun in 1963 Linda Gail Lewis recorded it, with Jerry backing her on piano. Live performances include Hollywood 1983 and Arnheim 1994.

First Release: 'The Mercury Sessions' (1985)

[530] **SIXTEEN CANDLES** (1985)
(Luther Dixon / Allyson Khent)

Originally released by The Crests (1958), 'Sixteen Candles' was also covered by Bobby Vee (1961), The Four Seasons (1964), The Jackson 5 (1971), Sha Na Na (1973) and Donny Osmond (1974). All of those are quite sweet and innocent, which is more than can be said about the then fifty-year-old Jerry Lee Lewis version (when he sings *"Sixteen Candles, make my dream come true!"*, it is clear that he is after a bit more than a slice of cake!). Not a song that was performed much live despite it being a minor Country hit, a rare exception was in Burlington, Vermont in 1986.

First Release: 'Class of '55' (1986) + Single A-side (1986)

Sixteen Candles / Rock and Roll (Fais-Do-Do)
(No. 61 Country)

[531a] **SIXTY MINUTE MAN** (1957)
(Rose Marks / Billy Ward)

Originally released by Billy Ward and The Dominoes in 1951, Jerry cut three quite similar Rockin' takes around June 1957, though they stood no more chance of '50s release than 'Big Legged Woman' and 'Birthday Cake'. Not a concert regular, the handful of live performances include Genk (Belgium) 1980, Nashville 1980 and Jerry's 66th Birthday concert in Memphis in 2001.

First Release: 'Rockin' and Free' (1974)

[531b] **SIXTY MINUTE MAN** (1973)

A little slower than the Sun cuts, this Bluesy version from a January 1973 session is nevertheless highly enjoyable. The sessions in London ran for 4 days from the 8th to the 11th of January, and this was the *only* song from the very first day to end up on the album, suggesting a less than great start to the proceedings!

First Release: 'The Session' (1973)

[532] **SKID ROW** (1965)
(John T. Axton / Mae Boren Axton / Harold Smith)

A great Country song about a man down on his luck *("I guess I'm doomed to die, on old skid row!")* this features a unique baritone saxophone solo, something that would be impossible to imagine on the less adventurous late '60s recordings. It was taped during the January 1965 'The Return Of Rock' sessions, but instead of being included on the follow-up 'Country Songs For City Folks', it went unheard until turning up on an early '80s bootleg EP.

First Release: 'The Killer: 1963-1968' (box-set, 1986)

[533] **SLIPPIN' AND SLIDIN'** (1975)
(Eddie Bocage / Al Collins / Richard Penniman / James Smith)

Originally released by Eddie Bo as 'I'm Wise' in 1956 and adapted by Little Richard the same year, cover versions include Mickey Gilley (1961), Wanda Jackson (1961), The Crickets (1964), Gene Vincent and The Shouts (1964), Gene Simmons (1964) and The Everly Brothers (1965). Lasting almost 9 minutes long and with Jerry playing an electric piano, this is an interesting but *way* too lengthy studio jam.

First Release: '30th Anniversary Album' (1986)

[534a] **SLIPPIN' AROUND** (1958)
(Floyd Tillman)

Originally released by Floyd Tillman in 1949, Jerry transforms this rather average Country song into a powerful mid-tempo Blues. Like so much of Jerry's Sun stuff, it slipped out only half-noticed on a compilation, this time via The Netherlands in 1974.

First Release: 'Collectors' Edition' (1974)

[534b] **SLIPPIN' AROUND** (1968)

Far closer to the pure Country of the original, Jerry's Mercury cut was first released as the B-side of 'She Still Comes Around', making its album debut on 'The Best of Jerry Lee Lewis' in 1970. The song got a rare live outing at a show in Reno in 1990.

Single B-side (1969)

[535] **SMOKE GETS IN YOUR EYES [INSTRUMENTAL]** (1970) (L)
(Otto Harbach / Jerome Kern)

Original released by Gertrude Niesen in 1933 and made more famous by The Platters in 1958, Jerry's version is a nice but impromptu live instrumental. It's not the first time he'd performed the song, as he also played it, again as an instrumental, in Keanesburg in 1962.

First Release: 'The Killer: 1969-1972' (box-set, 1986)

[536] SO LONG I'M GONE (1958)
(Roy Orbison)

Originally released by Warren Smith in 1957, Jerry's version is OK, but sounds a bit slap-dash and untogether compared to the great original.

First Release: 'Rockin' and Free' (1974)

[537a] SOFTLY AND TENDERLY (1980) *
(William L. Thompson)

Originally released by Miss Hinkle and Mr. MacDonough in 1906, this Gospel ballad was covered by Eddy Arnold (1950), Carl Smith with The Carter Sisters and Mother Maybelle (1952), The Prisonaires (1953), Tennessee Ernie Ford (1956), Ray Price (1960), Loretta Lynn (1972), Johnny Cash (1975) and Jimmy Swaggart (1977). Jerry's 1980 version features some wonderful piano and fiddle, and lasts a full 5 minutes.

First Release: 'The Caribou Ranch Sessions, 1980-1986' (2012) (bootleg)

[537b] SOFTLY AND TENDERLY [with Webb Pierce] (1984)

This beautifully-sung duet is by far the highlight of the 'Four Legends' album, and was apparently even played at Webb Pierce's funeral in 1991.

First Release: 'Four Legends' (1985)

[538a] SOMEDAY (YOU'LL WANT ME TO WANT YOU) (1958)
(Jimmie Hodges)

Originally released by Elton Britt in 1945 and covered by The Drifters featuring Clyde McPhatter (1954), Jerry's Sun cut was taped at the legendary 'Elvis songs' February 1958 session, featuring the same solid but more basic drumming that indicates that Russell Smith rather than Jimmy Van Eaton is on drums.

First Release: 'Jerry Lee Lewis and His Pumping Piano' (1974)

[538b] SOMEDAY (YOU'LL WANT ME TO WANT YOU) (1971)

With Jerry's more mature but not yet worn-out voice and some nice fiddle, this probably has the edge over the Sun cut, even if it doesn't quite swing in the same way. The song was performed live in Las Vegas in 1992.

First Release: 'The Mercury Sessions' (1985)

[539] **SOMEONE WHO CARES FOR YOU** (1970) (L)
(Jimmie Davis)

First recorded by Jimmie Davis as 'Someone To Care' in 1951, this slow Gospel song was featured on 1970's Memphis Church recording.

First Release: 'The Killer: 1969-1972' (box-set, 1986)

[540] **SOMETIMES A MEMORY AIN'T ENOUGH** (1973)
(Stan Kesler)

Starting off ominously with a strings and steel guitar intro, 'Sometimes A Memory Ain't Enough' is a far better title than song, though as it got as high as No. 6 in the Country charts, others may disagree! There is no record of the song ever being performed live: unlike 1972 and to a lesser extent 1974, live audios and set-lists from 1973 are relatively scarce, but *if* it was performed, then it didn't stick around for long.

First Release: 'Sometimes A Memory Ain't Enough' (1973) + Single A-side (1973)

Sometimes A Memory Ain't Enough / I Think I Need To Pray
(No. 6 Country)

[541] **SPEAK A LITTLE LOUDER TO US JESUS** (1974)
(Marijohn Wilkin)

A good rockin' Gospel song from the 'Boogie Woogie Country Man' album sessions, it is a bit too similar to the superior 'Jesus Is On The Mainline' for both songs to be included, so was kept in the can. Occasional live performances include Cincinnati 1975, Wheeling 1975 and South Amboy 1987.

First Release: '30th Anniversary Album' (1986)

[542] STAGGER LEE (1970) (L)
(Lloyd Price / Harold Logan)

An old song that was first released by Ma Rainey as 'Stack O' Lee Blues' in 1926 and reworked and made famous Lloyd Price in 1958, cover versions include Bill Haley and His Comets (1960), Dion (1962), The Isley Brothers (1963), Shirley Ellis (1964), P.J. Proby (1965), James Brown (1967) and Wilson Pickett (1967). Jerry's live version from Las Vegas has a great mid-tempo shuffle beat. It was later performed in Las Vegas in 1985.

First Release: 'The Killer: 1969-1972' (box-set, 1986)

[543] STEPCHILD (2008-2010)
(Bob Dylan)

A Bob Dylan song that was first released by Solomon Burke in 2002, 'Stepchild' is a mid-tempo Blues-Rock shuffle that wouldn't have sounded out of place on 'The Session' decades earlier. A version without the Doyle Bramhall II and Daniel Lanois overdubs circulates unofficially.

First Release: 'Rock & Roll Time' (2014)

[544] STICKS AND STONES (1966)
(Titus Turner)

Originally released by Ray Charles in 1960, 'Sticks and Stones' was covered by Wanda Jackson (1961), Joey Dee and The Starliters (1961), Billy Fury and The Tornados (1963), The Zombies (1965) and The Righteous Brothers (1965). As with 1963's 'Hit The Road Jack', Jerry's fine version of 'Sticks and Stones' was another attempt at recapturing the relative success of 'What'd I Say' in 1961, but despite an appearance on 'Upbeat' (his only networked TV appearance that year) it failed to chart. Live appearances include Lausanne in 1966 and Toronto in 1967.

First Release: 'Memphis Beat' (1966) + Single A-side (1966)

Sticks and Stones / What A Heck Of A Mess
(Not a hit)

[545] SUNDAY MORNING COMING DOWN (2008-2010)
(Kris Kristofferson)

Originally released by Ray Stevens in 1969, 'Sunday Morning Coming Down' will forever be associated with Johnny Cash thanks to his memorable 1970 hit. Jerry's lengthy, slow version is made all the more poignant by the decision to not enhance his aged vocals with duetting singers or backing vocalists, and is an unexpected triumph.

First Release: 'Mean Old Man' (2010)

[546] SWANEE RIVER HOP [INSTRUMENTAL] [with Fats Domino and Ray Charles] (1986) (L)
(Stephen Foster)

Published in 1851 and first recorded by Len Spencer as 'The Old Folks At Home' in 1892, Fats Domino probably based his 1956 'Swanee River Hop' on Albert Ammons' 'Swanee River Boogie' from a decade earlier. Fats, Jerry and Ray all jam on this song, and the end result is far more musically satisfying than the usual 'all star' get-togethers.

First Release: 'Fats Domino & Friends' (VHS, 1986)

'Fats Domino & Friends' (1986)

[547] SWEET DREAMS (1969)
(Don Gibson)

Originally released by Don Gibson in 1956, cover versions of this timeless classic include George Jones (1956), Patsy Cline (1963), The Everly Brothers (1963), Brenda Lee (1966), Tommy McLain (1966) and Roy Orbison (1967). Jerry's version is vocally superb, if a little predictable musically.

First Release: 'Sings The Country Music Hall of Fame Hits, Vol. One' (1969)

[548] SWEET GEORGIA BROWN (1970)
(Ben Bernie / Kenneth Casey / Maceo Pinkard)

Originally released by Ethel Waters in 1925, cover versions include Cab Calloway (1931), Bing Crosby (1932), The Coasters (1957), Freddy Cannon (1960), Ray Charles (1961), Tony Sheridan and The Beat Brothers (1962), Conway Twitty (1964), Ella Fitzgerald (1966) and Nancy Sinatra (1967). Jerry's unbelievably fast version features some incredible piano that is matched by Kenny's fiddle, as well as a wonderfully expressive vocal *("Jerry Lee don't lie, not much!")*. 'Sweet Georgia Brown' was performed live occasionally up until around 2001.

First Release: 'There Must Be More To Love Than This' (1970)

[549a] SWEET LITTLE SIXTEEN (1961)
(Chuck Berry)

Originally released by Chuck Berry in 1959, Jerry's first recording from June 1961 is one of the best, with Ace Cannon on honking saxophone. Yet it is relatively unheard in comparison to later versions, not even being released until 1983.

First Release: 'The Sun Years' (Box-Set, 1983)

[549b] SWEET LITTLE SIXTEEN (1962)

Another 4 takes were taped the following January, with by far the slowest, albeit with a great vocal, being selected for single release. Jerry promoted the record on 'American Bandstand', his first major TV appearance in 3 years and his first time on the show since 1958. Not that it helped much, stalling at No. 95 in the Pop charts. The song remained a regular part of Jerry's concerts well into the 21st century, while a much faster and more exciting alternate take first surfaced on 1969's 'Rockin' Rhythm & Blues' album.

First Release: Single A-side (1962)

Sweet Little Sixteen / How's My Ex Treating You
(No. 95 Pop)

[549c] **SWEET LITTLE SIXTEEN** (1977)

A very good remake, it is close in pace and arrangement to the 1962 alternate take on 'Rockin' Rhythm & Blues', and is spoilt only slightly by the unnecessary backing vocals.

First Release: 'Keeps Rockin'' (1978)

[549d] **SWEET LITTLE SIXTEEN** [with Ringo Starr] (2003-2006)

The Beatles spoke fondly of Jerry Lee Lewis' music, with John Lennon even kissing The Killer's feet after a 1973 performance. So it was a no-brainer to invite Ringo Starr. His voice is highly suited to the song, complimenting Jerry's perfectly, and the song is taken at a very brisk pace. One of the 'Last Man Standing' highlights!

First Release: 'Last Man Standing' (2006)

[550] **SWEET THANG** [with Linda Gail Lewis] (1969)
(Nat Stuckey)

Originally released by Nat Stuckey in 1966 and covered by Mel Tillis (1967), Ernest Tubb and Loretta Lynn (1967) and George Jones (1967), 'Sweet Thing' (sometimes spelled 'Sweet Thang') is up there with 'Jackson' as one of Jerry and Linda's most irresistibly fun duets. Jerry performed the song with Dottie West on 1982's '25 Years Of Jerry Lee Lewis' TV special (presumably Linda Gail was unavailable), and even performed a slow solo version in Birmingham, Alabama in 1974.

First Release: 'Sings The Country Music Hall of Fame Hits, Vol. Two' (1969) + 'Together' (1969)

[551] **SWEET VIRGINIA** [with Keith Richards] (2008-2010)
(Mick Jagger / Keith Richards)

Originally released by The Rolling Stones in 1972, this Country Rock song works quite well, with suitably ragged Keith Richards harmonies and excellent (though over-loud) guitar work.

First Release: 'Mean Old Man' (2010)

[552] **SWING DOWN SWEET CHARIOT** [with The Rust College Quintet] (1969) (L)
(Wallis Willis)

For the aptly-named 'The Many Sounds of Jerry Lee' TV specials (filmed at the Holiday Inn in Memphis), Jerry included a couple of Gospel numbers. One of these was The Golden Gate Quartet's 1947 'Swing Down Sweet Chariot', performed away from the piano whilst backed by vocal group The Rust College Quintet.

First Release: 'The Many Sounds of Jerry Lee' (DVD, 2010)

[553] SWING LOW SWEET CHARIOT [with The Rust College Quintet] (1969) (L)
(Wallis Willis)

Basically the same song as 'Swing *Down* Sweet Chariot', 'Swing *Low* Sweet Chariot' dates back further, to The Fisk University Jubilee Quartet in 1910.

First Release: 'The Many Sounds of Jerry Lee' (DVD, 2010)

[554a] SWINGING DOORS (1966)
(Merle Haggard)

Originally released by Merle Haggard earlier the same year, Jerry's version from the 'Memphis Beat' sessions is excellent, even if it didn't quite fit in with the other material he was recording at the time. Finally released 5 years on 'Would You Take Another Chance On Me', it was an album highlight. Live performances include Reno 1976, Stockholm 1977, Margate 1978, Nottingham 1983, Skien 1989, Las Vegas 1989, Paris 1989 and Munich 1991.

First Release: 'Would You Take Another Chance On Me' (1971)

[554b] SWINGING DOORS [with Merle Haggard and James Burton] (2008-2010)

Although they inevitably both sound older and frailer, it doesn't really matter here, and they're clearly having a lot of fun (*"Thanks to ol' Jerry Lee's piano playing, I'm always here till closing time!"* sings Merle).

First Release: 'Mean Old Man' (2010)

[555] TAKE ME OUT TO THE BALL GAME [with Neil Sedaka] (1965) (L)
(Jack Norworth / Albert Von Tilzer)

On 'Shindig!' in 1965, producer Jack Good came up with the innovative idea of having Jerry Lee Lewis and Neil Sedaka perform a duet of Harvey Hindermeyer's 1908 song 'Take Me Out To The Ball Game' (in celebration of the opening of the Baseball season), with one piano on top of the other! A few years later, for 1969's '33⅓ Revolutions per Monkee' TV special, Jack Good took this idea to an extreme, with Jerry Lee Lewis, Fats Domino, Little Richard and Brian Auger ALL piled up on top of each other.

First Release: 'Shindig! Presents Jerry Lee Lewis' (VHS, 1992)

[556] TAKE YOUR TIME (1973)
(unknown)

A hesitant version of a mediocre ballad by an unknown writer, 'Take Your Time' is one of the 'Southern Roots' sessions' weaker tracks, and it was rightly left in the can.

First Release: 'The Killer: 1973-1977' (box-set, 1987)

[557] **TEENAGE LETTER** (1963)
(Renald Richard)

Originally released by Big Joe Turner in 1957 and covered by Billy Lee Riley in 1961, 'Teenage Letter' is a very exciting version of a not particularly great song, and unusually features a Little Richard-styled saxophone solo with Jerry pounding along to it. He performed the song at least once during his 1963 UK tour.

First Release: Single A-side (1963)

Teenage Letter / Seasons Of My Heart
(Not a hit)

[558] **TEENAGE QUEEN** (1983)
(B. Firman)

When Jerry appeared 'Austin City Limits' in October 1983, he included an interesting Rock 'n' Roll song called 'Teenage Queen', that was unheard elsewhere. So, there was much excitement 8 years later when fans learnt that this unreleased MCA track would finally be issued. We were in for a disappointment, as Jerry's very obvious vocal overdub is both out of time and lethargic. Indeed, a probably superior vocal can be clearly heard beneath it.

First Release: 'Honky Tonk Rock & Roll Piano Man' (1991)

[559] **TELL TALE SIGNS** (1973)
(Alex Zanetis)

A reasonable enough Country song about a woman cheating on her man, fortunately the strings aren't quite as insufferable as on most of the July 1973 Stan Kesler sessions. 'Tell Tale Signs' was performed in Memphis in 1974.

First Release: 'I-40 Country' (1974) + Single A-side (1974)

Tell Tale Signs / Cold, Cold Morning Light
(No. 18 Country)

[560] **TENNESSEE SATURDAY NIGHT** (1977)

(Billy Hughes)

Originally released by Red Foley in 1948 and covered by Johnny Bond (1949), Ella Mae Morse (1951) and Pat Boone (1955), in Jerry's hands it's a very good Rock 'n' Roll song, though the mix is poor on the studio version. He performed it live occasionally up until the late '90s, often changing the line *"They get crazy on a Saturday Night!"* to *"They get naked on a Saturday night!"*.

First Release: 'Country Memories' (1977)

'Country Memories' (1977)

[561] **TENNESSEE WALTZ** (1980) *
(Redd Stewart / Pee Wee King)

Originally released by Pee Wee King in 1948 and popularized by Patti Page in 1958, Jerry had been performing 'Tennessee Waltz' very occasionally for years, including Keanesburg in 1962 and Toronto in 1967. For his 1980 studio recording however, he gave it an inappropriate but exciting Rock 'n' Roll makeover. Jerry performed the song once more, in traditional ballad style, at his 40th Anniversary Show in Memphis in 1996.

First Release: 'The Caribou Ranch Sessions, 1980-1986' (2012) (bootleg)

[562] **THANKS FOR NOTHING** (1975)
(Rayburn Anthony / Gene Dobbins)

A good Country song with old time chord changes, co-writer Rayburn Anthony had recorded for Sun and may have first bumped into Jerry there.

First Release: 'Boogie Woogie Country Man' (1975)

[563a] **THAT KIND OF FOOL** (1973/1974)
(Mack Vickery)

Although just a run-through performed alone at the piano, this has a poignancy missing from the fuller later versions.

First Release: 'The Knox Phillips Sessions: The Unreleased Recordings' (2014)

[563b] **THAT KIND OF FOOL** (1975)

By the time Jerry got around to recording the song properly at a January 1975 session, Mack Vickery had released his own version of the song under the name Atlanta James. That didn't prevent Jerry from putting in a fine performance of his own though, with Kenny's fiddle and Jerry's world-weary voice just adding to the charm.

First Release: 'Odd Man In' (1975) + Single B-side (1975)

[563c] **THAT KIND OF FOOL** [with Keith Richards] (2003-2006)

With Jerry in surprisingly good voice, nice piano playing and otherwise sympathetic backing, this could've been *the* version of the song. Unfortunately, Keith Richards' over-loud guitar and out-of-time vocal renders it far from great. Never a song that was performed much in the '70s, Jerry performed it a handful of times during 2005-2007.

First Release: 'Last Man Standing' (2006)

[564a] **THAT LUCKY OLD SUN** (1958)
(Haven Gillespie / Beasley Smith)

Originally released by Vaughn Monroe and His Orchestra in 1949 and covered by Frankie Laine (1949), Dean Martin (1949), Frank Sinatra (1949), Louis Armstrong (1949) and LaVern Baker (1955), Jerry's touching version of 'That Lucky Old Sun' is played alone at the piano. It was long thought to have been taped sometime in 1957, but is now thought more likely to come from the lengthy 'solo' session from around July 1958.

First Release: '16 Songs Never Issued Before 2' (1975)

[564b] **THAT LUCKY OLD SUN** (1988)

Jerry told everyone who'd listen that he could beat the originals when cutting the 'Great Balls of Fire!' movie soundtrack, and in 'That Lucky Old Sun', he did just that. The best was yet to come though: On the 'Last Man Standing Live' TV special and DVD, following a particularly noisy duet with Kid Rock, the other musicians departed the stage, leaving just Jerry and Kenny. They played an *extremely* touching version of 'That Lucky Old Sun'. Other live performances have been rare, but include San Jose 1979, Indianapolis 1996 and New York 1996.

First Release: 'Great Balls Of Fire!' (1989)

[565] **THAT OLD BOURBON STREET CHURCH** (1973)
(Mack Vickery)

Although not really a Gospel song as such, lines like *"Your dirty old clothes won't bother the lord, 'cause he's used to the smell of that wine!"* are clearly Christian-minded, and together with a delicious old-time melody plus some Ragtime horns, this is one of the highlights of 'Southern Roots'.

First Release: 'Southern Roots' (1973)

[566a] **THAT WAS THE WAY IT WAS THEN** (1980) *
(Mickey Newbury)

A Country-Pop ballad about nostalgia, Jerry's 1980 cut features a guitar intro and no piano, giving it an almost 'Middle Age Crazy' feel. Writer Mickey Newbury would release his own version in 1985, and Brenda Lee would release it in 1985.

First Release: 'The Caribou Ranch Sessions, 1980-1986' (2012) (bootleg)

[566b] **THAT WAS THE WAY IT WAS THEN** (1983)

Quite different from the earlier unreleased cut, this time there's a piano (but no solo) and strings. Jerry performed 'That Was The Way It Was Then' in New York in 1986.

First Release: 'I Am What I Am' (1984) + Single B-side (1984)

[567] THAT'S MY DESIRE (1956)
(Loveday / Kresa)

Originally released by Russell Wooding and His Grand Central Red Caps in 1931, and popularized by Frankie Laine in 1946, Jerry played a brief solo version of 'That's My Desire' at the end of the famed 'Million Dollar Quartet' session on 4th December 1956.

First Release: 'The Complete Million Dollar Session' (1987)

[568] THE ALCOHOL OF FAME (1973)
(Buzz Rabin)

Although not the greatest of songs, 'The Alcohol Of Fame' is an album highlight for the simple fact that there are *no strings!* If only the rest of 'I-40 Country' was unadorned in this way.

First Release: 'I-40 Country' (1974)

[569] THE BALLAD OF BILLY JOE (1959)
(Charlie Rich)

A Western-style Country ballad with lines like *"I'll be hung tomorrow just because I had to kill that little rat!"*, 'The Ballad of Billy Joe' would've suited Johnny Cash or Marty Robbins more than it did Jerry, though he certainly doesn't do a bad job on it. Charlie Rich's 1958 solo demo would be released in 1974, while covers include Georgie Fame and Alan Price (1971) and Tom Jones (1973). In 1967, Bobbie Gentry released 'Ode To Billie Joe', a kind of sequel to 'The Ballad of Billy Joe', and had a million seller with the song.

First Release: Single B-side (1959)

[570] THE CLOSEST THING TO YOU (1975)
(Bob McDill)

Originally released by Dickey Lee in 1975, 'The Closest Thing To You' is a classy Country-Pop ballad. It was promoted on 'The Midnight Special', but there were no other confirmed live performances.

First Release: 'Country Class' (1976) + Single A-side (1976)

The Closest Thing To You / You Belong To Me
(No. 27 Country)

'The Midnight Special' (1977)

[571a] **THE CRAWDAD SONG (1956)**
(Traditional)

An absolute stormer, complete with Gene Vincent and The Blue Caps-styled screams, 'The Crawdad Song' has been a fan favorite ever since it was first released in 1970. It is unclear where exactly Jerry found the song: It was first released by Honeyboy and Sassafras in 1930, while later versions include those by Burl Ives, Woody Guthrie, Cisco Houston and Big Bill Broonzy, all in 1953-1954.

First Release: 'Ole Tyme Country Music' (1970)

[571b] **THE CRAWDAD SONG (1973/1974)** *

For his 1975 'Odd Man In' album, Jerry re-cut the song with a slower, High Heel Sneakers-type rhythm, but a circulating unreleased and low quality tape from the 1973/1974 Knox Phillips sessions reveals that he'd been playing around with a similar arrangement for some time.

First Release: bootleg only

[571c] **THE CRAWDAD SONG** (1975)

While inevitably over-shadowed by the Sun version, the slower 1975 cut shouldn't be over-looked either, particularly the prominent pounding piano work. Subsequent live performances include Rome 1987, Paris 1989, Babenhausen (Germany) 1991 and the 66th Birthday Concert in Memphis 2001.

First Release: 'Odd Man In' (1975)

[572] **THE FIFTIES** (1976)
(Jerry Foster / Bill Rice)

A contrived fake-Rock 'n' Roll song written by writers who don't understand the genre, 'The Fifties' is even worse than the similar 'Jerry Lee's Rock 'n' Roll Revival Show'.

First Release: 'The Mercury Sessions' (1985)

[573] **THE FIRE MEGAMIX!** (1989)
(Sunny David / David Williams) + (Bob Feldman / Jerry Goldstein / Richard Gottehrer) + (Otis Blackwell / Jack Hammer) + (Otis Blackwell)

One place where the 'Great Balls Of Fire' movie soundtrack album was particularly successful was Spain, so much so that he did several lucrative tours and TV appearances there over the next couple of years. Perhaps because of this, 'The Fire Megamix!' was released exclusively in that country. A cut-and-paste medley of 'Whole Lotta Shakin' Goin' On', 'I'm On Fire', 'Great Balls Of Fire' and 'Breathless', it is sacrilege of course, but if released in Britain in 1989, it could've given 'Jive Bunny' a bit of competition!

First Release: Single A-side (1989)

[574] **THE GODS WERE ANGRY WITH ME** (1973)
(Roma Wilkinson / Watt Watkins)

Originally by released by Jim Reeves in 1957, 'The Gods Were Angry With Me' was covered by Ferlin Husky (1959), Bobby Bare (1967) and Jim Ed Brown (1969). Though not a particularly great song, this has the distinction of being the only number from the Stan Kesler sessions that wasn't released at the time, and the sparse production is *far* superior to anything on those albums, thanks to being overdubs-free.

First Release: 'From The Vaults' (1986)

[575] **THE GOODBYE OF THE YEAR** (1971)
(Dallas Frazier / A.L. Owens)

From the same team that wrote 'Touching Home', this song isn't quite so memorable, despite a strong vocal by Jerry.

First Release: 'Would You Take Another Chance On Me' (1971)

[576] **THE HAUNTED HOUSE** (1973)
(Robert Geddins)

Originally released by Johnny Fuller in 1958 and covered by Gene Simmons (1964), Ray Sharpe (1964), Sam The Sham and The Pharaohs (1964), Lynn Anderson (1970) and Roy Buchanan (1972), 'The Haunted House' is a light-hearted song that made a refreshing break from all those maudlin ballads *("Had one big eye and two big feet!)*. Released on 'Southern Roots', a vastly extended version with some incredible piano was released on 1987's 'The Killer: 1973-1977' box-set. Live performances include 'In Concert' 1974 and the 40th Anniversary Show in Memphis in 1996.

First Release: 'Southern Roots' (1973)

[577] **THE HOLE HE SAID HE'D DIG FOR ME** (1963)
(Marion Turner)

Originally released by Allen Curtis in 1963, 'The Hole He Said He'd Dig For Me' is an excellent Charlie Rich-styled Bluesy ballad, and was released as the B-side to 1964's 'She Was My Baby (He Was My Friend)'. An inferior alternate take was issued on a French-only compilation in 1969, and Mickey Gilley revived the song in 1975. A poor quality recording survives of Jerry performing the it in Greenville, Mississippi, in 1964.

First Release: Single B-side (1964)

[578a] **THE HOUSE OF BLUE LIGHTS** (1975)
(Don Raye / Freddie Slack)

Originally released by Freddie Slack and Ella Mae Morse with Don Raye in 1946 and covered by The Andrews Sisters (1946), Merrill Moore (1953), Chuck Berry (recorded 1958, released 1974) and Freddy Cannon (1960), 'The House Of Blue Lights' is a song Jerry has visited several times in the studio. From the 'Odd Man In' sessions, his 1975 version is typical of those sessions; shot voice, prominent piano, and harmonica. It would've made a great inclusion, but was instead kept in the can for over a decade.

First Release: 'From The Vaults' (1986)

[578b] **THE HOUSE OF BLUE LIGHTS** (1986)

Although a little on the short side, this performance is excellent, with well-mixed voice and piano, and no backing vocals. Taped in September 1986, it was released on 1988's 'Rocket'.

First Release: 'Rocket' (1988)

[578c] **THE HOUSE OF BLUE LIGHTS** (1994)

For 'Young Blood' Jerry recorded another version of 'The House Of Blue Lights', but this time with a fun Rock 'n' Swing arrangement, and it made a fine finish to a flawed but highly enjoyable album. Sales were disappointing though (not helped by Jerry's minimal promotion), and it would be another 11 years before he released a new album. The song was performed very occasionally well into the '90s.

First Release: 'Young Blood' (1995)

[578d] **THE HOUSE OF BLUE LIGHTS** (2008-2010) *

Jerry recorded two more than acceptable and rather fast run-throughs at the 'Mean Old Man' / 'Rock & Roll Time' sessions, but none of them have been officially released at time of writing.

First Release: 'Come Sundown' (2014) (bootleg)

[579] **THE HURTIN' PART** (1971)
(Thomas LaVerne / Bill Taylor)

'The Hurtin' Part' is a rather mediocre Country song, despite coming from the pen of Bill Taylor, someone who wrote/co-wrote such goodies as 'Invitation To Your Party', 'One Minute Past Eternity', 'There Must Be More To Love Than This' and 'I Am What I Am'.

First Release: 'Would You Take Another Chance On Me' (1971)

[580] **THE KILLER** [with T.G. Sheppard] (2008)
(Bobby Tomberlin / Jerry Lee Lewis / Kelly Lang / T.G. Sheppard)

Basically a Jerry Lee Lewis tribute on which The Killer himself makes a cameo, the song starts as gentle acoustic ballad with nostalgic lyrics *("It was 1957, seems like yesterday...")*, then develops into a loud and raucous modern Country-Rock song. Jerry is in good voice, and he is clearly enjoying the experience.

First Release: 'Partners In Rhyme' (2009)

'Partners in Rhyme' (2009)

[581a] THE LAST CHEATER'S WALTZ (1977)
(Sonny Throckmorton)

A Pop ballad that is far closer to Engelbert Humperdinck's 'The Last Waltz' than it is to Hank and Merle, Jerry nevertheless sings it well, even if there isn't any piano. Sonny Throckmorton released his own version in 1978, and it was also covered by Johnny Duncan (1979) and Emmylou Harris (1981), but most significant was T.G. Sheppard's 1979 version, which topped the Country charts. Jerry performed the song in Cardiff in 1983.

First Release: 'Keeps Rockin'' (1978)

[581b] THE LAST CHEATER'S WALTZ (2006)

Although in a lower key and with inevitably more aged vocals, the 21st century re-cut includes some beautiful piano playing. The backing vocalists Stacy Michelle and Bernard Fowler are a bit over-prominent at times though, and it was probably a wise decision not to put the song on 'Last Man Standing', saving it as a bonus track instead.

First Release: Target (exclusive download) + 'Rock 'n' Roll Resurrection' (2007) (bootleg)

[582a] THE LAST LETTER (1970)
(Rex Griffin)

Originally released by Rex Griffin in 1937, 'The Last Letter' was covered by Wanda Jackson (1961), Willie Nelson (1963), Ernest Tubb (1963), Ray Price (1965), Dottie West (1967), Connie Smith (1967), Glen Campbell (1968) and Marty Robbins (1968). Jerry tackled the song at three different sessions over the years, none of which were released at the time, with this first one being notable for Jerry overdubbing himself as a duet.

First Release: 'The Killer: 1969-1972' (box-set, 1986)

[582b] THE LAST LETTER (1977)

A 'Keeps Rockin'' outtake, this is played at a rather sprightly pace. Probably a bit *too* sprightly!

First Release: 'The Mercury Sessions' (1985)

[582c] THE LAST LETTER (1980) *

Although a little ragged and unrehearsed, this version is probably the best of the three, thanks to some excellent piano, fiddle and steel guitar breaks. The song was performed live in Knoxville in 1981 and Goldston in 1996.

First Release: 'The Caribou Ranch Sessions, 1980-1986' (2012) (bootleg)

[583a] **THE LILY OF THE VALLEY** (1970)
(Charles Fry / William Shakespeare Hays)

Originally released by the Happy Valley Family in 1935, Jerry's mid-paced version is one of the highlights of his 1970 Gospel album. The song was performed live several times on the 1972 European Tour.

First Release: 'In Loving Memories: The Jerry Lee Lewis Gospel Album' (1970)

[583b] **THE LILY OF THE VALLEY** [with Jimmy Swaggart] (2022)

A little faster than the cut from over half a century earlier, the harmonies are ragged and Jimmy Swaggart's baritone is an acquired taste, but you can be sure that every word is sung with feeling and sincerity.

First Release: 'The Boys From Ferriday' (2022)

[584] **THE LOVE-IN** (1968) (L) *
(Sheb Wooley)

For the 1968 'Innocence, Anarchy and Soul' aborted TV show, Jerry was asked to perform a Sheb Wooley song from the previous year called 'The Love-In', with lyrics like *"Society spurners, card burners, liberal thinkers love-in near our town!"*. It's actually a lot better than expected, and fortunately a rough recording survives. See 'Give Me Some Action' for more on 'Innocence, Anarchy and Soul'!

First Release: bootleg only

[585] **THE MARINE'S HYMN [INSTRUMENTAL]** (1956)
(Jacques Offenbach)

A famous US Marines marching song based on Jacques Offenbach's 'Couplets Des Deux Hommes D'armes' from 1867, if they tried marching to Jerry's boogie woogie version, it would be more of a run than a march!

First Release: '16 Songs Never Issued Before 2' (1975)

[586] **THE MERCY OF A LETTER** (1972)
(Jerry Foster / Bill Rice)

It had already started to creep in over the previous couple of albums, but by 1972's 'Who's Gonna Play This Old Piano', the hard honky Tonk Country of the late '60s had largely been (temporarily) forgotten in favor of string-covered ballads, where the emphasis was far more on Pop than Country. 'The Mercy Of A Letter' is one such song.

First Release: 'Who's Gonna Play This Old Piano' (1972) + Single B-side (1972)

[587] **THE MORNING AFTER BABY LET ME DOWN** (1973)
(Ray Griff)

Original released by Loretta Lynn in 1972, the same year writer Ray Griff released his own version, 'The Morning After Baby Let Me Down' is a memorable Country-Pop song with good lyrics *("There was nothin' to hold on to, but the sheets that fell around me!")* and production that isn't quite as over-blown as other songs on the album.

First Release: 'Sometimes A Memory Ain't Enough' (1973)

[588] **THE OLD COUNTRY CHURCH** (1976)
(John Whitfield Vaughan)

A song that was first published in 1934, and first released on record by The King's Sacred Quartet in 1950, 'The Old Country Church' is not a Gospel song as such, but a song *about* the church. A truly touching performance, when Jerry says *"Mama's gone home now, but her memory lingers on!"* he sounds genuinely upset. The song was performed live occasionally up until the mid '80s, and then revived for 'Kerrie Live!' in 2000.

First Release: 'Country Class' (1976)

'Country Class' (1976)

[589a] **THE OLD RUGGED CROSS** (1970)
(George Bennard)

Originally released by Mrs. William Asher and Homer Rodeheaver in 1921 and covered by Dinah Shore and Gene Autry (1950), Roy Rogers and Dale Evans (1950), Jo Stafford (1950), Ray Price (1960), Patti Page (1966), Ella Fitzgerald (1967), Burl Ives (1967) and Loretta Lynn (1968), 'The Old Rugged Cross' is a song that meant a lot to Jerry. So it was no surprise that he included a suitably respectful version on his 1970 Gospel album. Live performances have been relatively infrequent, but do include the Memphis Church recording in 1970 and 'Kerrie Live!' in 2000, and perhaps significantly, he closed concerts in London with the song in both 1972 and 1977.

First Release: 'In Loving Memories: The Jerry Lee Lewis Gospel Album' (1970)

[589b] **THE OLD RUGGED CROSS** (2022)

A song Jerry probably felt he *had* to do on what he no doubt expected to be his final album, his voice is frail, yet he somehow wills himself to hit notes that he probably hadn't reached in years. The combination is at the same time heart-warming and heart-breaking.

First Release: 'The Boys From Ferriday' (2022)

[590] **THE ONE ROSE THAT'S LEFT IN MY HEART** (1975)
(Del Lyon / Lani McIntire)

Originally recorded by Jimmie Rodgers with Lani McIntire's Hawaiians in 1930, it was not released until 1937, the same year that Gene Autry covered the song. Jerry first attempted the it during the 'Odd Man In' sessions, a take that wasn't released until 1987, and then cut a longer and superior version for 'Country Class' 6 months later. Beautifully sung, this is matched by the superb piano and fiddle. The song was performed occasionally well into the New Millennium.

First Release: 'Country Class' (1976)

[591] **THE PILGRIM** [with Kris Kristofferson] (2003-2006)
(Kris Kristofferson)

Originally released by Kris Kristofferson (as 'The Pilgrim - Chapter 33') in 1971 and covered by Teresa Brewer with Oily Rags [aka Chas 'n' Dave] (1973) and Willie Nelson (1979), 'The Pilgrim' with lyrics like *"He's a poet he's a picker he's a prophet he's a pusher!"* is a song about contradictions, which is probably why Jerry could clearly identify with it. There's no piano, but it doesn't need it, and Jerry and Kris' duet is a real highlight of 'Last Man Standing'.

First Release: 'Last Man Standing' (2006)

[592] **THE RETURN OF JERRY LEE** (1958)
(Jack Clement / Barbara Pittman)

Following the May 1958 scandal (basically, the British establishment getting into a right old tizzy over Jerry's personal life), Sun producer Jack Clement came up with the idea of compiling a 'joke' record as his next release. Featuring Memphis DJ George Klein (as 'Edward R. Edward') and snippets of previous recordings, it went something along the lines of (GK): *"What did Queen Elizabeth say about you?"*, (JLL): *"Goodness gracious, Great Balls of Fire!"*. Only mildly amusing when heard once, it doesn't bear too many repeated plays, and did nothing whatsoever to revive Jerry's career. If only DJ's had flipped the record over and played 'Lewis Boogie' instead!

First Release: Single A-side (1958)

The Return Of Jerry Lee / Lewis Boogie
(Not a hit)

[593] **THE REVOLUTIONARY MAN** (1973)
(Doug Sahm)

Written by rockin' hippy Doug Sahm (very much a revolutionary man, though perhaps in a different way to Jerry Lee Lewis), 'The Revolutionary Man' is a mid-tempo Soul-Rock song, which Jerry really gets into (*"I'm a revolutionary mother-humper, I don't give a damn what they say!"*), even if the backing singers' *"Jerry is a rebel"* contribution is a bit cringing.

First Release: 'Southern Roots' (1973)

[594] **THE URGE** (1966)
(Donnie Fritts)

A dirty little Rhythm 'n' Blues ditty with lines that rival 'Big Legged Woman' (*"Don't try to make it hard, just do like you're told!"*), Memphis Beat' album-closer 'The Urge' deserves more acclaim.

First Release: 'Memphis Beat' (1966)

[595a] **THE WILD SIDE OF LIFE** (1960)
(Arlie Carter / William Warren)

Originally released by Jimmy Heap and The Melody Masters in 1951 and made famous by Hank Thompson in 1952, Jerry's Sun recording from late 1960 is played mid-tempo, and features some excellent saxophone.

First Release: 'From The Vaults of Sun' (1974)

[595b] **THE WILD SIDE OF LIFE** (1965)

Re-cut for his first Country album, the 1965 Smash version is slower, and with some additional chord changes thrown in. The song was performed live in Stockholm 1977, Strasbourg 1977, Vienna 1977, St. Louis 1980, Augusta 1985, Reykjavik 1986 and Gothenburg 2007.

First Release: 'Country Songs For City Folks' (1965)

[596] **THERE MUST BE MORE TO LOVE THAN THIS** (1970)
(Thomas LaVerne / Bill Taylor)

A deceptively simple Country song in the Hank Williams mold, 'There Must Be More To Love Than This' is one of the more enduring early '70s Country hits. Promoted on 'The Andy Williams Show' early the following year, it was clearly a favorite of Jerry's, remaining a fairly regular concert inclusion until the late '90s. The song was covered by The Wilburn Brothers in 1971.

First Release: 'There Must Be More To Love Than This' (1970) + Single A-side (1970)

There Must Be More To Love Than This / Home Away From Home
(No. 1 Country)

'There Must Be More To Love Than This' (1971)

[597a] **THERE STANDS THE GLASS** (1968)
(Audrey Greisham / Russ E. Hull / Mary Jean Shurtz)

Originally released by Blaine Smith in 1952 and covered by Webb Pierce (1953), Conway Twitty (1966) and Wanda Jackson (1968), 'There Stands The Glass' had long been a favorite of Jerry's, with live performances at least as early as his 1962 concerts in Keanesburg, New Jersey. Jerry's 1968 cut is superb, with his superlative vocals making one overlook the Nashville assembly-line production. The song was performed very occasionally up until the mid '90s.

First Release: 'She Still Comes Around' (1969)

[597b] **THERE STANDS THE GLASS** (1984)

Though good, the re-cut of 'There Stands The Glass' is very short, being part of a longer medley (the other song segments don't feature Jerry).

First Release: 'Four Legends' (1985)

[598] **THINGS** (1994)
(Bobby Darin)

Originally released by Bobby Darin in 1962, the Pop-Rocker 'Things' isn't a song one would've thought suitable for Jerry, but it is unexpectedly excellent, and a real highlight of his 1995 album.

First Release: 'Young Blood' (1995)

[599] **THINGS THAT MATTER MOST TO ME** (1971)
(Thomas LaVerne / Bill Taylor)

'Things That Matter Most To Me' is a spoken-word song which was written specially for 'The Jerry Lee Lewis Show' pilot in 1971, where it is heard accompanied by footage of Jerry walking around outside. The song was also performed live on the '25 Years of Jerry Lee Lewis' TV special in 1982.

First Release: 'Would You Take Another Chance On Me' (1971)

[600] **THINK ABOUT IT, DARLIN'** (1972)
(Jerry Foster / Bill Rice)

With an almost 'classical' soaring strings introduction, and with part-crooned, part-spoken vocals, 'Think About It, Darlin'' is a *long* way from Jimmie Rodgers and Hank Williams. Yet it is quite impressive in its own way. Promoted in stripped-down (and superior) form on the UK's 'The Old Grey Whistle Test' the same year, the song was performed live occasionally until around 1987.

First Release: 'Who's Gonna Play This Old Piano' (1972) + Single Double-A-side (1972)

[601] **THIRTEEN AT THE TABLE** (1971)
(Buddy Emmons)

A religious song about The Last Supper *("He broke the bread and poured the blood red wine!")*, 'Thirteen At The Table' was Jerry's first Gospel recording since his mercifully-brief decision to give up 'worldly music' six months earlier.

First Release: 'Would You Take Another Chance On Me' (1971)

[602] **THIRTY NINE AND HOLDING** (1980)
(Jerry Foster / Bill Rice)

One of those 'middle-aged' songs that Jerry excelled at during the late '70s and early '80s *("He still thinks he's the man that he used to be!")*, 'Thirty-Nine and Holding' is one of his better post-Mercury Country recordings. Promoted on 'The Tomorrow Show', it was still performed occasionally into the New Millennium.

First Release: 'Killer Country' (1980) + Single A-side (1981)

Thirty Nine and Holding / Change Places With Me
(No. 4 Country)

'The Tomorrow Show' (1981)

[603] **THIS LAND IS YOUR LAND** [with Linda Gail Lewis, Carl Perkins and Jackie Wilson] (1971) (L)
(Woody Guthrie)

Originally released by Woody Guthrie in 1944, 'This Land Is Your Land' was covered by The Weavers (1958), The Kingston Trio (1961), Lester Flatt and Earl Scruggs (1962), The New Christy Minstrels (1962), Peter, Paul and Mary (1963), The Seekers (1965) and Country Joe McDonald (1969), and has long been considered a Left-Wing folkie anthem. So why Jerry Lee Lewis and guests performed it is unknown!

First Release: 'The Jerry Lee Lewis Show' (VHS, 1991)

[604] **THIS MUST BE THE PLACE** (1965)
(Dennis Lambert / Neil Levenson)

An otherwise excellent rocker, it is all-but-ruined by a very clumsy edit just after the piano intro (this author can't be the only one who thought his record was jumping when he first heard it!). Sadly a full uncut version of the song has never surfaced.

First Release: Single B-side (1965)

[605] **THIS TRAIN** [with Johnny Cash, June Carter-Cash, Carl Perkins and Roy Orbison] (1977) (L)
(Traditional)

First recorded by The Florida Normal Industrial Institute Quartet in 1924, 'This Train' was also covered by Sister Rosetta Tharpe (1939), Hank Thompson (1955), Louis Armstrong (1958), Peter, Paul and Mary (1962), Big Bill Broonzy (1962), The Seekers (1963) and The Staple Singers (1965). The whole cast performed a lively version on 1977's 'The Johnny Cash Christmas Show'.

First Release: 'Johnny Cash - Christmas Special 1977' (DVD, 2008)

'The Johnny Cash Christmas Show' (1977)

[606] **THIS WORLD IS NOT MY HOME** (2000) (L)
(Albert E. Brumley)

First released by Stove Pipe No. 1 [aka Sam Jones] as 'Lord Don't You Know I Have No Friend Like You' in 1924, 'This World Is Not My Home' was covered by The Carter Family (1931), The Monroe Brothers (1936), Roy Acuff (1958), The Chuck Wagon Gang (1959) and Jim Reeves (1962). Jerry performed it very occasionally throughout the '70s, '80s and '90s, but the only *official* release is on 'Kerrie Live!', a VHS tape that was available direct from Jerry's wife Kerrie.

First Release: 'Kerrie Live!' (VHS, 2001)

'Kerrie Live!' (2000)

[607] TIME CHANGES EVERYTHING (1971)
(Tommy Duncan)

Originally released by Bob Wills and His Texas Playboys in 1940, 'Time Changes Everything' was covered by Roy Rogers (1940), Johnny Cash (1960), Bill Monroe and His Blue Grass Boys (1961), Ray Price (1962), George Jones (1962), Webb Pierce (1966) and Merle Haggard (1970). Jerry's excellent Swing version features prominent piano and he is suitably supported by fiddle and steel guitar. It got a rare live outing in Montreal in 1986.

First Release: 'Touching Home' (1971)

[608] TO MAKE LOVE SWEETER FOR YOU (1968)
(Jerry Kennedy / Glenn Sutton)

After a couple of very near misses, in early 1968 Jerry finally did it, he scored his first Country chart-topper since 'Great Balls of Fire'! It had been a long, hard 10 years. And the record that got him there was 'To Make Love Sweeter For You', a truly beautiful and impeccably-played Country ballad. It was promoted on 'This Is Tom Jones' and 'Hee Haw', but later live performances were relatively rare, probably because it was a bit of a challenge to sing. They include Attica, Indiana, 1971, Slough 1972, Copenhagen 1977, Manchester 1977, Stockholm 1985, Rome 1987 and Goldston 1996. George Morgan covered the song in 1969.

First Release: 'She Still Comes Around' (1969) + Single A-side (1968)

To Make Love Sweeter For You / Let's Talk About Us
(No. 1 Country)

'This is Tom Jones' (1969)

[609] **TODAY I STARTED LOVING YOU AGAIN** (1968)
(Bonnie Owens / Merle Haggard)

Originally released by Merle Haggard earlier the same year, Jerry's version of this great song is amongst his very best late '60s Country recordings. It was performed live very occasionally until the late '80s.

First Release: 'She Still Comes Around' (1969)

[610] **TOGETHER AGAIN** (1964) (L)
(Buck Owens)

Originally released by Buck Owens in 1964, 'Together Again' on 'The Greatest Live Show on Earth' is hard Country played to a Rock 'n' Roll crowd, and just like 'Your Cheatin' Heart' on 'Live at The Star Club, Hamburg', it goes down a storm! Very occasional later performances include Toronto 1967, St. Louis 1980, Toronto 1986, Trondheim 1993 and Las Vegas 1995.

First Release: 'The Greatest Live Show on Earth' (1964)

[611] **TOMORROW MAY MEAN GOODBYE** (1970) (L)
(James B. Coats)

A slow Gospel song from the 1970 Memphis Church recording, his *"Listen to ol' Jerry and today, fall down upon your knees and pray!"* isn't *that* different *from "I want you to get down on your knees one time, and shake for Jerry Lee Lewis honey!"* in 'Sexy Ways', it's just that on one he's encouraging prayer, and on the other he's encouraging...

First Release: 'The Killer: 1969-1972' (box-set, 1986)

[612] **TOMORROW NIGHT** (1957)
(Sam Coslow / Wilhelm Grosz)

First released by Henry Russell and His Romancers (1939), 'Tomorrow Night' was covered by Jimmy Dorsey and His Orchestra (1939), Lonnie Johnson (1948), Patti Page (1948), LaVern Baker (1954) and Elvis Presley (recorded 1954, released 1965). Jerry's version is amongst the slowest of his earliest Sun recordings, and the most interesting thing about it is the piano solo.

First Release: 'Rockin' and Free' (1974)

[613] **TOMORROW'S TAKING BABY AWAY** (1973)
(Thomas LaVerne / Bill Taylor)

A not particularly great song from the July 1973 sessions and with the usual smothering of strings and backing vocalists, what *is* largely noticeable about these recordings is how good Jerry's singing is, despite the scarcity of strong material. So why *did* Stan Kesler feel the need to put so much junk on top of it? 'Tomorrow's Taking Baby Away' was performed at least once, at a show in Memphis in 1974.

First Release: 'I-40 Country' (1974) + Single B-side (1974)

[614] **TOO MANY RIVERS** (1972)
(Harlan Howard)

Originally released by Brenda Lee in 1965, Jerry's version is well-sung and played, even if he does overdo the ad-libs a little bit. He performed it live in Dalton 1979, a show that has been much bootlegged (and often wrongly dated as 1978, 1980 and even 1984).

First Release: 'Who's Gonna Play This Old Piano' (1972

[615] **TOO MUCH TO GAIN TO LOSE** (1970)
(Dottie Rambo)

Originally released by The Singing Rambos in 1968, 'Too Much To Gain To Lose' is a Gospel ballad in ¾ time, and like much of the 'In Loving Memories' album, the mixing is excellent with very prominent piano.

First Release: 'In Loving Memories: The Jerry Lee Lewis Gospel Album' (1970)

[616] **TOO WEAK TO FIGHT** (1980)
(Chuck Howard)

An interesting Country-Pop song, the opening line is *"Being the humanitarian I am!"*, not a phrase many would associate with Jerry Lee Lewis! It was performed at a concert in Rhode Island in 1981.

First Release: 'Killer Country' (1980)

[617] **TOO YOUNG** (1965)
(Sylvia Dee / Sidney Lippman)

Originally released by Victor Young and His Orchestra in 1950, covers of 'Too Young' include Nat 'King' Cole (1951), Frankie Lymon (1957), The Clovers (1960), Sam Cooke (1960), Marty Robbins (1961) and Marvin Gaye (1965). Not a song particularly suited to him, the best thing about Jerry's version is an extraordinary piano solo that lasts almost a full minute!

First Release: 'Memphis Beat' (1966)

[618] **TOOT, TOOT, TOOTSIE GOODBYE** (1979)
(Ernie Erdman / Ted Fiorito / Gus Kahn)

Jerry always insisted that there were only four true musical 20th century stylists: Jerry Lee Lewis was one of them of course, as was Hank Williams and ('30s Country-Blues man) Jimmie Rodgers - with master showman Al Jolson being the 4th. Despite this, he didn't cover many Al Jolson songs, so a version of his 1922 recording 'Toot, Toot, Tootsie (Goodbye)' (also covered by Brenda Lee in 1959 and Jackie Wilson in 1961) was very welcome indeed. He doesn't disappoint either, with piano that successfully combines Ragtime with 'Rock 'n' Roll, and backing that include banjo, electric guitar and Dixieland brass. The song was performed live in Oslo in 1985.

First Release: 'When Two Worlds Collide' (1980)

[619] **TOSSIN' AND TURNIN'** (1979) *
(Ritchie Adams / Malou Rene)

Originally released by Bobby Lewis in 1961, 'Tossin' and Turnin' was covered by The Marvelettes (1963), Dave Berry and The Cruisers (1963), Dee Dee Sharp (1963), Lulu (1966), The Supremes (1972) and Bill Haley and The Comets (1973). Jerry's version is fine, but without adding a great deal to the original.

First Release: 'Alive and Rockin'' (1986) (bootleg)

[620] **TOUCHING HOME** (1971)
(Dallas Frazier / A.L. Owens)

Originally released by Whitey Shafer in 1968, 'Touching Home' is a hard Country song with just the tiniest hint of Blues. In some ways it was also the end of an era, being his last significant single before the more orchestrated Pop of 'Would You Take Another Chance On Me', 'Think About It Darlin'', etc. The song was performed live occasionally into the New Millennium.

First Release: 'Touching Home' (1971) + Single A-side (1971)

Touching Home / Woman, Woman (Get Out Of Our Way)
(No. 3 Country)

[621] **TRAVELIN' BAND** [with John Fogerty] (2003-2006)

(John Fogerty)

A Little Richard-type rocker originally recorded by Creedence Clearwater Revival in 1970 and covered by Bill Haley and The Comets the following year, Jerry's incredibly fast-paced version featuring duetting vocals from the song's composer is a lot of fun, with some excellent piano and saxophone. Lil' sis Linda Gail Lewis had previously released the song in 1991.

First Release: 'Last Man Standing' (2006)

[622] **TREAT HER RIGHT** (1967)

(Roy Head)

Originally released by Roy Head in 1965 and covered by Chris Farlowe (1965), Len Barry (1965) and Otis Redding (1966), this tough Soulful Rhythm 'n' Blues song is ideal for Jerry, with him bringing it down low and then rockin' hard in true 'Whole Lotta Shakin' Goin' On'/'Mean Woman Blues' style, and although it's far down in the mix, listen out for that pumpin' piano during the closing 30 seconds!

First Release: Soul My Way (1967)

[623a] **TROUBLE IN MIND** (1973)

(Richard M. Jones)

A song that dates back to at least Thelma La Vizzo (as 'Trouble In Mind Blues') in 1924, other possible influences are Amos Milburn (1952), Big Bill Broonzy (1954) and Big Joe Turner in (1957), while Rock 'n' Roll era covers include Conway Twitty (1960), Sam Cooke (1961), Fats Domino (1961) and The Everly Brothers (1962). A slow Country-Blues, *Jerry* really shows off during his final solo! 'Trouble In Mind' remained a concert favorite for the rest of his career.

First Release: 'The Session' (1973)

[623b] TROUBLE IN MIND [with Eric Clapton] (2003-2006)

A couple of minutes shorter than the earlier version, this is still impressive stuff. Unfortunately Eric Clapton's albeit excellent playing is mixed *way* too loud, at times almost drowning out both Jerry's vocals and his piano. And that's the problem with these later day 'all star' collaborations; whereas in the past, such pickers as James Burton, Steve Cropper and Albert Lee blended in to help create a satisfying whole, modern day producers and engineers feel that any guests need to have a starring role.

First Release: 'Last Man Standing' (2006)

[623c] TROUBLE IN MIND (2006)

This live-in-the-studio performance is a typically good version, just like those generally heard in latter day concerts.

First Release: Napster (exclusive download) + 'Rock 'n' Roll Resurrection' (2007) (bootleg)

[624] TUPELO COUNTY JAIL [with Webb Pierce, Mel Tillis and Faron Young] (1984)
(Webb Pierce / Mel Tillis)

First recorded by Webb Pierce in 1958, Jerry, Webb, Mel and Faron are clearly loving every minute of this and the other 'Four Legends' tracks.

First Release: 'Four Legends' (1985)

[625] TURN AROUND (1957)
(Carl Perkins)

Originally released by Carl Perkins in 1955, Jerry's version features prominent Roland Janes guitar, a Jimmy Van Eaton shuffle beat, and trademark Jerry Lee Lewis pumpin' piano. It was released on his first EP in late 1957, while cousin Mickey Gilley covered it 3 years later.

First Release: 'The Great Ball of Fire' EP (1957)

[626] TURN ON YOUR LOVE LIGHT (1967)
(Deadric Malone / Joseph Scott)

Originally released by Bobby Bland in 1961 and covered by Gene Chandler (1962), Them (1966), Mitch Ryder (1966), The Righteous Brothers (1966) and Long John Baldry (1966), this frantic Soul-rocker is a highlight of the under-rated 'Soul My Way', despite the lack of piano. Released as a single, 5 years later it was put on an album again as filler on 'The Killer Rocks On', as well as issued as a B-side, where it finally charted in its own right at No. 95 in the Pop charts. Jerry closed a couple of shows with the song in Toronto in 1967, played it at the aborted 'Innocence, Anarchy and Soul' taping in 1968, and performed it on 'The Many Sounds of Jerry Lee' in 1969 whilst playing drums!

First Release: Soul My Way (1967) + Single A-side (1967) + 'The Killer Rocks On' (1972) + Single B-side (1972)

Turn On Your Love Light / Shotgun Man
(Not a hit)

'The Many Sounds of Jerry Lee' (1969)

[627] **TURN YOUR RADIO ON** (1987)
(Albert E. Brumley)

Originally released by Lulu Belle and Scotty in 1939 and a single for Ray Stevens 1971, thanks to the use of a proper piano and sympathetic backing that includes a vocal group, this Gospel song is one of the few really listenable tracks from the December 1987 Hank Cochran sessions. Jerry had performed the song live at least a couple of times, including at an undated and unknown USA gig circa 1974, and New York just a few months before he recorded it in the studio.

First Release: 'At Hank Cochran's' (1995)

[628] **TUTTI FRUTTI** (1962) (L) *
(Dorothy LaBostrie / Joe Lubin / Richard Penniman)

Originally released by Little Richard in 1955 and covered by Pat Boone (1956), Elvis Presley (1956) and Carl Perkins (1958), a very poor quality live version from Keansburg in 1962 appeared on a bootleg 10 years later. The song has been performed a great many times since, though usually only as parts of lengthier medleys.

First Release: 'With Jerry Lee Rock and Roll' (1972) (bootleg)

[629] **TWENTY FOUR HOURS A DAY** (1966)
(Bobby Lee Trammell)

Originally released by Bobby Lee Trammell in 1965, Jerry's version of this Pop-Rocker had strings on when the song first surfaced on a bootleg EP in the early '80s. The un-enhanced version was released on a box-set a few years later.

First Release: 'The Killer: 1963-1968' (box-set, 1986)

[630] **TWILIGHT** [with Robbie Robertson] (2003-2006)
(Robbie Robertson)

Originally released by The Band in 1976, 'Twilight' is a lovely song, but perhaps not one that particularly suits Jerry, with the whole thing sounding a little out-of-sync. Jerry is far better on the officially unreleased 'Up On Cripple Creek'!

First Release: 'Last Man Standing' (2006)

[631] **UBANGI STOMP** (1958)
(Charles Underwood)

A song that would be considered 'racist' in these more censored days, 'Ubangi Stomp' is in fact just a light-hearted and fun Rock 'n' Roll song. Originally released by Warren Smith in 1956, Jerry's version is very exciting, except that the piano is largely inaudible apart from the intro and the solo! Despite this lapse on the engineer's part, it made a highly worthwhile track on his debut album. Live performances include Toronto 1967, 'The Many Sounds of Jerry Lee' 1969, Las Vegas 1970, Birmingham 1977, Berlin 1977, Hamburg 1977, Essen 1977, Plymouth 1983, Northampton 1987, Las Vegas 1989 and the 66th Birthday Show in Memphis 2001. Fellow Sun artist Carl Mann covered the song in 1960, though it wasn't released until 1977.

First Release: 'Jerry Lee Lewis' (1958)

[632] UNTIL THE DAY FOREVER ENDS (1974)
(Jerry Foster / Bill Rice)

From the October 1974 'Boogie Woogie Country Man' sessions, this is fairly typical of the recordings from this period; hoarse and ravaged vocals, but with lighter production and more prominent piano. The song is fairly mediocre, and was rightly left off the album.

First Release: 'From The Vaults' (1986)

[633] UP ON CRIPPLE CREEK (2008-2010) *
(Robbie Robertson)

Originally released by The Band in 1969, Jerry does a great job on this song (complete with yodeling!), and is clearly enjoying himself. The lack of piano doesn't really matter, and probably wouldn't have suited the song anyway.

First Release: 'Come Sundown' (2014) (bootleg)

[634a] WAITING FOR A TRAIN (1962)
(Jimmie Rodgers)

Originally released by Jimmie Rodgers in 1929 and covered by Gene Autry the following year 'Waiting For A Train' (sometimes called 'All Around The Watertank') was a long time favorite of Jerry's. He attempted it at two separate 1962 sessions, initially cutting two sprightly takes in January, and several, more relaxed, takes in September, with the latter session being distinguished by the presence of a honking saxophone. A take from the January session was the first to be released, on 'Ole Tyme Country Music' and on a single in 1970, with a September 1962 'saxophone' take sneaking out on the 2nd pressings of the single.

First Release: 'Ole Tyme Country Music' (1970) + Single A-side (1970)

Waiting For A Train (All Around The Watertank) / Big Legged Woman
(No. 11 Country)

[634b] **WAITING FOR A TRAIN** (1969)

Relaxed and beautifully sung, the light strings actually enhance rather than distract from the song. 'Waiting For A Train' was performed live occasionally up until around 2000.

First Release: 'She Even Woke Me Up To Say Goodbye' (1970)

[635] **WAKE UP LITTLE SUSIE** (1986)
(Boudleaux Bryant / Felice Bryant)

The Everly Brothers aren't an act that Jerry usually covered, but his version of their 1957 classic is well worth checking out, despite the intrusive backing vocals, thanks to some inspired and nifty piano playing.

First Release: 'Rocket' (1988)

[636] **WALK A MILE IN MY SHOES** (1972)
(Joe South)

Originally released by Joe South in 1969, 'Walk A Mile In My Shoes' was covered by Ray Stevens (1970), Elvis Presley (1970) and Brenda Lee (1970). Jerry's strong vocals and piano *almost* manage to transcend the overbearing strings. The song was performed live occasionally until around 1993.

First Release: 'The Killer Rocks On' (1972)

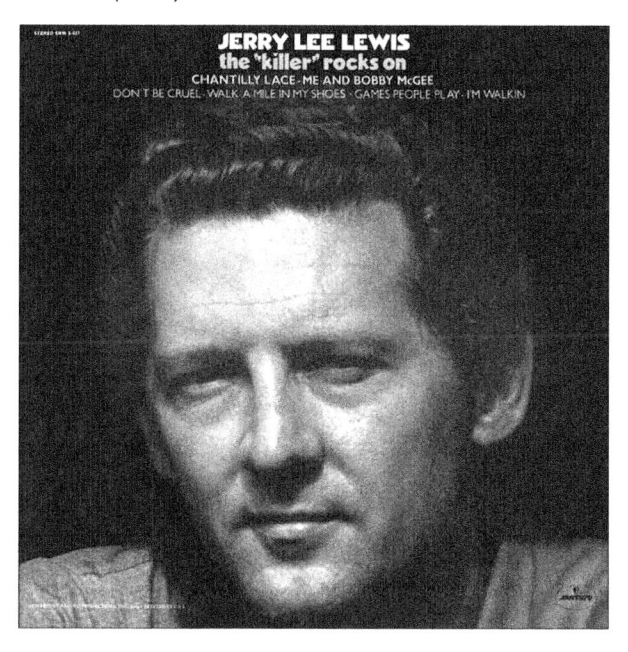

'The Killer Rocks On' (1972)

[637] **WALK RIGHT IN** (1965)
(Gus Cannon / Hosea Woods)

Originally recorded by Cannon's Jug Stompers in 1930, 'Walk Right In' was popularized by The Rooftop Singers in 1962. As with a couple of other songs on the album such as 'King Of The Road' and 'Ring Of Fire', Jerry sings it well without adding much to the original, something that is not helped by the lack of piano.

First Release: 'Country Songs For City Folks' (1965)

[638] **WALKIN' THE DOG** [with Webb Pierce, Mel Tillis and Faron Young] (1984)
(Tex Grimsley / Cliff Grimsley)

Not the Rufus Thomas song sadly, 'Walkin' The Dog' was originally released by Tex Grimsley and His Texas Showboys in 1950 and covered by Webb Pierce in 1953. As enjoyable (and samey) as the rest of the 'Four Legends' album, the best bit is Jerry's voice singing the opening line *"Here's my friend my good ol' Buddy, Faron Young from Louisiana, sing it son!"* (Faron Young was several years older than Jerry!).

First Release: 'Four Legends' (1985)

[639] **WALKING THE FLOOR OVER YOU** (1968)
(Ernest Tubb)

Originally released by Ernest Tubb in 1941, 'Walking The Floor Over You' was covered by Georgia Gibbs (1957), Glen Campbell (1963), Charlie Walker (1965), Merle Haggard (1965), Junior Parker (1966) and Hank Thompson (1967). With fast and impressive piano and fiddle, it is by far the most exciting thing on the 'Another Place, Another Time' album. It was even better live though, and was generally performed in a higher key and with more urgency, as witnessed on 'Hee Haw' in 1969, as well as in Gloucester 1972, Hamburg 1972, Atlantic City 1988, Memphis 1993, Sarpsborg 1993 and Trondheim 1993.

First Release: 'Another Place, Another Time' (1968) + Single B-side (1968)

[640] **WALL AROUND HEAVEN** (1972)
(Cecil Harrelson / Carmen Holland)

A Country song with lyrics that Jerry could identify with such as *"Before she went to heaven I promised her I'd change, but my life's become a shame and disgrace!"*, this is yet more proof of how good a lyricist his old buddy Cecil Harrelson had become, even if he did tend to be a bit on the maudlin side.

First Release: 'Who's Gonna Play This Old Piano' (1972)

'Who's Gonna Play This Old Piano' (1972)

[641] **WAYMORE'S BLUES** [with Johnny Cash, Carl Perkins and Roy Orbison] (1985)
(Waylon Jennings / Curtis Buck)

Originally released by Waylon Jennings in 1975, 'Waymore's Blues' is one of the better songs on 'Class of '55', with lighter production and the kind of acoustic guitar riff Johnny Cash was playing at Sun.

First Release: 'Class of '55' (1986)

[642] **WE BOTH KNOW WHICH ONE OF US WAS WRONG** (1972)
(Dallas Frazier / A.L. Owens)

The nearest thing to a Rocker on the 'Who's Gonna Play This Old Piano' album, 'We Both Know Which One Of Us Was Wrong' is a mid-tempo song with old time chord changes and some good piano.

First Release: 'Who's Gonna Play This Old Piano' (1972)

[643] **WE LIVE IN TWO DIFFERENT WORLDS** [with Linda Gail Lewis] (1968)
(Fred Rose)

Originally released by Tex Ritter in 1944, 'We Live In Two Different Worlds' was covered by Roy Acuff (1945), Red Foley (1961), Carl Smith (1962), Slim Whitman (1962), Don Gibson (1962) and The Louvin Brothers (1967). Jerry and Linda never harmonized better than on this song, and they both spoke fondly of it in later years. Performed very occasionally in the early days including in Attica, Indiana in 1971, they attempted it years later in Newport (Wales) in 1987, but sadly it was a bit of a mess.

First Release: 'Another Place, Another Time' (1968) + 'Together' (1969) + Single B-side (1969)

[644] **WE REMEMBER THE KING** [with Johnny Cash, Carl Perkins and Roy Orbison] (1985)
(Paul Kennerley)

With lyrics like *"We will treasure all of the gifts that he did bring, we remember the King!"*, it isn't clear who this song is about, but it was *implied* at the time that it's a tribute to Elvis Presley. Whatever, Johnny Cash is the main participant on this slow ballad, with the others in little more than supporting roles.

First Release: 'Class of '55' (1986)

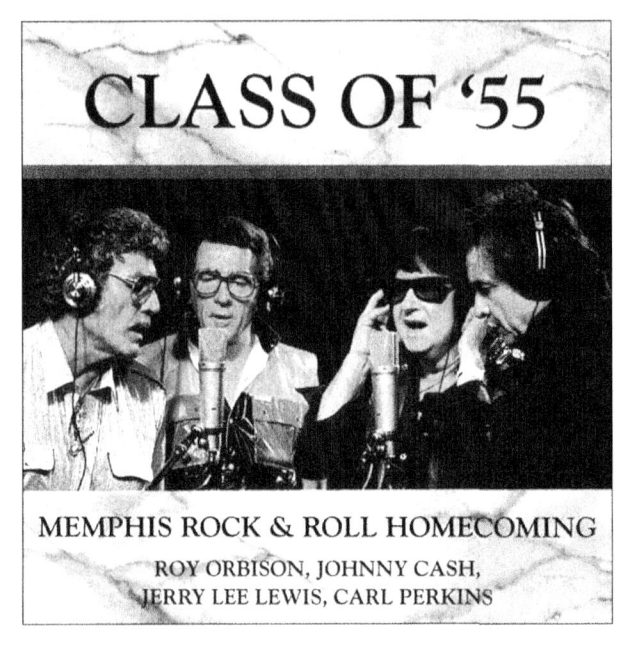

'Class of '55' (1986)

[645] **WE THREE (MY ECHO, MY SHADOW AND ME)** (1961) (L) *
(Dick Robertson / Nelson Cogane / Sammy Mysels)

In 1972, a bootleg LP appeared, called 'With Jerry Lee Rock and Roll', and amongst the highlights of this was a ropey but listenable live audience recording of a song called 'We Three'. Originally released by The Ink Spots in 1940, later research revealed that it was taped at Li'l Abner's Rebel Room in Memphis, circa February 1961. Two things about the performance are remarkable: (a) It is highly polished and obviously very well-rehearsed, and (b) Jerry says beforehand *"This is one we intend to have coming out on record pretty soon!"*... Which raises the question, was the song also recorded at Sun? Obviously, if it had been found in the vaults, it would've been released, but could it be in a misplaced or mislabeled tape box somewhere? You never know! Incidentally, Jerry's 2-piece 'band' at Li'l Abner's Rebel Room was his cousin (and father-in-law) J.W. Brown on bass and Gene Chrisman on drums. Two decades later, Gene Chrisman would reunite with Jerry, as the drummer on the MCA 'My Fingers Do The Talkin'' album.

First Release: 'With Jerry Lee Rock and Roll' (1972) (bootleg)

[646a] **WEDDING BELLS** (1963)
(Claude Boone)

Originally released by Bill Carlisle in 1947 and covered by Hank Williams in 1949, 'Wedding Bells' was first recorded at the September 1963 'Golden Hits' sessions, where it featured a very prominent guitar riff. Strangely, this was eventually released on 'Soul My Way', where it couldn't have sounded more out of place (Jerry also cut a version at a May 1965 session, but that is unissued and apparently lost).

First Release: Soul My Way (1967)

[646b] **WEDDING BELLS** (1976)

Far sparser and with steel guitar and fiddle accompaniment, the 1976 re-make probably has the edge. The song was performed in Rotterdam in 1982 and at the 67th birthday show in Memphis in 2002.

First Release: 'Country Class' (1976)

[647] **WHAT A FRIEND WE HAVE IN JESUS** (1980) *
(Charles C. Converse / Joseph M. Scriven)

First recorded by J.J. Fisher in 1899, and later revived by Sister Rosetta Tharpe (1951), Bing Crosby (1951), Tennessee Ernie Ford (1958), Cliff Richard (1967) and Ray Price (1976), 'What A Friend We Have In Jesus' is a typically good Gospel recording from his unreleased Elektra sessions.

First Release: 'The Caribou Ranch Sessions, 1980-1986' (2012) (bootleg)

[648] **WHAT A HECK OF A MESS** (1966)
(Jerry Lee Lewis)

Jerry didn't write many songs, least of all weepy Country ballads, but this song about a messy divorce is surprisingly good. First attempted during the 'Country Songs For City Folks' sessions in a version now lost, this B-side of 'Sticks and Stones' was covered by Hank Williams Jr. in 1967, perhaps as a *"Thank you"* for Jerry recording so many of his daddy's compositions.

First Release: Single B-side (1958)

[649] **WHAT AM I LIVING FOR** (1987) *
(Chuck Willis)

A bluesy ballad, 'What Am I Living For' was originally released by Chuck Willis in 1958, with the many covers including Jack Scott (1959), Conway Twitty (1960), Carl McVoy (1962), Clyde McPhatter (1962), Wanda Jackson (1963), Billy Fury (1963), The Everly Brothers (1965), The Animals (1966), Solomon Burke (1969) and Ray Charles (1971). Jerry's version from March 1987 is super, but remains only available on unofficial releases. He performed the song live in Cambridge, Bridlington and Stavanger on the April 1987 European tour, in South Amboy later in 1987, and at a benefit concert for Rockabilly pioneer Charlie Feathers in Memphis in 1988. Incidentally, this writer once had breakfast with Charlie Feathers, along with Linda Gail Lewis, in a Norfolk (UK) hotel. Quite a character, though his offer of chewing tobacco was politely declined, despite Linda Gail's urging *"Go on Peter, be adventurous!!"*...

First Release: 'The Caribou Ranch Sessions, 1980-1986' (2012) (bootleg)

[650] **WHAT MAKES THE IRISH HEART BEAT** [with Don Henley] (2003-2006)
(Van Morrison)

Originally released by Van Morrison as 'Irish Heartbeat' in 1983, 'What Makes The Irish Heart Beat' is a very odd choice of song for Jerry to record, though he did live in Dublin with Kerrie and Lee for a while in 1993-1994, so probably feels some affinity to the country. A Celtic Folk-type track with Irish pipes and played in ¾ 'waltz' time, it's just a shame that Van Morrison wasn't there instead of Don Henley. Maybe Van was keeping his distance after his 2000-2001 collaboration with Linda Gail Lewis ended in acrimony!

First Release: 'Last Man Standing' (2006)

[651] **WHAT MY WOMAN CAN'T DO** (1973)
(George Jones / Earl Montgomery / Billy Sherrill)

Originally released by George Jones earlier the same year, Jerry's version is only partially a success, perhaps because he appears to be trying to sing it George Jones instead of Jerry Lee Lewis style.

First Release: 'Sometimes A Memory Ain't Enough' (1973)

[652a] **WHAT'D I SAY** (1960)
(Ray Charles)

Originally released by Ray Charles in 1959, Jerry attempted 'What'd I Say' at two 1960 sessions. In January, he cut two takes, and then another one in June, with the latter being distinguished by the hoarse vocals and honking saxophone. All are more than acceptable, but were left in the can until much later.

First Release: 'The Sun Years' (Box-Set, 1983)

[652b] WHAT'D I SAY (1961)

Recorded at his first ever Nashville session in February 1961, Jerry at last cut a version of the song that everyone was happy with (despite the session singers being no Raelettes!). They must've been happy with its success too, as it got to No. 30 in the Pop charts, and did even better at No. 10 in the UK, his biggest hit since 'Breathless' three years earlier. It is on stage where the song *really* came to life though, and never more so than with the extended version on 'Live at The Star Club, Hamburg' *("Play that thing right boy!")*. A regular throughout the '60s, it was played with less frequency as the decades progressed, though Jerry did dig it out during the finale of his last ever UK gig in Glasgow in 2015.

First Release: Single A-side (1961) + 'Jerry Lee's Greatest!' (1961)

What'd I Say / Livin' Lovin' Wreck
(No. 30 Pop, No. 27 Country)

[652c] WHAT'D I SAY (1973)

Playing an electric piano and featuring female backing vocalists Thunderthighs (the only occurrence of both of these during the January 1973 'The Session' recordings), it's a very good version despite being a little over-long. A marginally longer edit sneaked out on the Japanese Quadrophonic 'Rock 'n' Roll Supersession' release.

First Release: 'The Session' (1973)

[652d] WHAT'D I SAY (1980) *

A fast, wild, but slightly ragged version (it sounds very odd with the drums coming in straight away!), this was probably a studio warm-up rather than a serious attempt at cutting a releasable track.

First Release: 'The Caribou Ranch Sessions, 1980-1986' (2012) (bootleg)

[653a] WHAT'S MADE MILWAUKEE FAMOUS (HAS MADE A LOSER OUT OF ME) (1968)
(Glenn Sutton)

The all-important follow-up single to the big comeback hit 'Another Place, Another Time', 'What's Made Milwaukee Famous' was even more memorable and more successful. Uniquely for the time, a simple promotional video appears to have been made, featuring Jerry miming to the song alone at the piano with no band or audience (its only known broadcast was on French TV's 'Point Chaud' on 30th May 1970). Other performances include 'Hee Haw' and 'The Many Sounds of Jerry Lee', and it was occasionally performed live well into the New Millennium.

First Release: 'Another Place, Another Time' (1968) + Single A-side (1968)

What's Made Milwaukee Famous / All The Good Is Gone
(No. 94 Pop, No. 2 Country)

Mercury Promo Video (1968)

[653b] WHAT'S MADE MILWAUKEE FAMOUS (HAS MADE A LOSER OUT OF ME) [with Rod Stewart] (2003-2006)

In 1972, Rod Stewart covered the song in a Country-Rock style, even having a UK hit with it, so it seemed like a great idea to include him on 'Last Man Standing'. Unfortunately, Jerry's re-cut is just a rough run-through without a band, and Rod Stewart's very obviously overdubbed vocal is in too low a key for him. A definite low-light of the album!

First Release: 'Last Man Standing' (2006)

[654] WHAT'S SO GOOD ABOUT GOODBYE (1977)
(Bob McDill)

'What's So Good About Goodbye' is a mediocre song from a generally very good album, and features Hargus 'Pig' Robbins on Floyd Cramer-style piano.

First Release: 'Country Memories' (1977)

[655] WHEN A MAN LOVES A WOMAN (1973)
(Calvin Lewis / Andrew Wright)

Originally released by Percy Sledge in 1966 and covered by Esther Phillips (1966), The Spencer Davis Group(1966), Ketty Lester (1966), Johnny Rivers (1967), Jerry Butler (1967) and Lou Rawls (1969) amongst many others, 'When A Man Loves A Woman' doesn't suit Jerry *at all*. Sure, he gives it his best shot, with some creative piano, but he sounds way out of his comfort zone. A rehearsal was released in 1987.

First Release: 'Southern Roots' (1973)

[656] WHEN BABY GETS THE BLUES (1971)
(Charles R. Phipps)

A song that is basically about his woman suffering with bi-polar, Jerry's *"When baby get's the blues my life turns over!"* isn't exactly sympathetic (of course, it could just be about a tart who drinks too much!).

First Release: 'Touching Home' (1971)

[657] WHEN HE WALKS ON YOU (LIKE YOU HAVE WALKED ON ME) (1971)
(Dallas Frazier / A.L. Owens)

Although a bit like 'Touching Home' from the same sessions, what lifts this above the ordinary are Jerry's adventurous and involved vocals.

First Release: 'Touching Home' (1971) + Single A-side (1971)

When He Walks On You (Like You Have Walked On Me) / Foolish Kind Of Man
(No. 11)

[658a] WHEN I GET MY WINGS (1980) *
(Billy Joe Shaver)

First released by Billy Joe Shaver in 1976, this otherwise fine recording would be better without the syncopated and rather slow beat. The song was performed live in Orlando 1986, Milan 1987 and Las Vegas 1989.

First Release: 'The Caribou Ranch Sessions, 1980-1986' (2012) (bootleg)

[658b] WHEN I GET MY WINGS (1987) *

The 1987 version is played as a straight ahead pumpin' piano Rock 'n' Roll song, and works far better. The live performance in Milan that same year was performed in a similar style, but sadly never made it onto any of the 'Live in Italy' releases.

First Release: 'The Caribou Ranch Sessions, 1980-1986' (2012) (bootleg)

[659] WHEN I GET PAID (1960)
(Henry Sledd / York Wilburn)

Recorded in October 1960 with Larry Muhoberac on piano and with backing that includes tinny guitars and saxophone, this already sounds a long way from the glory days with Roland and Jimmy at 706 Union Avenue. Yet on its own merits, this Pop-Rocker isn't *that* bad, at least in comparison to the god-awful 'Love Made A Fool Of Me' on the B-side. Cliff Bennett and The Rebel Rousers liked the song enough to cover it for a Joe Meek-produced single the following year.

First Release: Single A-side (1960)

When I Get Paid / Love Made A Fool Of Me
(Not a hit)

[660] **WHEN I TAKE MY VACATION IN HEAVEN** (1974)
(Herbert Buffum / R.E. Winsett)

Originally released by Ruth Donaldson and Helen Jepsen in 1927 and covered by Johnny Cash in 1962, 'When I Take My Vacation In Heaven' is a Gospel standard that Jerry had over-looked during his spate of spiritual recordings in 1970. He more than makes up for it here, with a nice ¾ time arrangement, and Jerry clearly meaning every word *("Jesus! Jesus! Jesus! Jesus! You're number one with Jerry Lee!")*. It was played occasionally into the 21st Century, with the last known performance, very appropriately, being at a show in Jacksonville on the day Johnny Cash died, and dedicated to his departed friend.

First Release: 'Odd Man In' (1975) + Single B-side (1975)

[661] **WHEN JESUS BECKONS ME HOME** (1970) (L)
(Gene Arnold)

Originally released by Gene Arnold in 1933, this slow Gospel song from 1970's Memphis Church recording is sometimes called 'What Will My Answer Be', and was recorded by Jimmy Swaggart under that title in 1974. He also performed it live on 'The Midnight Special' in 1977 and as part of a lengthy Gospel medley in Long Beach in 1978.

First Release: 'The Killer: 1969-1972' (box-set, 1986)

662] **WHEN MY BLUE MOON TURNS TO GOLD AGAIN** (1960)
(Gene Sullivan / Wiley Walker)

Originally released by Wiley Walker and Gene Sullivan in 1941 and covered by Hank Snow (1943), Eddy Arnold (1951), Tex Ritter (1952) and Elvis Presley (1956), Jerry cut two hoarse but good saxophone-led takes in June 1960. The song was performed live in Sarpsborg, Norway in 1993.

First Release: 'Rockin' and Free' (1974)

[663] WHEN THE GRASS GROWS OVER ME (1969)
(Don Chapel)

Originally released by George Jones in 1968 and covered by Conway Twitty the following year, this great song is made even greater by Jerry's full use of his vocal range. There really wasn't another Country singer in the world who could match up to him vocally circa 1969! It was performed live in Las Vegas in 1970.

First Release: 'She Even Woke Me Up To Say Goodbye' (1970)

[664] WHEN THE SAINTS GO MARCHING IN (1957)
(Traditional)

A song whose origins are lost, the earliest known recording was by The Paramount Jubilee Singers as 'When All The Saints Come Marching In' in 1923, and Bill Haley and His Comets cut a Rock 'n' Roll version as 'The Saints Rock 'n Roll' in 1956. Just as he had with Country, Jerry had *always* recorded Gospel, with his rocked-up spiritual 'When The Saints Go Marching In' even appearing on his very first album in 1958. Also available without the overdubbed male chorus (though it somehow works better with it), other notable performances include BBC's 'Saturday Club' in 1964, and with Johnny Cash and Carl Perkins at 'The Survivors' taping in Stuttgart in 1981 (something that was a little *too* messy to appear on the album!).

First Release: 'Jerry Lee Lewis' (1958)

[665] WHEN THEY RING THOSE GOLDEN BELLS (1980) *
(Anthony Burger)

Published in 1887 and with the earliest known recording being by The Imperial Quartet in 1916, 'When They Ring Those Golden Bells' was also recorded by Mickey Gilley in 1978. Jerry's version kicks off with an intro that sounds just like his Sun cut of 'Be-Bop-A-Lula', and is a more that worthy performance, if a tad over-long.

First Release: 'The Caribou Ranch Sessions, 1980-1986' (2012) (bootleg)

[666] WHEN TWO WORLDS COLLIDE (1979)
(Bill Anderson / Roger Miller)

Originally released by Roger Miller in 1961, 'When Two Worlds Collide' was covered and made famous by Jim Reeves in 1962. A Country-Pop song with plush strings, Jerry's version works better than expected thanks to some prominent good piano work. He performed the song live fairly often for a short while, but after around 1983 it disappeared.

First Release: 'When Two Worlds Collide' (1980) + Single A-side (1980)

When Two Worlds Collide / Good News Travels Fast
(No. 11 Country)

[667] **WHEN YOU WORE A TULIP AND I WORE A BIG RED ROSE** [with Linda Gail Lewis] (1970) (L)

(Jack Mahoney / Percy Wenrich)

Originally released by The American Quartet in 1914 and made famous by Judy Garland and Gene Kelly in 1942, Jerry and Linda's fast live version was a highlight of 1970's 'Live at The International, Las Vegas', and very occasionally performed live long after most of their other duets had been forgotten. These include 'The Jerry Lee Lewis Show' 1971, Attica, Indiana 1971, Burlington 1986, Houston 1987, Newport 1987, Sarpsborg 1993, Trondheim 1993 and the 40th Anniversary Show in Memphis 1996.

First Release: 'Live at The International, Las Vegas' (1970)

'The Jerry Lee Lewis Show' (1971)

[668] **WHENEVER YOU'RE READY** (1966)

(Cecil Harrelson)

Reputedly written about Linda Gail Lewis for whom Cecil was smitten, 'Whenever You're Ready' is a light-weight Pop-Rocker, and lyrics that weren't exactly his best *("I'll pack my clothes, and away we'll go!")*.

First Release: 'Memphis Beat' (1966)

[669] **WHERE HE LEADS ME** (1970)
(Ernest Blandy / John S. Norris)

A Gospel ballad that was published in 1898, recordings include Roy Rogers and Dale Evans (1950), Red Foley (1959), Jimmie Davis (1959) and Burl Ives (1962). Although not released until the mid '80s, Jerry's version circulated in poor quality on cassette for years before that. He performed it live on 'The Jerry Lee Lewis Show' pilot in 1971, where he played guitar and was accompanied by the four-piece Rust College Quintet (Linda Gail later recalled the missing 5th member being ill).

First Release: '30th Anniversary Album' (1986)

[670] **WHERE WOULD I BE** (1973)
(Ray Griff)

A Pop-Country ballad with heavy strings, this is one of the more forgettable songs on his most forgettable album.

First Release: 'I-40 Country' (1974)

[671] **WHISKEY RIVER** [with Willie Nelson] (2008-2010)
(Johnny Bush / Paul Stroud)

Originally released by Johnny Bush in 1972 and covered by Willie Nelson in 1973, 'Whiskey River' is a fabulous 'Outlaw' Country-Rock performance, and unlike many latter-day duets, is greatly enhanced by the presence of duet partner Willie.

First Release: 'Mean Old Man' (2010)

[672] **WHITE CHRISTMAS** (1964) *
(Irving Berlin)

Originally released by Bing Crosby in 1942, Rock 'n' Roll era cover versions of 'White Christmas' include The Drifters featuring Clyde McPhatter and Bill Pinckney (1954), Elvis Presley (1957), Connie Francis (1959), The Four Seasons (1962), Huey 'Piano' Smith (1962), The Platters (1963) and Darlene Love (1963). Proving his versatility, Jerry played a slow/fast version on BBC's 'Top Gear' in 1964, a performance that has appeared on several bootlegs over the years. It was played live very occasionally in later decades.

First Release: 'With Jerry Lee Rock and Roll' (1972) (bootleg)

[673a] WHO WILL THE NEXT FOOL BE (1964) (L)
(Charlie Rich)

Originally released by Charlie Rich in 1961 and covered by Bobby Bland in 1962, 'Who Will The Next Fool Be' is a superb Country-Soul-Blues ballad. On this 1964 live version, Jerry sings as if his life depends on it, putting in one of the greatest vocal performances ever captured on tape, complete with some great ad-libs *("You wouldn't be satisfied honey, if you had Elvis Presley!")*. He performed the song in the studio for BBC radio's 'Top Gear' in 1964 (with the even better line *"You wouldn't be satisfied with Elvis Presley, The Beatles, Jerry Lee Lewis, the whole bunch like that there!"*) and again in Paris in 1966, but by the late '60s the song had pretty much been forgotten... until 1979.

First Release: 'The Greatest Live Show on Earth' (1964)

[673b] WHO WILL THE NEXT FOOL BE (1979)

Although by 1979 Jerry wasn't quite the singer he'd been in 1964, instead of trying to recapture this, his approach was more mature, (perhaps) wiser and more world-weary, with a relaxed tempo and some wonderful musical interplay between Jerry, James Burton and Kenny Lovelace. Released in edited form as a single, it was a moderate Country hit. The song was played live fairly regularly from 1979 until around 1986, and then reprised for 'Last Man Standing Live' where it was performed with Solomon Burke.

First Release: 'Jerry Lee Lewis' (1979) + Single A-side (1979)

Who Will The Next Fool Be / Rita May
(No. 20 Country)

[674] **WHO'S GONNA PLAY THIS OLD PIANO** (1972)
(Ray Griff)

With drum intro, Ragtime brass and kazoo, 'Who's Gonna Play This Old Piano' has all the good-time party feel of a New Orleans Mardi Gras. Yet despite or because of this, it made it to No. 14 in the Country charts. Ray Griff released his own version in 1973, the same year British Skiffle pioneer Lonnie Donegan recorded it with Kenny Ball and His Jazzmen, and Jerry played the song live very occasionally into the New Millennium.

First Release: 'Who's Gonna Play This Old Piano' (1972) + Single A-side (1972)

Who's Gonna Play This Old Piano / No Honky Tonks In Heaven
(No. 14 Country)

[675] **WHO'S SORRY NOW** (1977)
(Bert Kalmar / Harry Ruby / Ted Snyder)

Originally released by Bob Thompson in 1923 and revived by Connie Francis in 1958, Jerry's version is part slow and part fast, though perhaps not slow enough and fast enough to have the same impact as (say) 'Mexicali Rose'. Live performances include Knoxville 1981, New York 1987, Memphis 1988, Hamar 1989 and Dublin 1995.

First Release: 'Country Memories' (1977) + Single B-side (1977)

[676a] WHOLE LOTTA SHAKIN' GOIN' ON (1957)
(Sunny David / David Williams)

Just as 'Blueberry Hill', 'Rock Around The Clock' and 'All Shook Up' will always be considered Fats Domino, Bill Haley and Elvis Presley songs, respectively, 'Whole Lotta Shakin' Goin' On' *always* be a Jerry Lee Lewis song. It really doesn't matter where he heard it first, or that Big Maybelle, Roy Hall and The Commodores all got there before him. Jerry actually recorded the song over two sessions, cutting at least 4 faster but inferior takes at the first session, and then the classic one-take single at a separate session weeks later. Initially selling poorly due to lack of airplay over its suggestive lyrics, it was only after he made his TV debut on 'The Steve Allen Show' on 28th July 1957 that things *really* took off, followed by August appearances on 'Alan Freed's Big Beat Party', 'American Bandstand' and a 2nd appearance on 'The Steve Allen Show'. Incidentally, the title of the original single is 'Whole *Lot Of* Shakin' *Going* On', with other spellings being later inventions. There have been many, many covers, but significant ones from the Rock 'n' Roll era include Ricky Nelson (1957), Carl Perkins (1958), Little Richard (1959), Cliff Richard and The Drifters (1959), Bill Haley and His Comets (1960), Conway Twitty (1960), Vince Taylor and The Play-Boys (with 'Twist' lyrics earlier than Jerry's, 1961) and Mickey Gilley (1962). Perhaps the most significant cover though, at least for Jerry Lee Lewis personally, was in 1973 when talented young trio The McCarver Sisters, featuring Sherry, Kerrie and Terri (later known as DeDe) recorded the song. Significant, because 11 years later Jerry married Kerrie, a marriage that produced a son and lasted for 21 years.

First Release: Single A-side (1957) + 'The Great Ball of Fire' EP (1957)

Whole Lot Of Shakin' Goin' On / It'll Be Me
(No. 3 Pop, No. 1 Country, No. 1 R&B)

'The Steve Allen Show' (1957)

[676b] WHOLE LOTTA TWISTIN' GOIN' ON (1962)

Although he wasn't the first person to think of it, at the height of the 'Twist' craze in early 1962, Jerry cut a twistin' version of his giant hit from nearly 5 years earlier. It's great fun too, with Jerry getting so into it he forgets what he's supposed to be singing *("Shake it, twist it, move it, c'mon baby!")*. Unlike 'I've Been Twistin'' from the same session, 'Whole Lotta Twistin' Goin' On' wasn't released until 1974.

First Release: 'Jerry Lee Lewis and His Pumping Piano' (1974)

[676c] WHOLE LOTTA SHAKIN' GOIN' ON (1963)

Far more mannered, polite and over-produced than either the 1957 hit single or the extended live versions he was doing at the time, interestingly, the basic arrangement owes more to the previous year's 'Whole Lotta Twistin' Goin' On' than it does the original.

First Release: 'The Golden Hits of Jerry Lee Lewis' (1964)

[676d] WHOLE LOTTA SHAKIN' GOIN' ON (1973)

The fade-in intro renders this January 1973 recording for 'The Session' a no-go almost before it starts (presumably someone screwed up somewhere), but get past that, and it's a highly spirited version, complete with impressive slide guitar by Rory Gallagher. How Jerry still sounded so inspired, in a cold London studio, performing a song he'd done thousands of times, is beyond the thinking of mere mortals!

First Release: 'The Session' (1973)

[676e] WHOLE LOTTA SHAKIN' GOIN' ON (1988)

Doing his best to prove that he could beat the original, Jerry at least almost matches it, with a remarkably enthusiastic 4 minute version. An outtake, nearly twice the length and with far more suggestive lyrics *("I know you folks didn't see that out there, but I was playing piano with my ass!")*, was included on 'The Killer's Private Stash' bootleg in 1991.

First Release: 'Great Balls Of Fire!' (1989)

> **"THE McCARVER SISTERS"**
>
> IN 1972, SHERRY, 12 YEARS OF AGE, KERRIE, 10, AND TERRI, 8, STARTED THEIR CAREERS. THEY WERE YOUNG, ENERGETIC, AND LOVED TO PERFORM.
>
> IN 1973, THEY RECORDED THEIR FIRST RECORD, "WHOLE LOTTA SHAKIN' GOING ON" AND "NASHVILLE OPEN YOUR GATES".
>
> IN 1974, THEY RECORDED THEIR SECOND RECORD WITH KERRIE SINGING "PAPER BOY BLUES" AND TERRI SINGING "RAGGEDY OLE MAN".
>
> THEY LEARNED TO PLAY INSTRUMENTS (Kerrie was taught to play drums by Tarp Tarrant, former drummer for Jerry Lee) AND STARTED PLAYING AS WELL AS SINGING. MANY SHOWS AND TOURS FOLLOWED.
>
> THEY HAVE PERFORMED ON STAGE WITH SUCH GREAT ARTISTS AS BARBARA MANDRELL, MEL TILLIS, CARL PERKINS, BILLY "CRASH" CRADDOCK, AND MANY MORE ALONG WITH THE "LIVING" KING OF ROCK AND ROLL, JERRY LEE LEWIS.
>
> IN 1980, THEY DID A SPECIAL PERFORMANCE WITH ROY ACUFF ON THE "55th" ANNIVERSARY OF THE "GRAND OLE OPRY" IN NASHVILLE, TN.
>
> TODAY (1988) SHERRY WORKS FOR THE SHELBY COUNTY SHERIFF'S DEPARTMENT. KERRIE (MRS. JERRY LEE LEWIS) TRAVELS WITH JERRY LEE AND TERRI, NOW KNOWN AS "DEDE" PERFORMS NIGHTLY AT DAD'S PLACE IN THE RAMADA INN.
>
> THEY STILL PERFORM TOGETHER FOR SPECIAL SHOWS AND OCCASIONS WHEN THEIR SCHEDULES ARE OPEN.

The McCarver Sisters 'Whole Lotta Shakin' Goin' On' single (reissue)

[677] **WHY DON'T YOU LOVE ME (LIKE YOU USED TO DO)** (1969)

(Hank Williams)

Originally released by Hank Williams in 1950, Jerry rarely disappointed when covering Hank Williams songs, and such was the case here, despite it only lasting 96 seconds (if *only* he'd cut a Hank Williams Tribute album in 1969!). Live performances include 'The Many Sounds of Jerry Lee' 1969, Farnworth 1983, Las Vegas 1985, Newport 1987 and Madrid 1990.

First Release: 'Sings The Country Music Hall of Fame Hits, Vol. Two' (1969)

[678] **WHY ME LORD** [with Moetta Hill] (1973)
(Kris Kristofferson)

Originally released by writer Kris Kristofferson the previous year, Jerry's version from the 'Jack Daniels Old No. 7' March 1973 session is a duet with singer and keyboardist Moetta Hill. She's a good singer, but the song's key is a little too low for her, and it was probably a correct decision not to release the recording at the time. Moetta would join Jerry's road band for a while in 1987, and again during the 1995-1997 period.

First Release: '30th Anniversary Album' (1986)

Peter Checksfield with Moetta Stewart (née Hill) (1987)

[679] **WHY SHOULD I CRY OVER YOU** (1957)
(Jimmie Short)

Originally released by Arthur Fields in 1922 and covered by Andy Williams (1954) and Frank Sinatra (1955), in reality the song is too poor to do with much with, though Jerry gives it his best shot.

First Release: 'The Sun Years' (Box-Set, 1983)

[680a] **WHY YOU BEEN GONE SO LONG** (1982)
(Mickey Newbury)

Originally released by Johnny Darrell in 1969 and covered by Tommy Cash (1969), Jessi Colter (1970), Jeannie C. Riley (1972), Mickey Newbury (1973) and Buffy Sainte-Marie (1973), this is a superior up-tempo Country-Rocker, with some great boogie woogie piano. The song was performed occasionally for the rest of Jerry's career, while an alternate take appeared on the 1991 'Honky Tonk Rock & Roll Piano Man' compilation.

First Release: 'My Fingers Do The Talkin'' (1982) + Single A-side (1983)

Why You Been Gone So Long / She Sings Amazing Grace
(No. 69 Country)

[680b] **WHY YOU BEEN GONE SO LONG** (2006)

The majority of the 'exclusive download' bonus tracks for 'Last Man Standing' were raw live-in-the-studio run-throughs with his road band, but this is anything but; a storming, fast performance and with Cajun accordion backing, featured prominently is session singer Stacey Michelle who almost duets with Jerry. One of the better 21st century remakes.

First Release: Best Buy (exclusive download) + 'Rock 'n' Roll Resurrection' (2007) (bootleg)

[681] **WILD AND WOOLY WAYS** (1977)
(Bob Morrison / Alan Rush)

Originally released by Rodney Lay and The Wild West in 1978, 'Wild and Wooly Ways' with its suitably rebellious lyrics *("I'm gonna make one more tequila memory, like an outlaw ridin' hard from Mexico!")* is an excellent 'Outlaw' up-tempo Country-Rock song that deserves to be more widely known. Oddly, it never quite came together on stage, but Jerry attempted it in Gothenburg 1978, Austin City 1983, Las Vegas 1989 and Berlin 1991.

First Release: 'Keeps Rockin'' (1978)

[682a] **WILD ONE (REAL WILD CHILD)** (1958)
(John Greenan / David Owens)

Originally released by Johnny O'Keefe in 1958, with a title like 'Wild One' it's perhaps not surprising that the Sun cuts (there were 3 of 'em, including one that surfaced *after* the release of 2015's 'The Collected Works' box-set!) are amongst Jerry's most frantic and uninhibited Sun recordings, and the song has been a firm fan favorite since first released in 1974. The Crickets' drummer Jerry Allison covered the song under the alias 'Ivan' the same year.

First Release: 'Rockin' and Free' (1974)

[682b] **WILD ONE (REAL WILD CHILD)** (1988)

Perhaps the most surprising of the 'movie soundtrack' remakes and amongst the most exciting, 'Wild One' (aka 'Real Wild Child') is *almost* as great as the Sun versions. The song was performed live occasionally from 1988 to 1995.

First Release: 'Great Balls Of Fire!' (1989)

[683a] **WILL THE CIRCLE BE UNBROKEN** (1959)
(Charles H. Gabriel / Ada Habershon)

Originally released by William McEwan in 1912, and popularized by The Carter Family (with a new composer credit) in 1935, Jerry's Sun version is suitably respectful and dignified. The song was performed occasionally well into the New Millennium, though perhaps most notably with Johnny Cash and Carl Perkins for 1981's 'The Survivors' taping.

First Release: 'Sunday Down South' (1970)

'The Survivors' (1982)

[683b] **WILL THE CIRCLE BE UNBROKEN** [with Mavis Staples, Robbie Robertson and Nils Lofgren] (2008-2010)

Lengthier, a little faster, and heavier in a very organic way, this sees the meeting of two Gospel giants, suitably supported by two guitar greats.

First Release: 'Mean Old Man' (2010)

[684] **WINE ME UP** (1969)
(Eddie Crandall / Faron Young)

Original released by Faron Young in 1969, Jerry's mid-tempo Swing version sees him *almost* Rockin', and almost certainly drinkin'! The performance is a real joy, right up to the yodeled ending.

First Release: 'She Even Woke Me Up To Say Goodbye' (1970)

[685] **WOLVERTON MOUNTAIN** (1965)
(Merle Kilgore / Claude King)

Originally released by Claude King in 1962 and covered by Nat 'King' Cole (1962), Roy Drusky (1962), Frank Ifield (1963) and Connie Francis and Hank Williams Jr. (1964), Jerry's version is notable for some excellent driving piano work, as well as a great vocal, and is a 'Country Songs For City Folks' highlight.

First Release: 'Country Songs For City Folks' (1965)

[686] **WOMAN, WOMAN (GET OUT OF OUR WAY)** (1970)
(Cecil Harrelson / Linda Gail Lewis)

A Bluesy Country song, 'Woman, Woman (Get Out Of Our Way)' made a great B-side, even if it wasn't *quite* hit material in its own right. With Cecil Harrelson, Linda Gail Lewis and Kenny Lovelace, Jerry had some very competent in-house writers (and I'm sure they all welcomed the publishing royalties!).

First Release: 'There Must Be More To Love Than This' (1970) + Single B-side (1971)

[687] **WON'T YOU RIDE IN MY LITTLE RED WAGON** (1987)
(Rex Griffin)

Original released by Hank Penny and His Radio Cowboys in 1940 and revived by Willie Nelson in 1981, the only thing worse than the horrible cheap Casio keyboard on Jerry's version is the fact that it goes on for well over 7 minutes - which is about 6 minutes longer than most listeners can take. For aural masochists only!

First Release: 'At Hank Cochran's' (1995)

[688] **WORKIN' MAN BLUES** (1969)
(Merle Haggard)

Originally released by Merle Haggard in 1969, Jerry's version kicks off with a Country-fied Blues guitar lick, and then quickly develops into a fabulous Rockin' Rhythm 'n' Blues track. Very occasional live performances include Nashville 1973, Chicago 1973 and Nottingham 1983.

First Release: 'She Even Woke Me Up To Say Goodbye' (1970)

Emma Connolly and Jerry Lee Lewis (1995)

[689] **WOULD YOU TAKE ANOTHER CHANCE ON ME** (1971)
(Jerry Foster / Bill Rice)

After the pure Country hits from early 1968 to mid 1971, 'Would You Take Another Chance On Me' saw a bit of a departure, with heavy orchestrated string arrangements and more Pop-like melodies - if it weren't for his passionate and involved vocal it could almost be labeled Easy Listening. *Not* that 'Country' record buyers and radio stations seemed to mind. The song was performed live very occasionally up until around 1987, and was covered by Kenny Price (1972), Carl Smith (1972) and Sonny James (1973).

First Release: 'Would You Take Another Chance On Me' (1971) + Single Double-A-side (1971)

[690a] **YOU ARE MY SUNSHINE** (1957)
(Jimmie Davis)

Originally released by The Pine Ridge Boys in 1939 and covered by Jimmie Davis (the song's composer, 1940) and Gene Autry (1941), Jerry cut two highly enjoyable pumpin' piano takes for Sun in 1957. The song was performed live very occasionally into the New Millennium.

First Release: 'Ole Tyme Country Music' (1970)

[690b] **YOU ARE MY SUNSHINE** [with Sheryl Crow and Jon Brion] (2008-2010)

Successfully combining Country with the Blues, this lengthy version features very good duet vocals by Sheryl Crow, as well as some suitably raunchy guitar and harmonica.

First Release: 'Mean Old Man' (2010)

[691a] **YOU BELONG TO ME** (1969)
(Pee Wee King / Chilton Price / Redd Stewart)

Originally released by Joni James in 1952, cover versions include Jo Stafford (1952), Dean Martin (1952), The Orioles (1952), Jim Reeves (1957), Gene Vincent and The Blue Caps (1958), The Duprees (1962), Patsy Cline (1962), Clyde McPhatter (1962) and Petula Clark (1965). The 1976 'Country Class' album featured clearer vocals than heard on the previous couple of albums, but on 'You Belong To Me' he sounded *particularly* youthful. It was only later that fans discovered it was actually recorded 7 years earlier! The song remained a concert regular for the next 40 years.

First Release: 'Country Class' (1976) + Single A-side (1976)

[691b] **YOU BELONG TO ME** (2006)

Ragged but right, this live-in-the-studio performance is fairly typical of Jerry's concert versions at the time.

First Release: Best Buy (exclusive download) + 'Rock 'n' Roll Resurrection' (2007) (bootleg)

[692] **YOU CALL EVERYBODY DARLING** (1977)
(Sam Martin / Ben Trace / Clem Watts)

Originally released by Smiley Wilson with The Crossroads Gang in 1947, 'You Call Everybody Darling' was covered by The Andrews Sisters (1948), Faron Young (1957) and Bill Haley and The Comets (1963). Jerry's sprightly version, taped at his final Mercury session in December 1977, was well worthy of release. Live performances include Dalton 1979, Cambridge 1987, New York 1987, Atlantic City 1988, Stuttgart 1991 and Las Vegas 1992.

First Release: 'The Mercury Sessions' (1985)

[693a] **YOU CAN HAVE HER** (1972)
(William S. Cook)

Originally released by Roy Hamilton in 1961, 'You Can have Her' was covered by Lenny Welch (1961), Johnny Rivers (1964), Gene Simmons (1964), Timi Yuro (1965), The Righteous Brothers (1965), Charlie Rich (1966) and Louis Armstrong (1970). Jerry's version is wonderful both vocally and on piano, but very soon those dreaded and totally unnecessary strings come in. Memorably seen in 'The London Rock 'n' Roll Show' film (a Rock 'n' Roll revival gig at Wembley Stadium in 1972 that seemingly combined greasy Teddy Boys with topless dancing hippy chicks), the song was performed fairly often until around the mid '90s.

First Release: 'The Killer Rocks On' (1972)

[693b] **YOU CAN HAVE HER** [with Eric Clapton and James Burton] (2008-2010)

Although inevitably not as strong vocally as on the earlier version and there's no piano, this is still highly worthwhile, with a brisker tempo, good duet vocals and stinging guitar licks.

First Release: 'Mean Old Man' (2010)

[694] **YOU DON'T MISS YOUR WATER** (1972)
(William Bell)

Originally released by William Bell in 1961, 'You Don't Miss Your Water' was covered by Otis Redding (1965), Percy Sledge (1967), The Byrds (1968), Otis Clay (1968), Taj Mahal (1968) and Alexis Korner (1970). Jerry's version is amongst his most Soulful recordings, with extraordinary powerful vocals, and even the strings somehow work on this. Live performances include Hamburg 1972, Amsterdam 1972, Berlin 1991 and Wolfen 1992.

First Release: 'The Killer Rocks On' (1972)

[695] **YOU DON'T HAVE TO GO** [with Neil Young] (2003-2006)
(Jimmy Reed)

Originally released by Jimmy Reed in 1954, Jerry's version is a tough Rhythm 'n' Blues shuffle, with some suitably grungy guitar and backing vocals by Neil Young. They performed the song live on 'The Late Show with David Letterman'.

First Release: 'Last Man Standing' (2006)

'The Late Show with David Letterman' (2006)

[696] **YOU HELPED ME UP (WHEN THE WORLD LET ME DOWN)** (1971)
(Cile Davis / Carmen Holland / Clyde Pitts)

A so-so Country song, on 'You Helped Me Up (When The World Let Me Down)' Jerry is in fine voice, just like on the rest of the 'Touching Home' album.

First Release: 'Touching Home' (1971)

[697] **YOU OUGHT TO SEE MY MIND** (1974)
(Carl Knight)

With its *"Baby, if you think my clothes look bad, you ought to see my mind!"* tagline, this is one of the more memorable Country songs from the mid '70s. Jerry performed it live in Cincinnati in 1975.

First Release: 'Odd Man In' (1975)

[698] **YOU WENT BACK ON YOUR WORD** (1963)
(Brook Benton / Bobby Stevenson)

The vast majority of 'The Return Of Rock' was taped in January 1965. However, this song (as well as 'Johnny B. Goode') hails from the less consistent 'Golden Hits' sessions in September 1963. That said, it's a sprightly performance of Clyde McPhatter's 1959 original, even if Jerry's voice sounds like it could do with a week's rest.

First Release: 'The Return of Rock' (1965)

[699] **YOU WENT OUT OF YOUR WAY (TO WALK ON ME)** (1969)
(Paul Craft)

A mid-tempo Honky Tonk song with pumpin' piano, 'You Went Out Of Your Way (To Walk On Me)' is a more than worthy track for what may well be Jerry's finest Country album.

First Release: 'She Even Woke Me Up To Say Goodbye' (1970) + Single B-side (1970)

[700a] **YOU WIN AGAIN** (1957)
(Hank Williams)

A Hank Williams song from 1952, Jerry recorded the song at two different sessions in 1957. In May, he cut 3 up-tempo versions, and while interesting, they don't do much more than prove that he could do it. Then in August, he cut the definitive slow single take, coming up with possibly the finest Hank Williams cover *ever*. Promoted on 'The Dewey Phillips Pop Show' and 'American Bandstand', 'You Win Again' has the distinction of being the *only* Hank Williams song that remained a concert regular throughout Jerry Lee Lewis' entire career.

First Release: Single B-side (1957)

'The Dewey Phillips Pop Show' (1957)

[700b] YOU WIN AGAIN (1963)

With the included final verse and subtle string accompaniment, the 1963 Smash re-cut of 'You Win Again' is in some ways as good as the 1957 cut.

First Release: 'The Golden Hits of Jerry Lee Lewis' (1964)

[701] (YOU'D THINK BY NOW) I'D BE OVER YOU (1977)

(Jerry Foster / Bill Rice)

Played very slowly and with piano that sounds like Hargus 'Pig' Robbins rather than Jerry Lee Lewis, this is the kind of Pop-Country that was dominating the Country charts by the late '70s (Hank Williams wouldn't have stood a chance if he was still around!).

First Release: 'Country Memories' (1977)

[702] YOU'RE ALL TOO UGLY TONIGHT (1977)

(Buzz Cason / Dan Penn)

Although a ¾ time waltz with amusing lyrics *("Girl you won't believe what's on the streets, I'm coming on home to you instead!")*, it was probably a wise decision not to release it until years later.

First Release: 'From The Vaults' (1986)

[703a] YOU'RE THE ONLY STAR (IN MY BLUE HEAVEN) (1956)

(Gene Autry)

First released by Gene Autry in 1935, 'You're The Only Star (In My Blue Heaven)' is a song he returned to numerous times at Sun. He recorded two slightly hesitant takes at his debut session on 14th November, from which take 2 was released on Charly's 1983 box-set. Along with both sides of his debut single plus a couple of other songs, Jerry played a brief solo version of this song at the tail end of the 'Million Dollar Quartet' session on 4th December 1956.

First Release: 'The Sun Years' (Box-Set, 1983)

[703b] YOU'RE THE ONLY STAR (IN MY BLUE HEAVEN) (1957)

With everyone involved sounding far more comfortable with the song, 3 takes were recorded circa June 1957, with the 3rd take released in 1970.

First Release: 'Ole Tyme Country Music' (1970)

[703c] YOU'RE THE ONLY STAR (IN MY BLUE HEAVEN) (1958)

Returning to the song in November 1958, 3 quick takes were tossed off during the sessions that produced 'I'll Sail My Ship Alone' and 'It Hurt Me So'. For a song that obviously meant a lot to Jerry in the '50s, it is something that has only rarely been performed since, with Sacramento 1976, Stockholm 1985 and the epic 66th Birthday show in Memphis in 2001 being 3 such occasions.

First Release: 'The Sun Years' (Box-Set, 1983)

[704] YOU'VE STILL GOT A PLACE IN MY HEART (1969)
(Leon Payne)

Originally released by Leon Payne in 1950, covers include Dean Martin (1967), Glen Campbell (1967), Merle Haggard (1968) and Don Gibson (1968). Proving that he could croon with the best of 'em, Jerry still couldn't resist showing off on piano (check out that intro!).

First Release: 'Sings The Country Music Hall of Fame Hits, Vol. One' (1969)

[705] YOUNG BLOOD (1994)
(Jerry Leiber / Mike Stoller)

First released by The Coasters in 1957, and later covered by The Beatles for the BBC, Jerry's 1994 recording rivals 'Sixteen Candles' for latter-day lechery! It is on the 1995 album of the same name.

First Release: 'Young Blood' (1995)

[706a] YOUR CHEATIN' HEART (1958)
(Hank Williams)

Originally released by Hank Williams in 1953, Jerry cut the song at two Sun sessions. The first one from March 1958 is played a bit too fast, and features some rather clumsy singing at the beginning.

First Release: 'A Taste of Country' (1970)

[706b] **YOUR CHEATIN' HEART** (1960)

From January 1960, this is still a little too rocked-up, though it does feature an interesting 'Break Up' type intro and some good boogie woogie piano.

First Release: 'Keep Your Hands Off Of It!' (1987)

[706c] **YOUR CHEATIN' HEART** (1963)

1964's 'The Golden Hits of Jerry Lee Lewis' was comprised of re-cuts of A's and B-sides of six of Jerry's early Sun singles - with one very notable exception: 'Your Cheatin' Heart' was included instead of 'It'll Be Me'. As none of his Sun versions of 'Your Cheatin' Heart' had been released yet, this song was new to most buyers, and is probably his best studio cut. The song was performed live regularly throughout the '60s (most notably in Hamburg in 1964), and very occasionally into the New Millennium, culminating in a lovely duet with Norah Jones for 'Last Man Standing Live'.

First Release: 'The Golden Hits of Jerry Lee Lewis' (1964)

[706d] **YOUR CHEATIN' HEART** (1975)

Kicking off with a 'Whole Lotta Shakin' Goin' On'-styled intro, performed fairly fast, and with prominent harmonica and lethargic vocals, this is clearly just a studio run-through that perhaps should've remained an outtake.

First Release: 'Odd Man In' (1975)

Peter Checksfield with Kerrie Lewis and Linda Gail Lewis (1992)

[707] **YOUR LOVING WAYS** (1963)
(Robert Chilton / Alton Harkins)

Recorded during Jerry's final Sun sessions in late August 1963, 'Your Loving Ways' is a frantic Gospel-influenced song with some fine piano, and backing singers who could've come straight out of a revival meeting. Incidentally, there has been some speculation on whether or not the prominent female backing vocalist is Linda Gail Lewis: This author once asked her this, but she couldn't recall ever hearing the song... And isn't this the way it will always be, with much of Jerry's recorded output remaining a mystery that can never be solved?

It's a hellava lotta fun tryin' though!

First Release: 'Original Golden Hits Volume III' (1971) + Single A-side (1972)

Your Loving Ways / I Can't Trust Me (In Your Arms Anymore)
(Not a hit)

SELECTED USA DISCOGRAPHY

Singles

12/1956: Crazy Arms / End Of The Road
04/1957: Whole Lotta Shakin' Goin' On / It'll Be Me
11/1957: Great Balls Of Fire / You Win Again
02/1958: Breathless / Down The Line
05/1958: High School Confidential / Fools Like Me
06/1958: The Return Of Jerry Lee / Lewis Boogie
08/1958: Break Up / I'll Make It All Up To You
11/1958: I'll Sail My Ship Alone / It Hurt Me So
02/1959: Lovin' Up A Storm / Big Blon' Baby
07/1959: Let's Talk About Us / The Ballad Of Billy Joe
11/1959: Little Queenie / I Could Never Be Ashamed Of You
03/1960: Baby, Baby Bye Bye / Old Black Joe
08/1960: Hang Up My Rock 'n' Roll Shoes / John Henry
10/1960: In The Mood / I Get The Blues When It Rains
12/1960: When I Get Paid / Love Made A Fool Of Me
03/1961: What'd I Say / Livin' Lovin' Wreck
07/1961: Cold, Cold Heart / It Won't Happen With Me
09/1961: Save The Last Dance For Me / As Long As I Live
12/1961: Money / Bonnie B.
02/1962: I've Been Twistin' / Ramblin' Rose
07/1962: Sweet Little Sixteen / How's My Ex Treating You
11/1962: Good Golly Miss Molly / I Can't Trust Me (In Your Arms Anymore)
04/1963: Teenage Letter / Seasons Of My Heart
10/1963: Pen and Paper / Hit The Road Jack
03/1964: I'm On Fire / Bread and Butter Man
06/1964: She Was My Baby (He Was My Friend) / The Hole He Said He'd Dig For Me
10/1964: High Heel Sneakers / You Went Back On Your Word
01/1965: Baby, Hold Me Close / I Believe In You
03/1965: Carry Me Back To Old Virginia / I Know What It Means
07/1965: Rockin' Pneumonia and The Boogie Woogie Flu / This Must Be The Place
10/1965: Green, Green Grass Of Home / Baby You've Got What It Takes
03/1966: Sticks and Stones / What A Heck Of A Mess
08/1966: Memphis Beat / If I Had It All To Do Over
07/1967: It's A Hang Up Baby / Holdin' On
10/1967: Turn On Your Love Light / Shotgun Man
02/1968: Another Place, Another Time / Walking The Floor Over You
05/1968: What's Made Milwaukee Famous / All The Good Is Gone
09/1968: She Still Comes Around (To Love What's Left Of Me) / Slipping Around

12/1968: To Make Love Sweeter For You / Let's Talk About Us
04/1969: Don't Let Me Cross Over / We Live In Two Different Worlds
06/1969: One Has My Name (The Other Has My Heart) / I Can't Stop Lovin' You
07/1969: Invitation To Your Party / I Could Never Be Ashamed Of You
10/1969: She Even Woke Me Up To Say Goodbye / Echoes
11/1969: Roll Over Beethoven / Secret Places
11/1969: One Minute Past Eternity / Frankie and Johnny
01/1970: Once More With Feeling / You Went Out Of Your Way (To Walk On Me)
03/1970: I Can't Seem To Say Goodbye / Goodnight Irene
07/1970: There Must Be More To Love Than This / Home Away From Home
09/1970: Waiting For A Train (All Around The Watertank) / Big Legged Woman
12/1970: In Loving Memories / I Can't Have A Merry Christmas, Mary (Without You)
03/1971: Touching Home / Woman, Woman (Get Out Of Our Way)
07/1971: When He Walks On You (Like You Have Walked On Me) / Foolish Kind Of Man
08/1971: Love On Broadway / Matchbox
10/1971: Me and Bobby McGee / Would You Take Another Chance On Me
02/1972: Your Lovin' Ways / I Can't Trust Me (In Your Arms Anymore)
03/1972: Chantilly Lace / Think About It Darlin'
06/1972: Lonely Weekends / Turn On Your Love Light
07/1972: Me and Jesus / Handwriting On The Wall
09/1972: Who's Gonna Play This Old Piano / No Honky Tonks In Heaven
01/1973: No More Hanging On / The Mercy Of A Letter
03/1973: Drinkin' Wine Spo-Dee O-Dee / Rock and Roll Medley
06/1973: No Headstone On My Grave / Jack Daniels (Old Number Seven)
09/1973: Sometimes A Memory Ain't Enough / I Think I Need To Pray
01/1974: I'm Left, You're Right, She's Gone / I've Fallen To The Bottom
03/1974: Meat Man / Just A Little Bit
05/1974: Tell Tale Signs / Cold, Cold Morning Light
09/1974: He Can't Fill My Shoes / Tomorrow's Takin' My Baby Away
01/1975: I Can Still Hear The Music In The Restroom / (Remember Me) I'm The One Who Loves You
07/1975: Boogie Woogie Country Man / I'm Still Jealous Of You
10/1975: A Damn Good Country Song / When I Take My Vacation In Heaven
01/1976: Don't Boogie Woogie / That Kind Of Fool
06/1976: Let's Put It Back Together Again / Jerry Lee's Rock and Roll Revival Show
11/1976: The Closest Thing To You / You Belong To Me
10/1977: Middle Age Crazy / Georgia On My Mind
02/1978: Come On In / Who's Sorry Now
05/1978: I'll Find It Where I Can / Don't Let The Stars Get In Your Eyes
03/1979: Rockin' My Life Away / I Wish I Was Eighteen Again
07/1979: Who Will The Next Fool Be / Rita May
01/1980: When Two Worlds Collide / Good News Travels Fast

05/1980: Honky Tonk Stuff / Rockin' Jerry Lee
08/1980: Over The Rainbow / Folsom Prison Blues
12/1980: Thirty Nine and Holding / Change Places With Me
03/1982: I'm So Lonesome I Could Cry / Pick Me Up On Your Way Down
09/1982: I'd Do It All Again / Who Will Buy The Wine
11/1982: My Fingers Do The Talkin' / Forever Forgiving
02/1983: Come As You Were / Circumstantial Evidence
06/1983: Why You Been Gone So Long / She Sings Amazing Grace
04/1984: I Am What I Am / That Was The Way It Was Then
??/1986: Get Out Your Big Roll Daddy / Honky Tonkin' Rock 'n' Rollin' Piano Man
07/1986: Sixteen Candles / Rock and Roll Fais Do Do
01/1989: Never Too Old To Rock and Roll / Rock and Roll Kiss
06/1989: Great Balls Of Fire / Breathless
04/1990: It Was The Whiskey Talkin' (Not Me) / It Was The Whiskey Talkin' (Not Me)
??/1995: Goosebumps / Crown Victoria Custom '51
??/2006: Pink Cadillac *(Download only)*
??/2007: Honky Tonk Woman *(Download only)*
??/2009: Mean Old Man *(Download only)*

EP

09/1957: The Great Ball of Fire

Albums

1958: Jerry Lee Lewis
1961: Jerry Lee's Greatest!
1964: Golden Hits of Jerry Lee Lewis
1964: The Greatest Live Show on Earth
1964: Live at The Star Club, Hamburg *(Not originally released in the USA)*
1965: The Return of Rock
1965: Country Songs for City Folks
1966: Memphis Beat
1966: By Request (More of The Greatest Live Show on Earth)
1967: Soul My Way
1968: Another Place, Another Time
1969: She Still Comes Around
1969: Sings the Country Music Hall of Fame Hits, Vol. 1
1969: Sings the Country Music Hall of Fame Hits, Vol. 2
1969: Together [with Linda Gail Lewis]
1970: She Even Woke Me Up to Say Goodbye
1970: Live at The International, Las Vegas
1970: In Loving Memories: The Jerry Lee Lewis Gospel Album

1971: There Must Be More to Love Than This
1971: Touching Home
1971: Would You Take Another Chance on Me?
1972: The Killer Rocks On
1972: Who's Gonna Play This Old Piano?
1973: The Session
1973: Sometimes a Memory Ain't Enough
1973: Southern Roots
1974: I-40 Country
1975: Boogie Woogie Country Man
1975: Odd Man In
1976: Country Class
1977: Country Memories
1978: Keeps Rockin'
1979: Jerry Lee Lewis
1980: When Two Worlds Collide
1980: Killer Country
1982: The Survivors Live [with Johnny Cash and Carl Perkins]
1982: My Fingers Do the Talkin'
1984: I Am What I Am
1985: Four Legends [with Faron Young, Mel Tillis and Webb Pierce]
1986: Class of '55 [with Johnny Cash, Carl Perkins and Roy Orbison]
1988: Rocket *(Not originally released in the USA)*
1989: Great Balls of Fire!
1995: Young Blood
2006: Last Man Standing
2010: Mean Old Man
2011: Live at Third Man Records
2014: Rock & Roll Time
2022: The Boys from Ferriday [with Jimmy Swaggart]

The best way to start building a Jerry Lee Lewis collection is via these magnificent box-sets.

www.bear-family.com

ABOUT THE AUTHOR

Peter Checksfield is the author of more than a dozen books, notably 'Shindig! America's Flat-Out Ass-Kickin' Rock 'n' Roll TV Show' and 'Let's Stomp! American Music that made The British Beat, 1954 – 1967' which both feature Jerry Lee Lewis, and two volumes on long-running British TV show 'Top Of The Pops' which do not feature Jerry Lee Lewis. He lives with his partner Heather on the Kent coast in the UK.

www.peterchecksfield.com

Printed in Great Britain
by Amazon